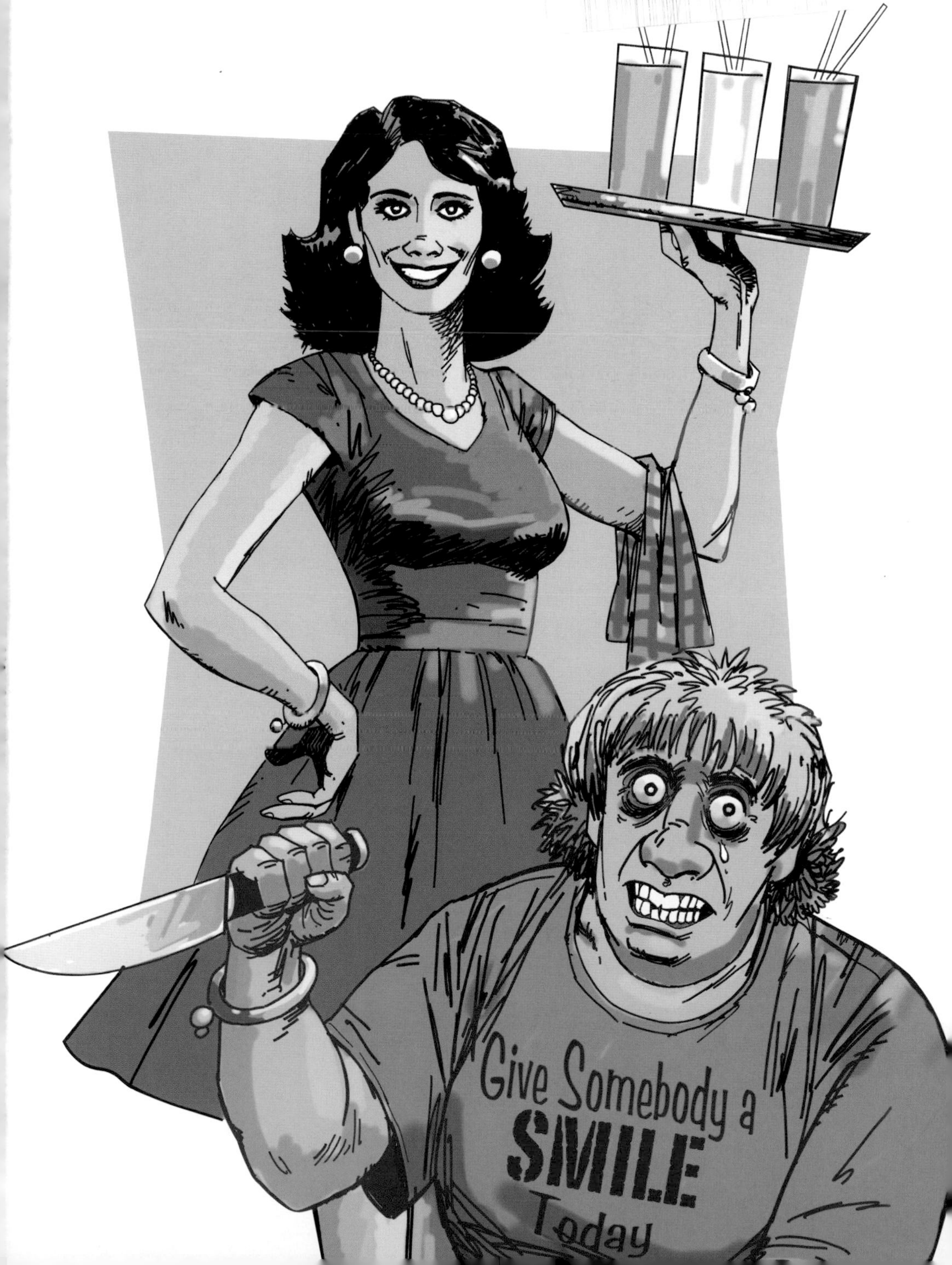
Give Somebody a
SMILE
Today

publisher MIKE RICHARDSON designer DARIN FABRICK art director LIA RIBACCHI

assistant editor MATT DRYER editor SCOTT ALLIE

The Milkman Murders, Published by Dark Horse Comics, Inc., 10956 SE Main Street, Milwaukie, OR, 97222. The Milkman Murders™ & ©2005 Joe Casey and Steve Parkhouse. All rights reserved. The stories, institutions, and characters in this publication are fictional. Any resemblance to actual persons (living or dead), events, institutions, or locales, without satiric intent, is purely coincidental. No portion of this book may be reproduced, by any means, without express written permission from the copyright holder. Dark Horse Books™ is a trademark of Dark Horse Comics, Inc. Dark Horse Comics® is a trademark of Dark Horse Comics, Inc., registered in various categories and countries. All rights reserved.

This volume collects issues one through four of the Dark Horse Comics mini-series, The Milkman Murders.

Published by Dark Horse Books, A Division of Dark Horse Comics, Inc.
10956 SE Main Street, Milwaukie, OR 97222

www.darkhorse.com

To find a comics shop in your area, call the Comic Shop Locator Service toll-free at 1-888-266-4226

First edition: April 2005 ISBN: 1-59307-080-2

1 3 5 7 9 10 8 6 4 2
Printed in China

DARK HORSE BOOKS™

THE MILKMAN MURDERS™

story
JOE CASEY

art
STEVE PARKHOUSE

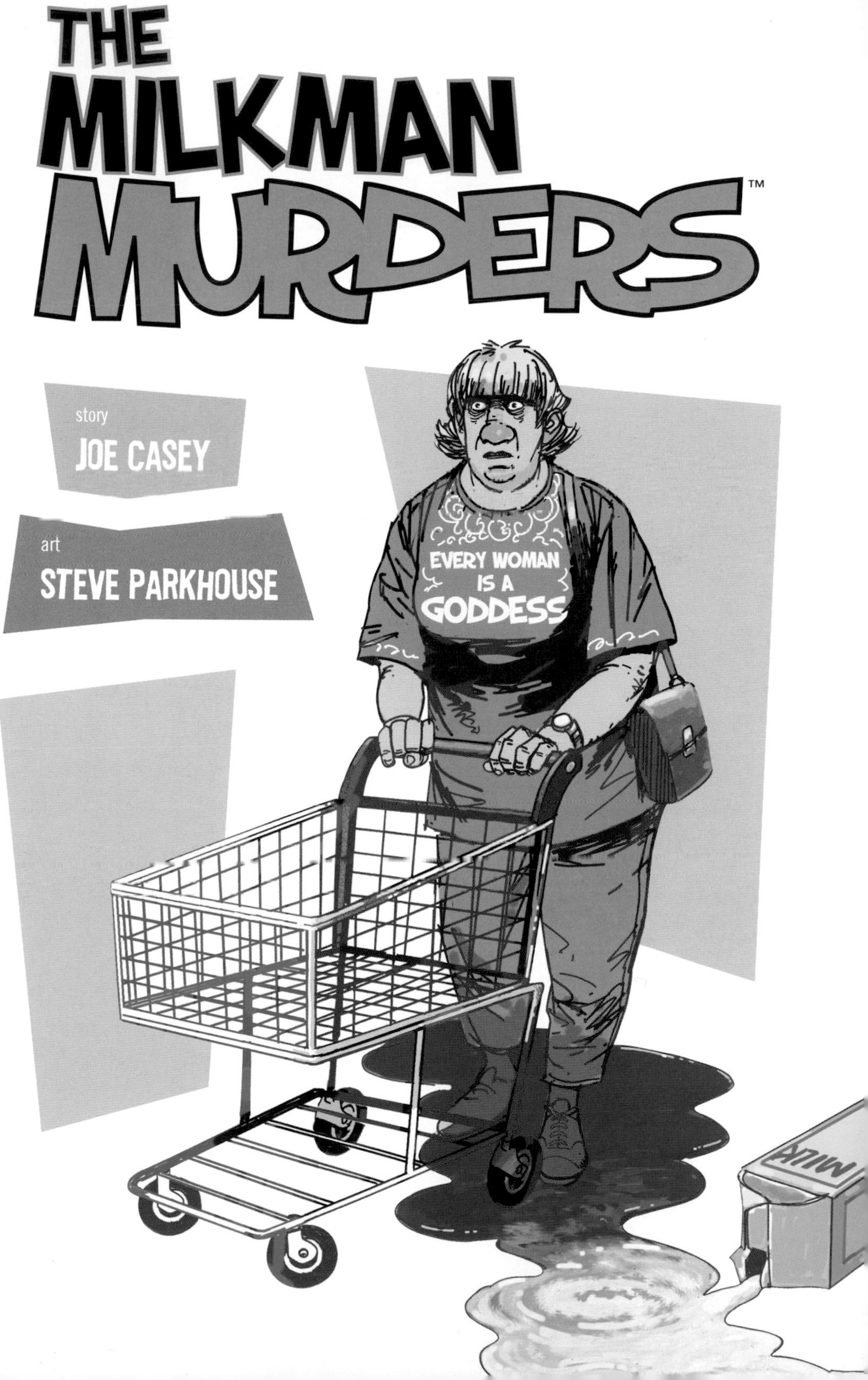
EVERY WOMAN IS A GODDESS

INTRODUCTION

I found my first comics in the basement of a friend's house, discarded copies of the horror books *Slow Death* and *Skull*. I'd never read anything like it. Horror fiction had been my passion since I was that little kid in New England, reading *'Salem's Lot* at the age of eight, feeling like those vampires were in my very own, then-rural New England town. Gentrification hit, and, as I grew, my sense of horror matured a little bit, while the town grew into its own little suburban nightmare. I still loved vampires and zombies, and, most of all, the monster from Mary Shelley's book, but I came to prefer the horror of *Apocalypse Now* and Carson McCullers's novels. The moral horror that you find in Eugene O'Neill. Horror's an emotion, not a genre, and I knew from an early age that what was scariest in *Rosemary's Baby* was not the devil, but Rosemary's betrayal by her husband, her whole world—for the most part a perfectly natural world—turning against her.

So when I started our horror line, I had every intention of *eventually* publishing more than stories about vampires and black magic. Those first horror comics I read, *Slow Death* in particular, were more concerned with the decay of society and humanity. Look at what we're doing to ourselves, our world, our children. We need all sorts of horror stories just to understand our own lives.

Milkman Murders trafficks in monstrosity with as much heart as the best of our monster books, and with far more persistence. Hellboy has never seen the likes of these nightmares. It's played broad, exaggerated, cartooned up for sure, but it's the real world this book is concerned with, and what the authors have to say about the real world—even about their own families—can't be written off as merely comic. Joe and Steve go deeper and deeper into what's wrong with these people, and I have to admit that when I saw where the story was heading, I flinched. When I read the script for chapter three, "What I'd Do for My Family," I took Joe to task. Was it just going to keep sliding downhill for these luckless bastards? Was there going to be any sense of redemption, any insight, any final humanity to this thing? The script so lacked artifice, was so unromantic, that I wasn't sure it was Art any longer. Steve liked it the way it was. We argued—I wanted an ending that would satisfy readers, characters with whom they could ultimately relate. I coughed up every cliché of genre writing, I'm sorry to say, trying to pull them closer to something conventional, something we'd seen before.

Joe never flinched, god bless him. We stuck with his ending, because I was dead wrong. There are enough stories out there following the conventional rules of reassuring us that it all ends well, that the world is ultimately knowable, and nurturing. That's what they're telling you when the monster is undone by a magic weed or a hero's undying love for his son.

Horror—the emotion of horror—thrives on mystery, and that kind of mystery provides no easy answers. Neither does this book.

Scott Allie
Horrified
November 2004

CHAPTER 1

"MEET THE VALE FAMILY..."

A MODERN SUBURBAN NIGHTMARE

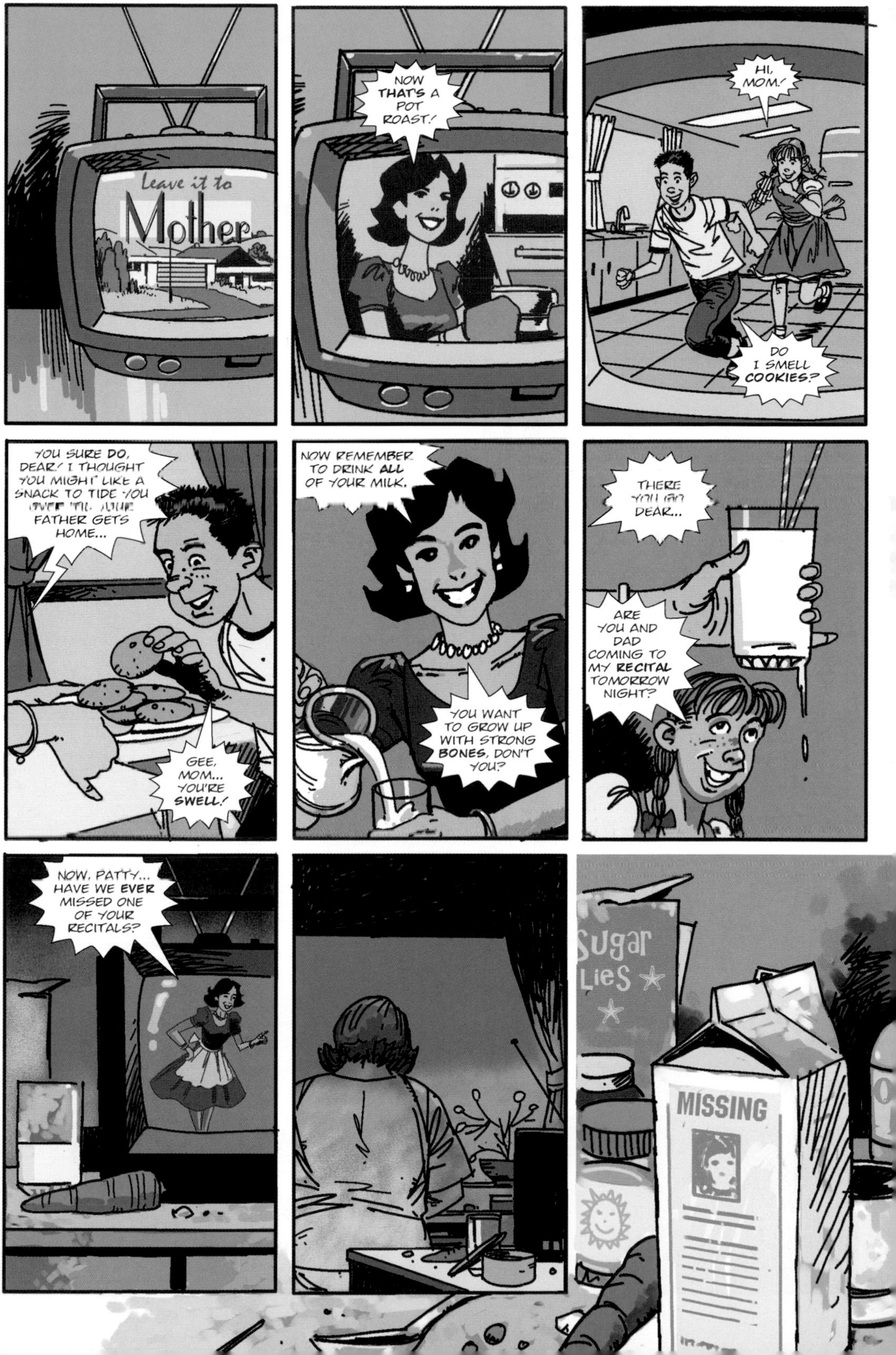

Leave it to Mother
NOW THAT'S A POT ROAST!
HI, MOM!
DO I SMELL COOKIES?
YOU SURE DO, DEAR! I THOUGHT YOU MIGHT LIKE A SNACK TO TIDE YOU
FATHER GETS HOME...
GEE, MOM... YOU'RE SWELL!
NOW REMEMBER TO DRINK ALL OF YOUR MILK.
YOU WANT TO GROW UP WITH STRONG BONES, DON'T YOU?
THERE YOU GO DEAR...
ARE YOU AND DAD COMING TO MY RECITAL TOMORROW NIGHT?
NOW, PATTY... HAVE WE EVER MISSED ONE OF YOUR RECITALS?
Sugar Lies
MISSING

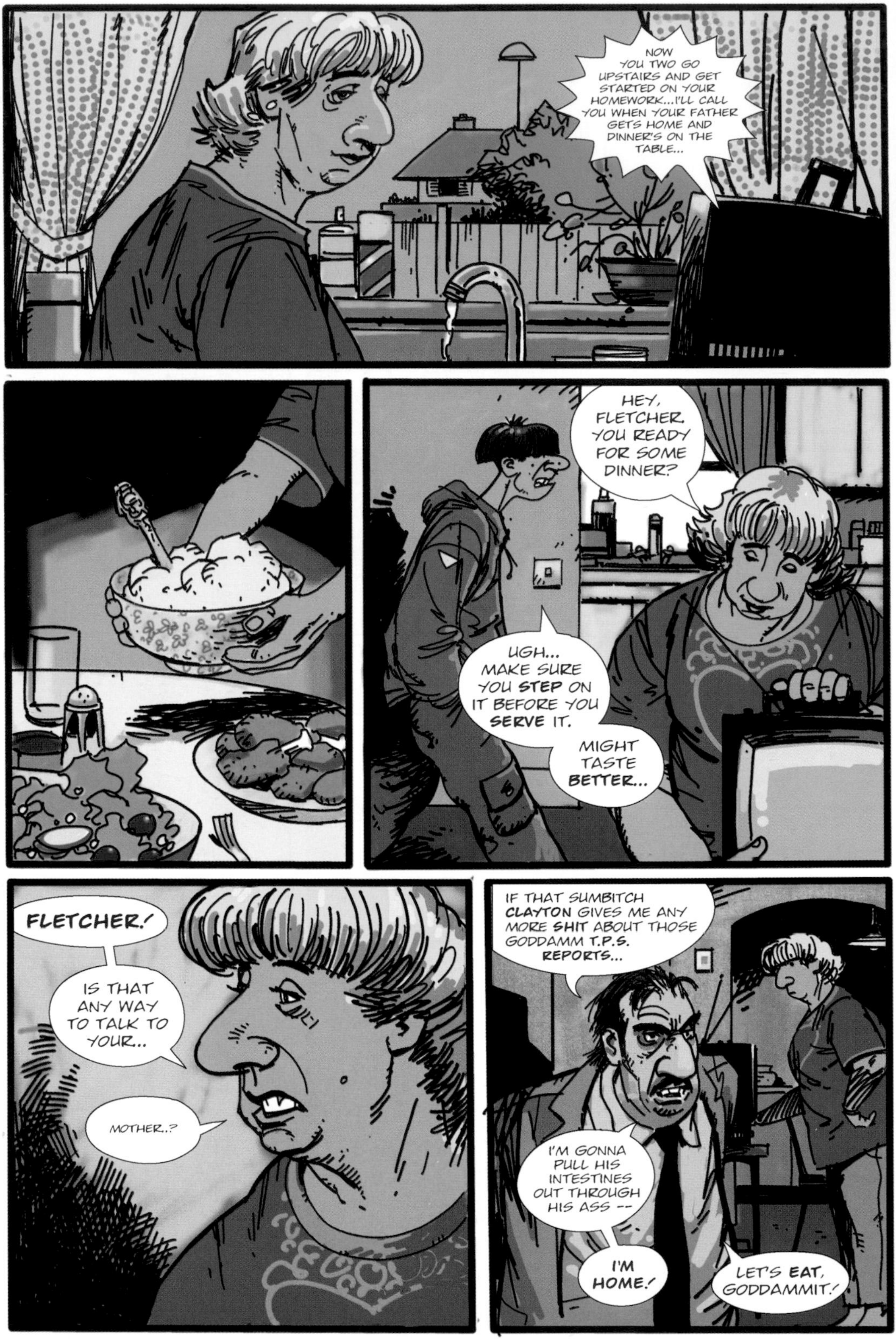
NOW YOU TWO GO UPSTAIRS AND GET STARTED ON YOUR HOMEWORK...I'LL CALL YOU WHEN YOUR FATHER GETS HOME AND DINNER'S ON THE TABLE...
HEY, FLETCHER. YOU READY FOR SOME DINNER?
UGH... MAKE SURE YOU STEP ON IT BEFORE YOU SERVE IT.
MIGHT TASTE BETTER...
FLETCHER!
IS THAT ANY WAY TO TALK TO YOUR...
MOTHER..?
IF THAT SUMBITCH CLAYTON GIVES ME ANY MORE SHIT ABOUT THOSE GODDAMM T.P.S. REPORTS...
I'M GONNA PULL HIS INTESTINES OUT THROUGH HIS ASS --
I'M HOME!
LET'S EAT, GODDAMMIT!

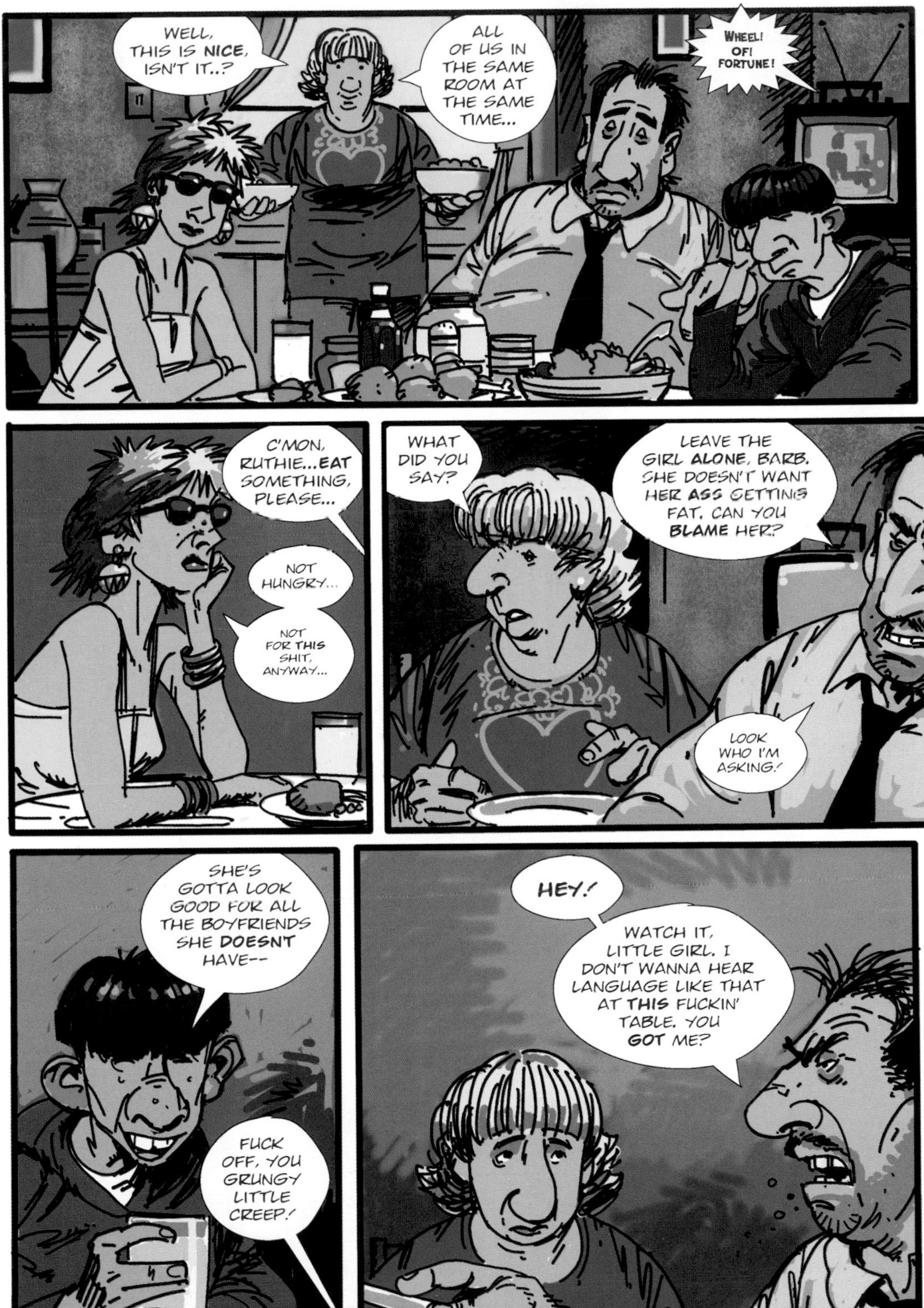
WELL, THIS IS **NICE**, ISN'T IT..?
ALL OF US IN THE SAME ROOM AT THE SAME TIME...
WHEEL! OF! FORTUNE!
C'MON, RUTHIE...**EAT** SOMETHING, PLEASE...
NOT HUNGRY...
NOT FOR **THIS** SHIT, ANYWAY...
WHAT DID YOU SAY?
LEAVE THE GIRL **ALONE**, BARB. SHE DOESN'T WANT HER **ASS** GETTING FAT. CAN YOU **BLAME** HER?
LOOK WHO I'M ASKING!
SHE'S GOTTA LOOK GOOD FOR ALL THE BOYFRIENDS SHE **DOESN'T** HAVE--
FUCK OFF, YOU GRUNGY LITTLE CREEP!
HEY!
WATCH IT, LITTLE GIRL. I DON'T WANNA HEAR LANGUAGE LIKE THAT AT **THIS** FUCKIN' TABLE. YOU **GOT** ME?

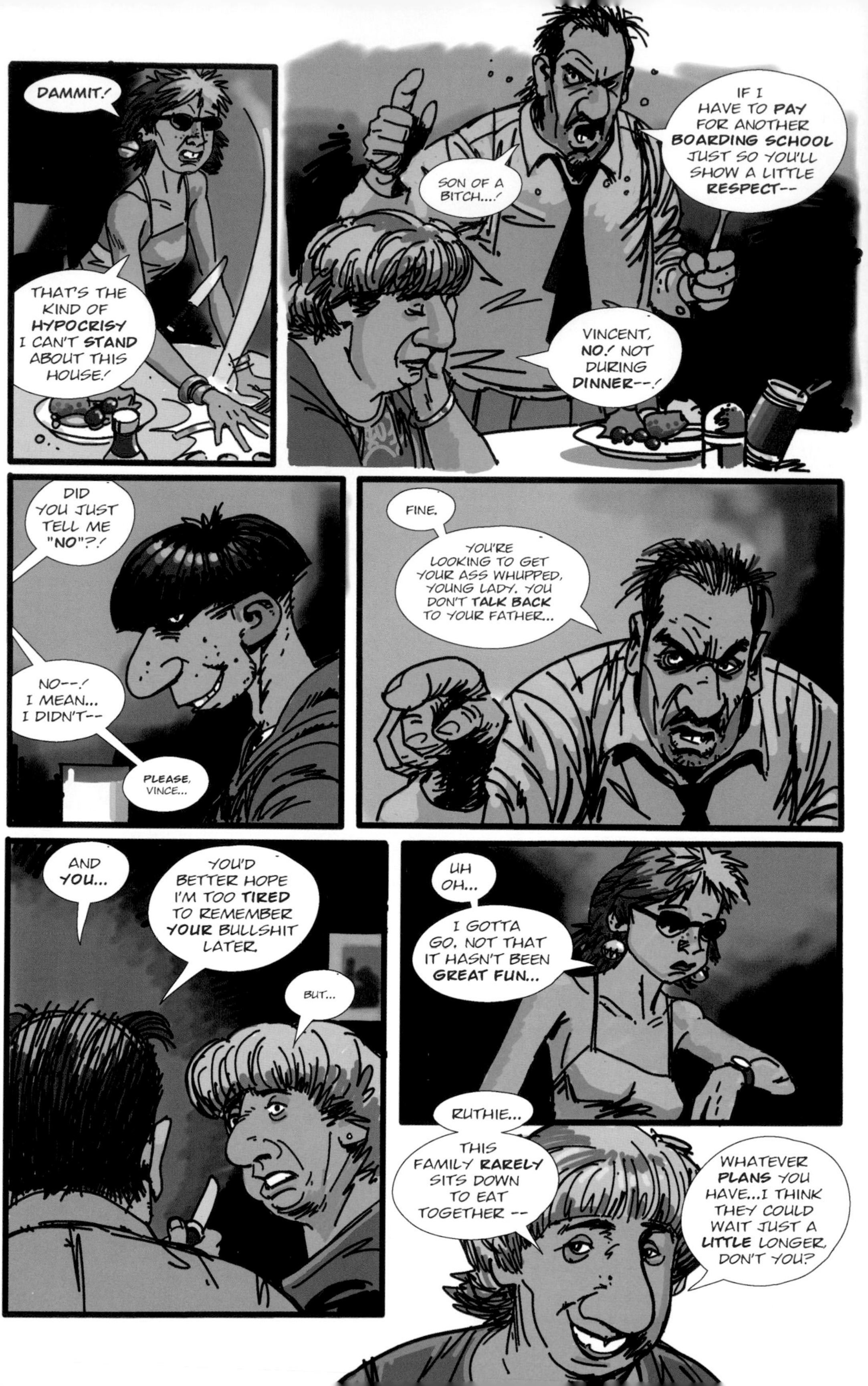
DAMMIT!
THAT'S THE KIND OF HYPOCRISY I CAN'T STAND ABOUT THIS HOUSE!
SON OF A BITCH...!
IF I HAVE TO PAY FOR ANOTHER BOARDING SCHOOL JUST SO YOU'LL SHOW A LITTLE RESPECT--
VINCENT, NO! NOT DURING DINNER--!
DID YOU JUST TELL ME "NO"?!
NO--! I MEAN... I DIDN'T--
PLEASE, VINCE...
FINE.
YOU'RE LOOKING TO GET YOUR ASS WHUPPED, YOUNG LADY. YOU DON'T TALK BACK TO YOUR FATHER...
AND YOU...
YOU'D BETTER HOPE I'M TOO TIRED TO REMEMBER YOUR BULLSHIT LATER.
BUT...
UH OH...
I GOTTA GO. NOT THAT IT HASN'T BEEN GREAT FUN...
RUTHIE...
THIS FAMILY RARELY SITS DOWN TO EAT TOGETHER --
WHATEVER PLANS YOU HAVE...I THINK THEY COULD WAIT JUST A LITTLE LONGER, DON'T YOU?

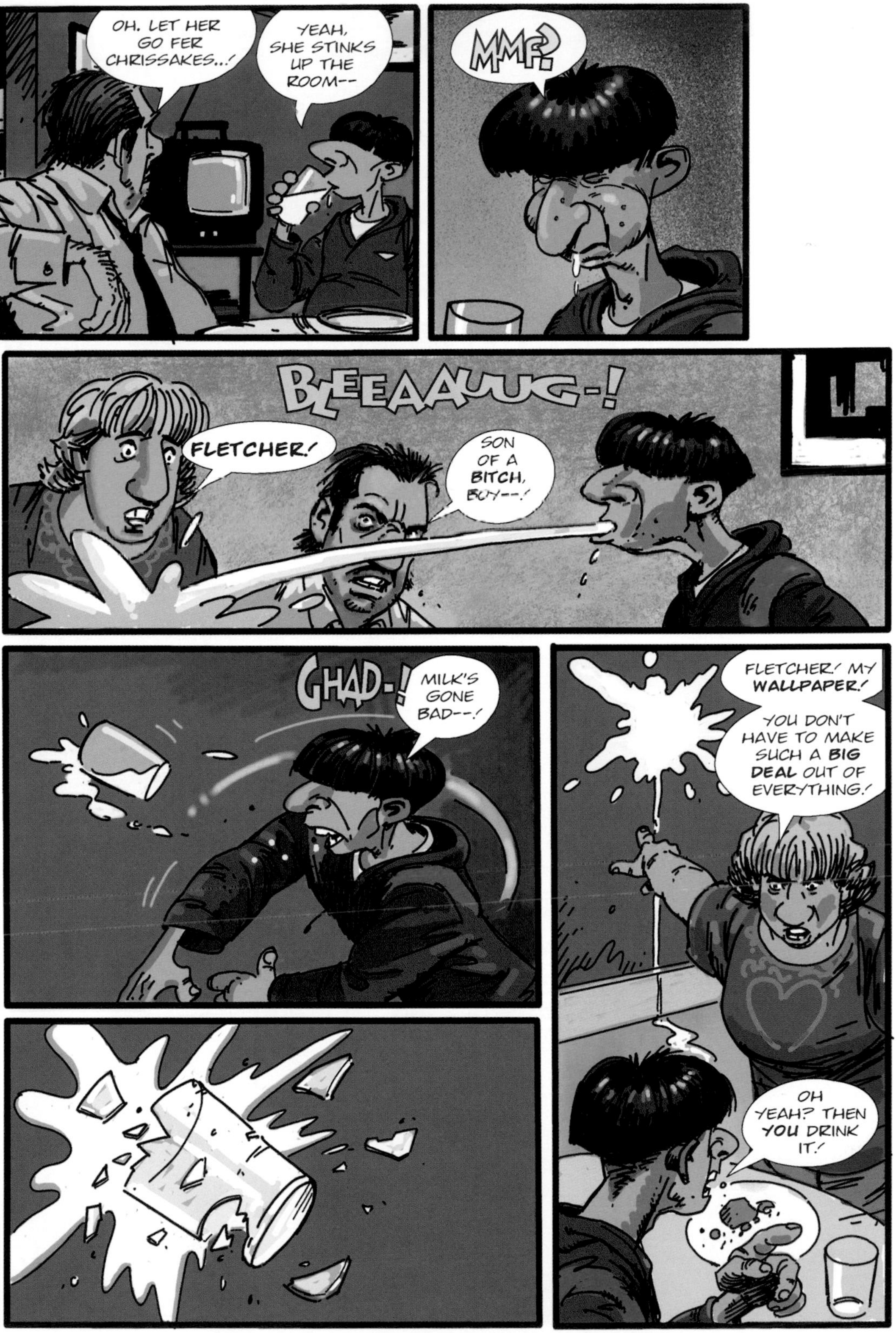
OH. LET HER GO FER CHRISSAKES...!
YEAH, SHE STINKS UP THE ROOM--
MMF?
BLEEAAUUG-!
FLETCHER!
SON OF A BITCH, BOY--!
GHAD-!
MILK'S GONE BAD--!
FLETCHER! MY WALLPAPER!
YOU DON'T HAVE TO MAKE SUCH A BIG DEAL OUT OF EVERYTHING!
OH YEAH? THEN YOU DRINK IT!

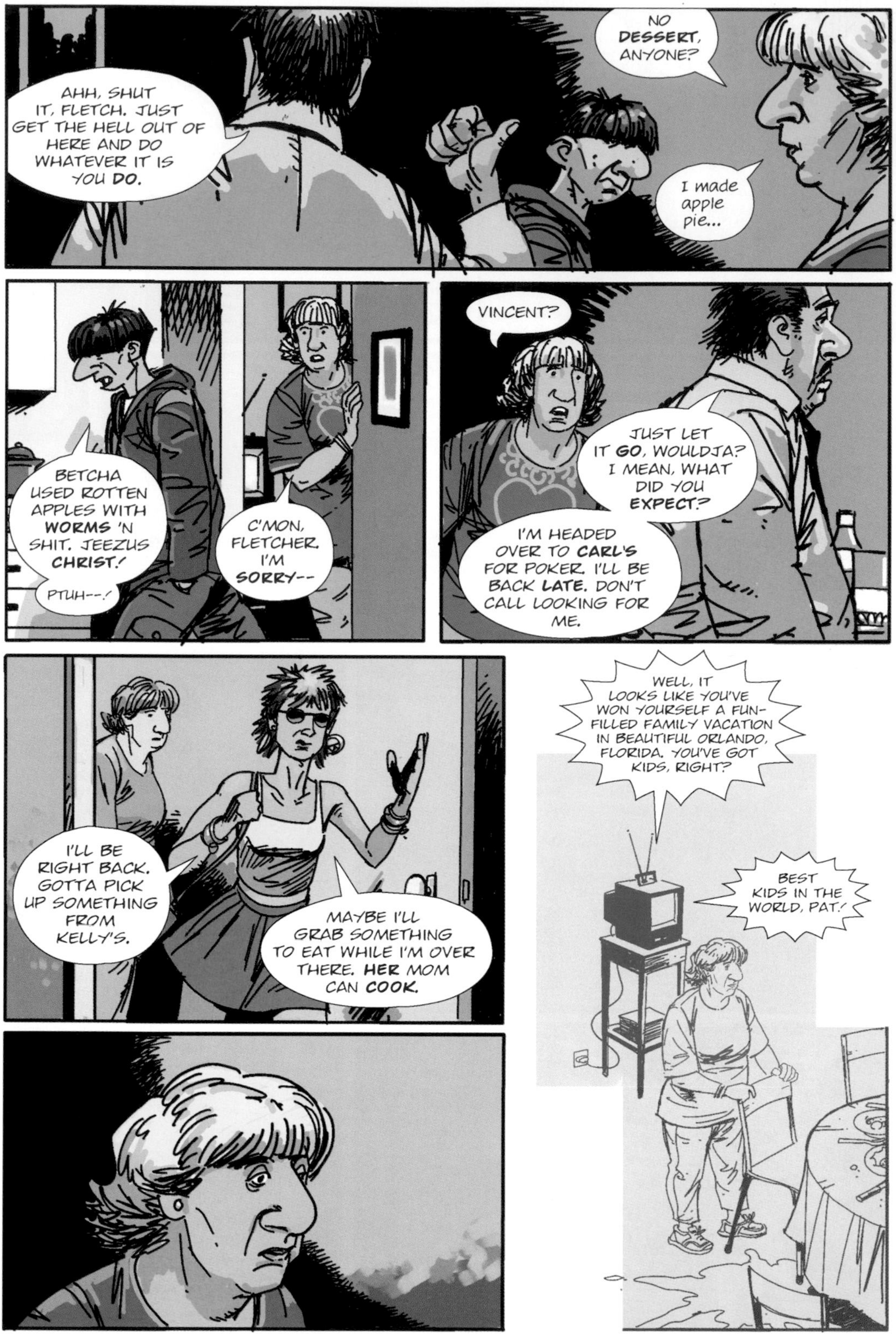

AHH, SHUT IT, FLETCH. JUST GET THE HELL OUT OF HERE AND DO WHATEVER IT IS YOU DO.
NO DESSERT, ANYONE?
I made apple pie...
BETCHA USED ROTTEN APPLES WITH WORMS 'N SHIT. JEEZUS CHRIST!
PTUH--!
C'MON, FLETCHER. I'M SORRY--
VINCENT?
JUST LET IT GO, WOULDJA? I MEAN, WHAT DID YOU EXPECT?
I'M HEADED OVER TO CARL'S FOR POKER. I'LL BE BACK LATE. DON'T CALL LOOKING FOR ME.
I'LL BE RIGHT BACK. GOTTA PICK UP SOMETHING FROM KELLY'S.
MAYBE I'LL GRAB SOMETHING TO EAT WHILE I'M OVER THERE. HER MOM CAN COOK.
WELL, IT LOOKS LIKE YOU'VE WON YOURSELF A FUN-FILLED FAMILY VACATION IN BEAUTIFUL ORLANDO, FLORIDA. YOU'VE GOT KIDS, RIGHT?
BEST KIDS IN THE WORLD, PAT!

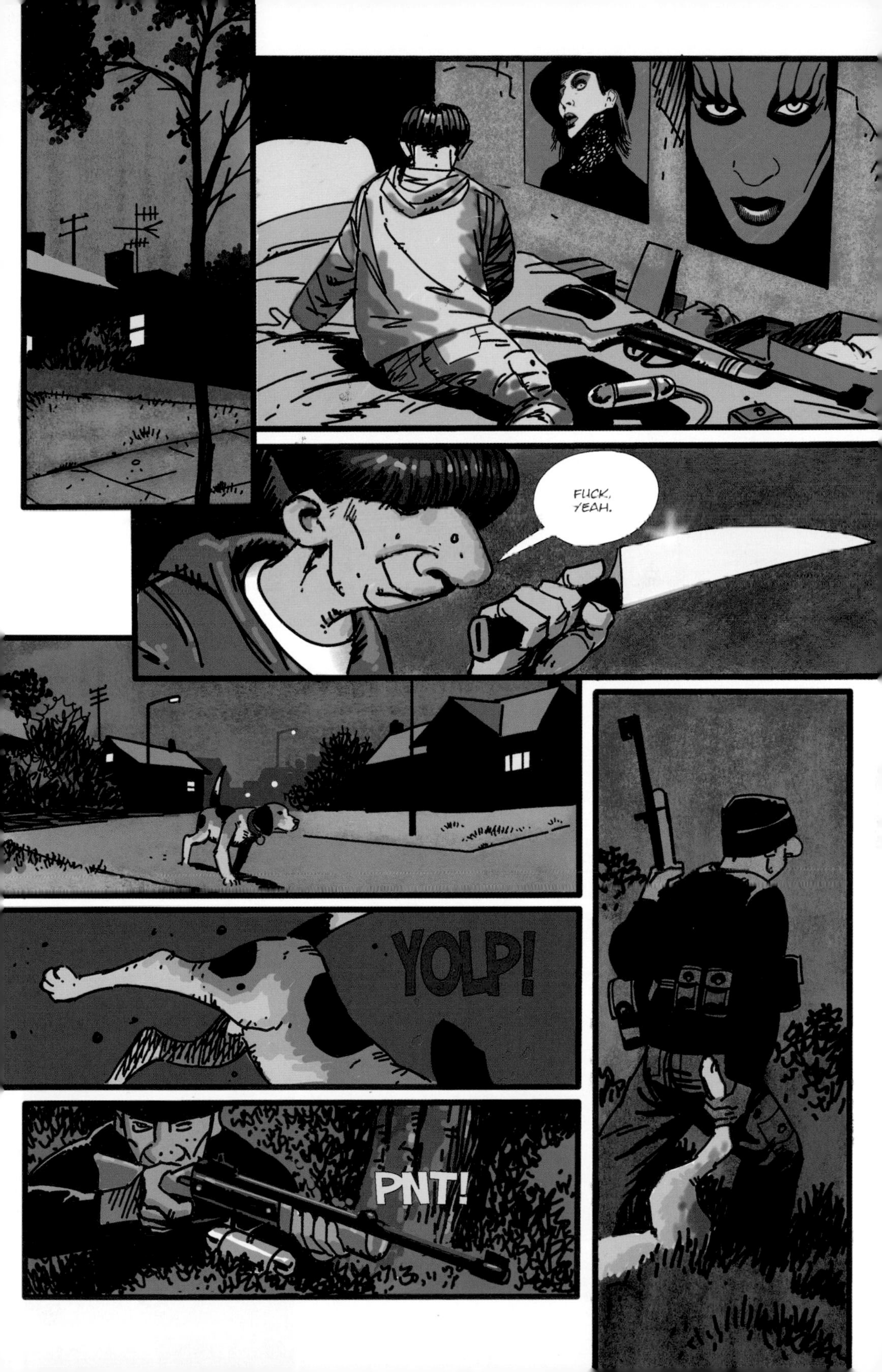
FUCK, YEAH.
YOLP!
PNT!

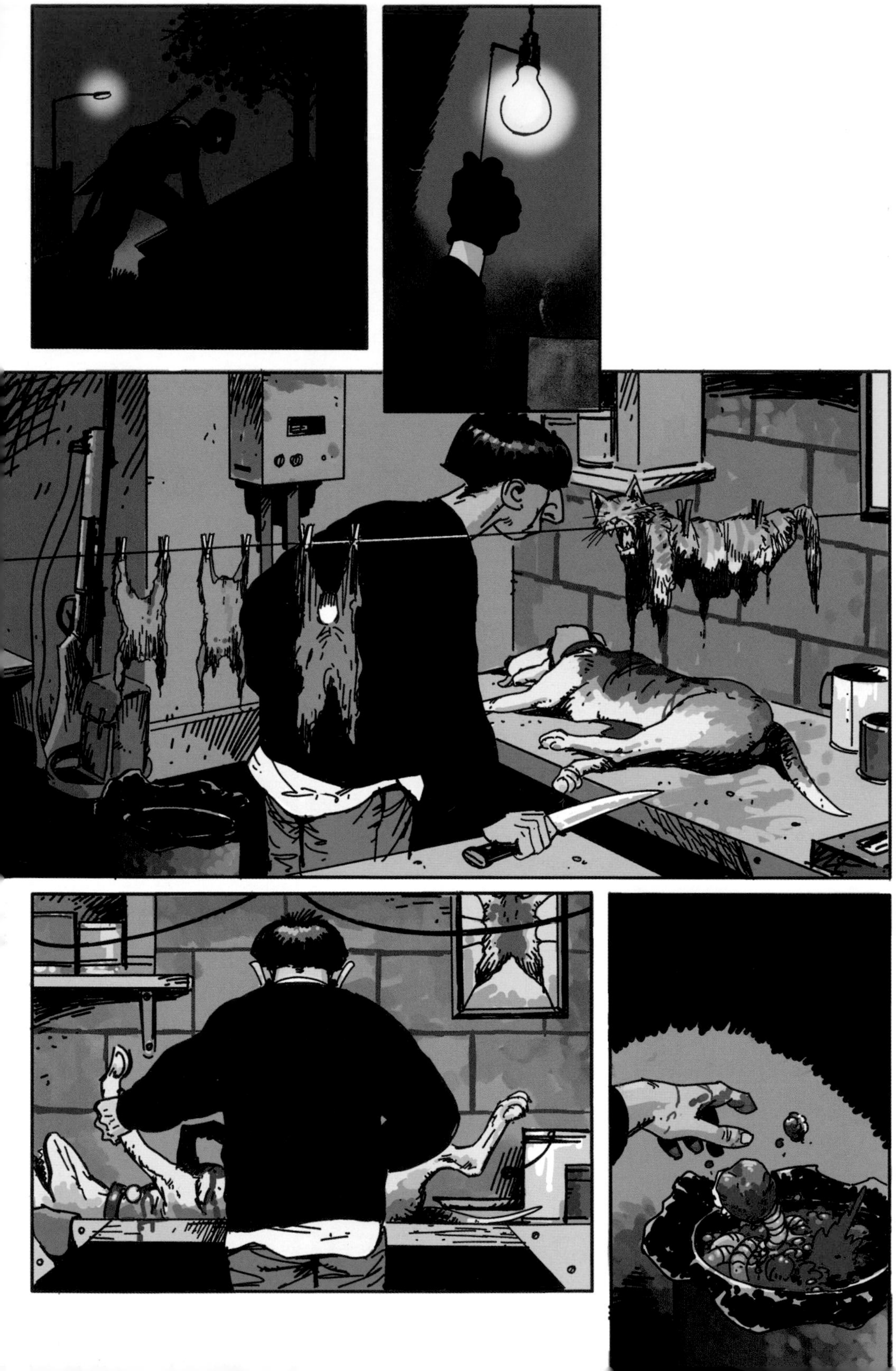

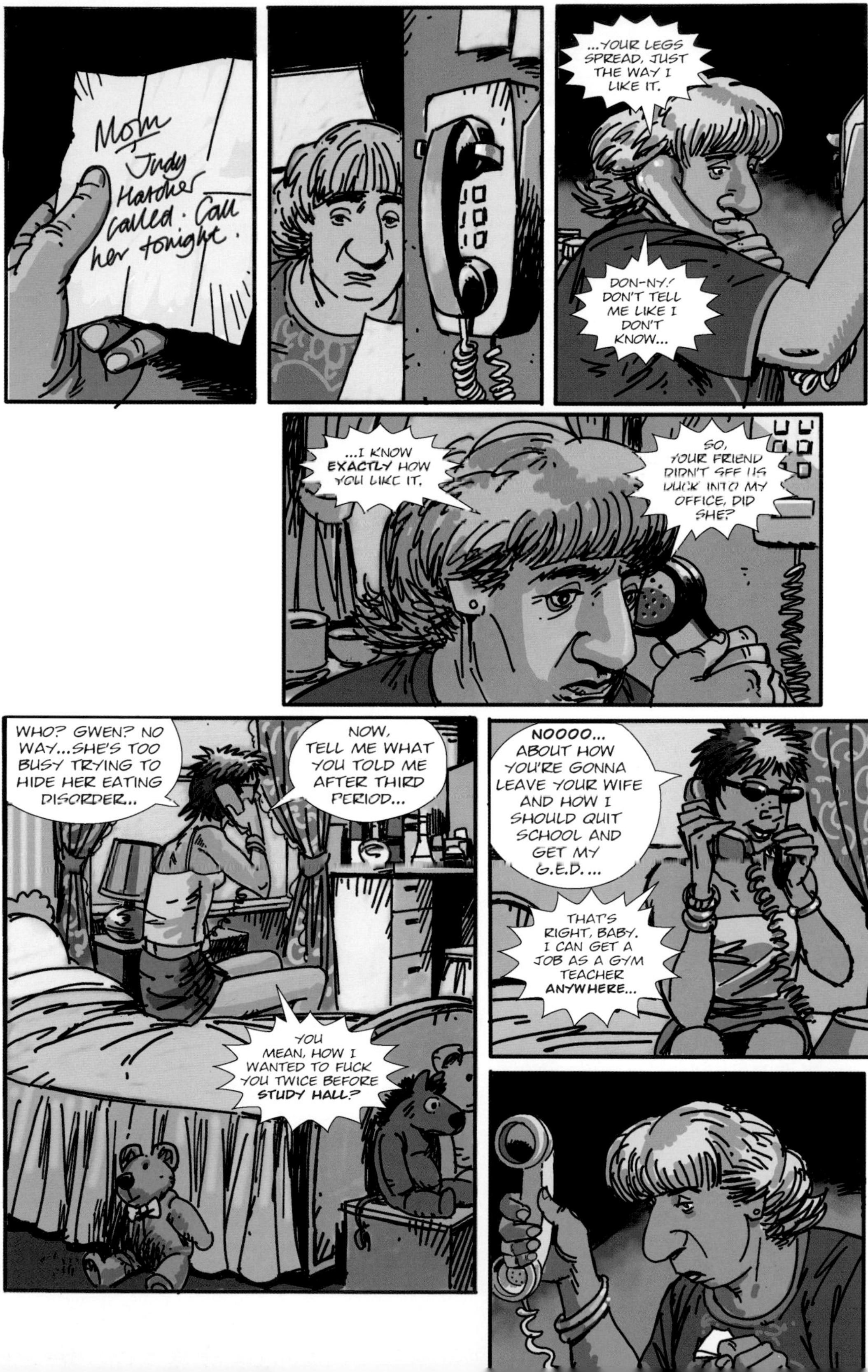
Mom,
Judy Hatcher called. Call her tonight.
...YOUR LEGS SPREAD, JUST THE WAY I LIKE IT.
DON-NY! DON'T TELL ME LIKE I DON'T KNOW...
...I KNOW **EXACTLY** HOW YOU LIKE IT.
SO, YOUR FRIEND DIDN'T SEE US DUCK INTO MY OFFICE, DID SHE?
WHO? GWEN? NO WAY...SHE'S TOO BUSY TRYING TO HIDE HER EATING DISORDER...
NOW, TELL ME WHAT YOU TOLD ME AFTER THIRD PERIOD...
YOU MEAN, HOW I WANTED TO FUCK YOU TWICE BEFORE **STUDY HALL?**
NOOOO... ABOUT HOW YOU'RE GONNA LEAVE YOUR WIFE AND HOW I SHOULD QUIT SCHOOL AND GET MY G.E.D....
THAT'S RIGHT, BABY. I CAN GET A JOB AS A GYM TEACHER **ANYWHERE...**

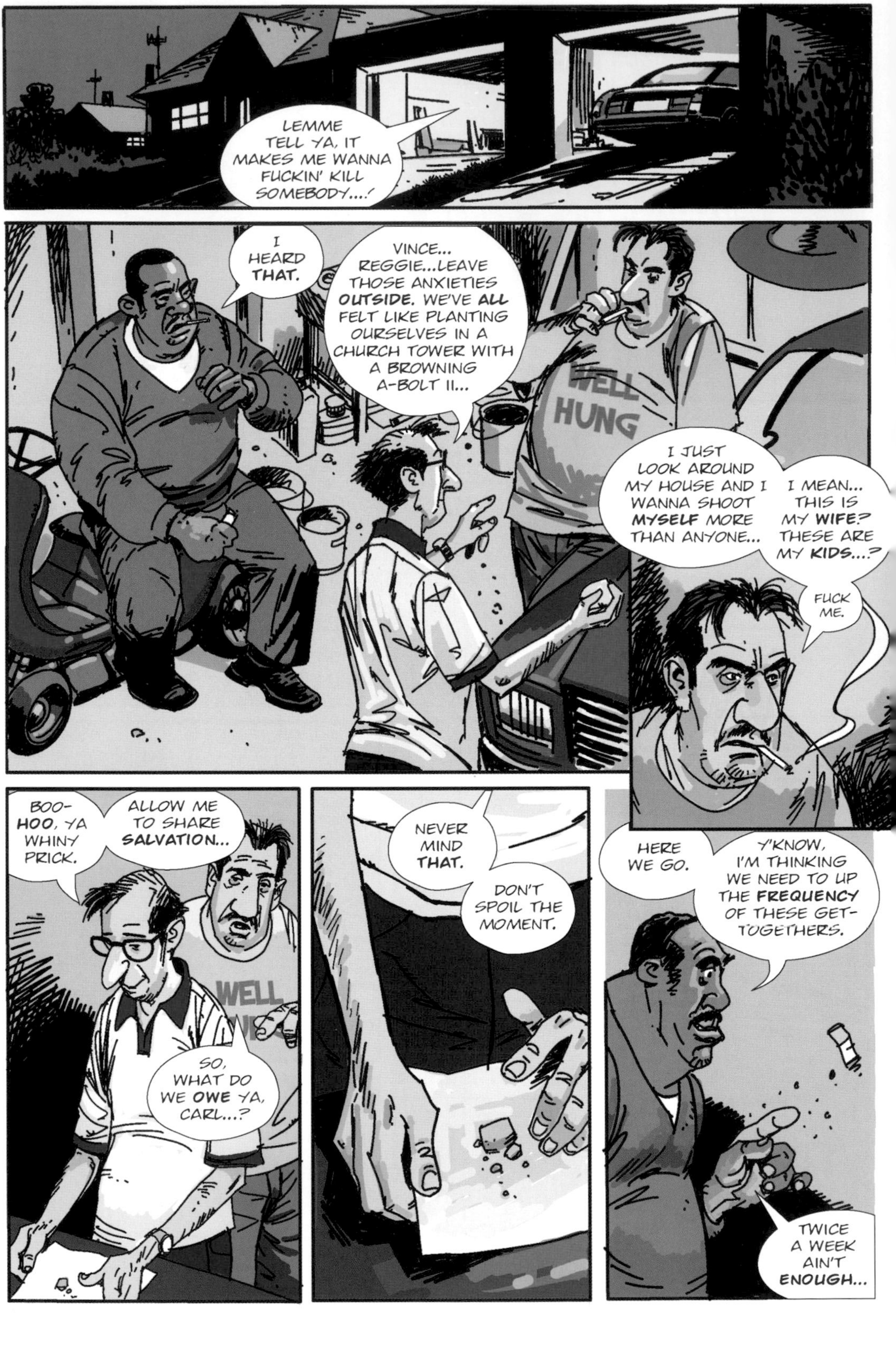

LEMME TELL YA, IT MAKES ME WANNA FUCKIN' KILL SOMEBODY...!
I HEARD **THAT.**
VINCE... REGGIE...LEAVE THOSE ANXIETIES **OUTSIDE.** WE'VE **ALL** FELT LIKE PLANTING OURSELVES IN A CHURCH TOWER WITH A BROWNING A-BOLT II...
I JUST LOOK AROUND MY HOUSE AND I WANNA SHOOT **MYSELF** MORE THAN ANYONE...
I MEAN... THIS IS MY **WIFE**? THESE ARE MY **KIDS**...?
FUCK ME.
BOO-**HOO**, YA WHINY PRICK.
ALLOW ME TO SHARE **SALVATION...**
SO, WHAT DO WE **OWE** YA, CARL...?
NEVER MIND **THAT.**
DON'T SPOIL THE MOMENT.
HERE WE GO.
Y'KNOW, I'M THINKING WE NEED TO UP THE **FREQUENCY** OF THESE GET-TOGETHERS.
TWICE A WEEK AIN'T **ENOUGH...**

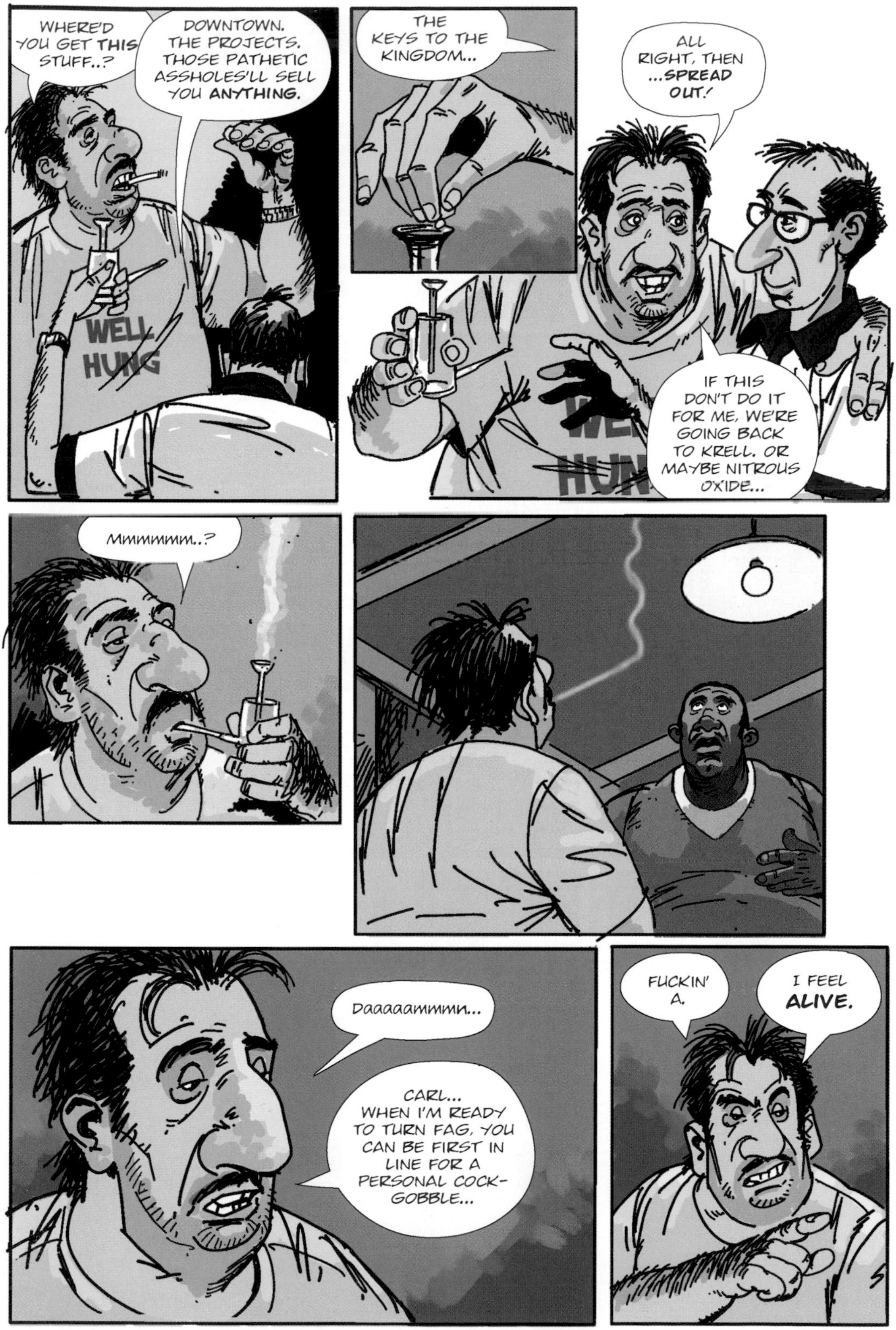
WHERE'D YOU GET THIS STUFF..?
DOWNTOWN. THE PROJECTS. THOSE PATHETIC ASSHOLES'LL SELL YOU ANYTHING.
WELL HUNG
THE KEYS TO THE KINGDOM...
ALL RIGHT, THEN ...SPREAD OUT!
IF THIS DON'T DO IT FOR ME, WE'RE GOING BACK TO KRELL. OR MAYBE NITROUS OXIDE...
Mmmmmm..?
Daaaaammmn...
CARL... WHEN I'M READY TO TURN FAG, YOU CAN BE FIRST IN LINE FOR A PERSONAL COCK-GOBBLE...
FUCKIN' A.
I FEEL ALIVE.

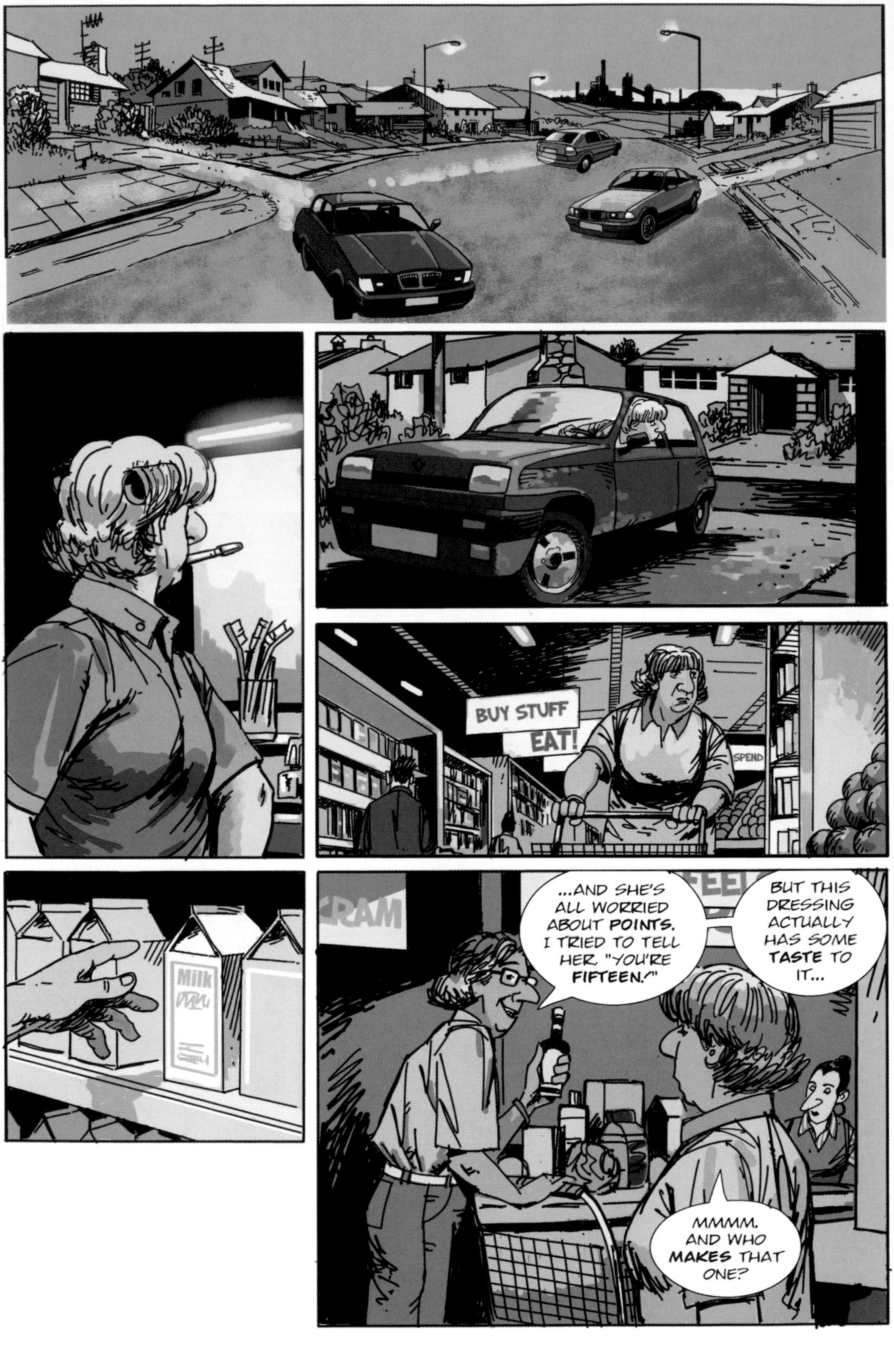

BUY STUFF
EAT!
SPEND
Milk
KRAM
...AND SHE'S ALL WORRIED ABOUT **POINTS.** I TRIED TO TELL HER, "YOU'RE **FIFTEEN.**"
BUT THIS DRESSING ACTUALLY HAS SOME **TASTE** TO IT...
MMMM. AND WHO **MAKES** THAT ONE?

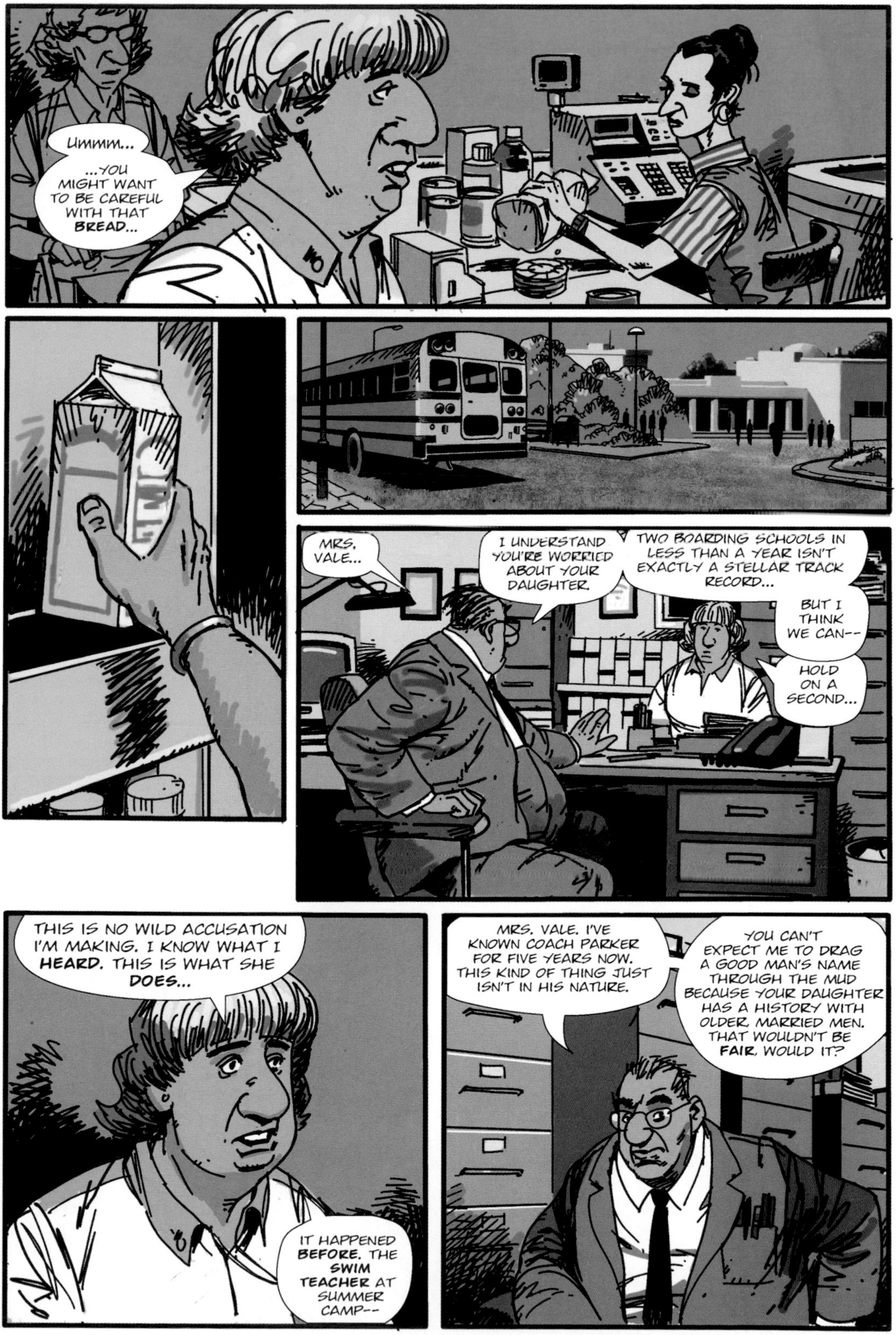
UMMM...
...YOU MIGHT WANT TO BE CAREFUL WITH THAT BREAD...
MRS. VALE...
I UNDERSTAND YOU'RE WORRIED ABOUT YOUR DAUGHTER.
TWO BOARDING SCHOOLS IN LESS THAN A YEAR ISN'T EXACTLY A STELLAR TRACK RECORD...
BUT I THINK WE CAN--
HOLD ON A SECOND...
THIS IS NO WILD ACCUSATION I'M MAKING. I KNOW WHAT I HEARD. THIS IS WHAT SHE DOES...
IT HAPPENED BEFORE. THE SWIM TEACHER AT SUMMER CAMP--
MRS. VALE. I'VE KNOWN COACH PARKER FOR FIVE YEARS NOW. THIS KIND OF THING JUST ISN'T IN HIS NATURE.
YOU CAN'T EXPECT ME TO DRAG A GOOD MAN'S NAME THROUGH THE MUD BECAUSE YOUR DAUGHTER HAS A HISTORY WITH OLDER, MARRIED MEN. THAT WOULDN'T BE FAIR, WOULD IT?

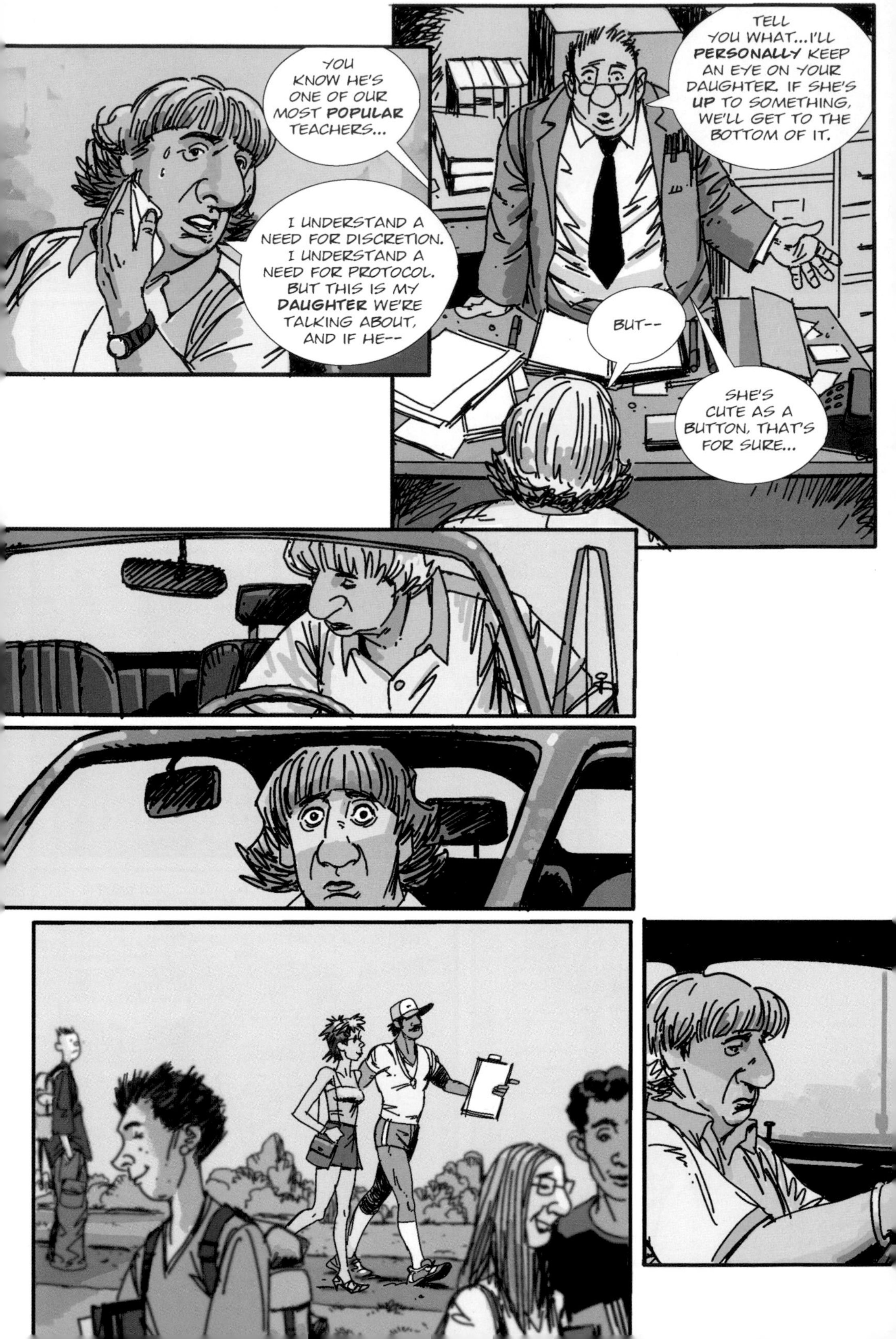
YOU KNOW HE'S ONE OF OUR MOST **POPULAR** TEACHERS...
I UNDERSTAND A NEED FOR DISCRETION. I UNDERSTAND A NEED FOR PROTOCOL. BUT THIS IS MY **DAUGHTER** WE'RE TALKING ABOUT, AND IF HE--
TELL YOU WHAT...I'LL **PERSONALLY** KEEP AN EYE ON YOUR DAUGHTER. IF SHE'S **UP** TO SOMETHING, WE'LL GET TO THE BOTTOM OF IT.
BUT--
SHE'S CUTE AS A BUTTON, THAT'S FOR SURE...

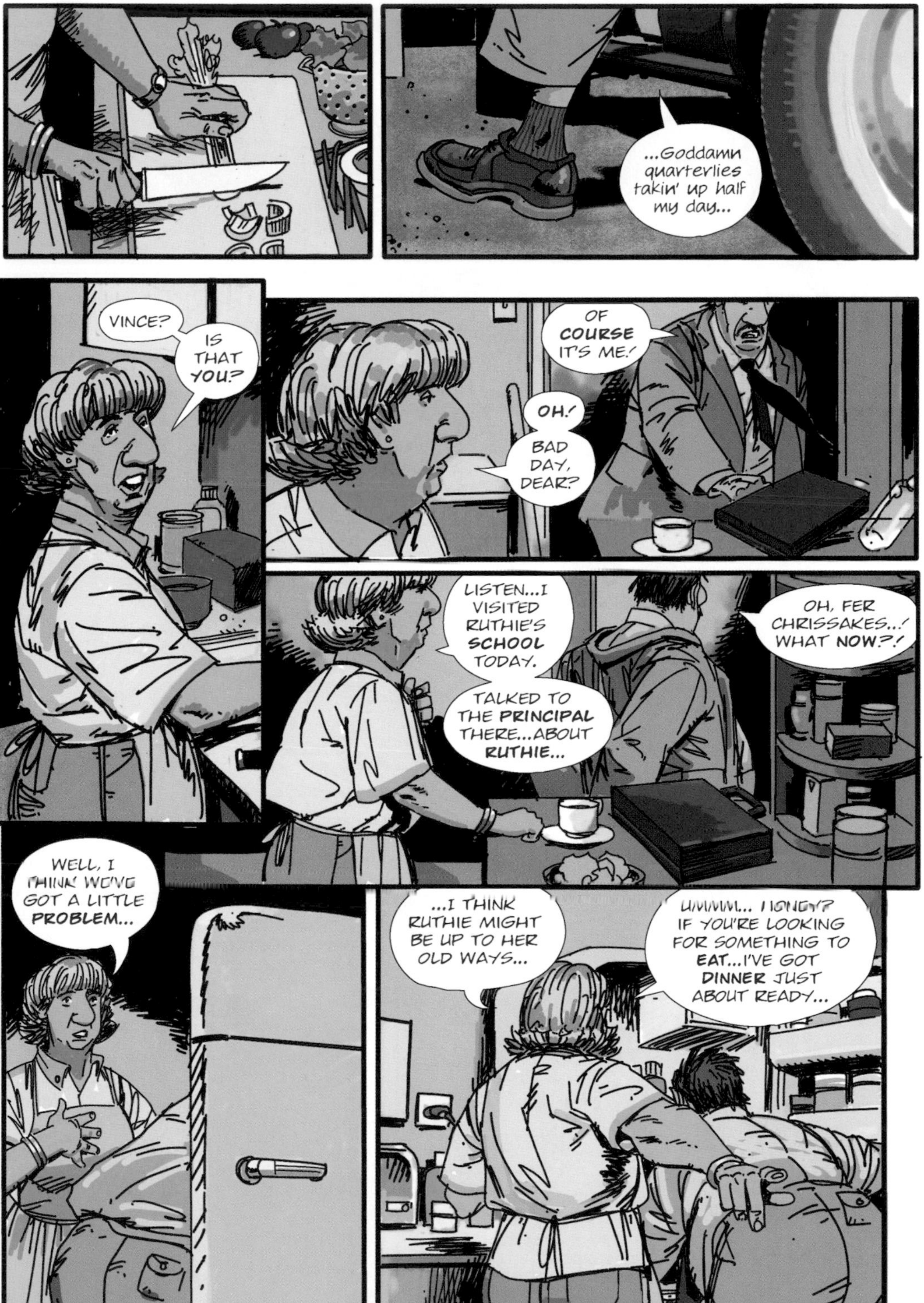
...Goddamn quarterlies takin' up half my day...
VINCE?
IS THAT YOU?
OF COURSE IT'S ME!
OH!
BAD DAY, DEAR?
LISTEN...I VISITED RUTHIE'S SCHOOL TODAY.
TALKED TO THE PRINCIPAL THERE...ABOUT RUTHIE...
OH, FER CHRISSAKES...! WHAT NOW?!
WELL, I THINK WE'VE GOT A LITTLE PROBLEM...
...I THINK RUTHIE MIGHT BE UP TO HER OLD WAYS...
UMMM... HONEY? IF YOU'RE LOOKING FOR SOMETHING TO EAT...I'VE GOT DINNER JUST ABOUT READY...

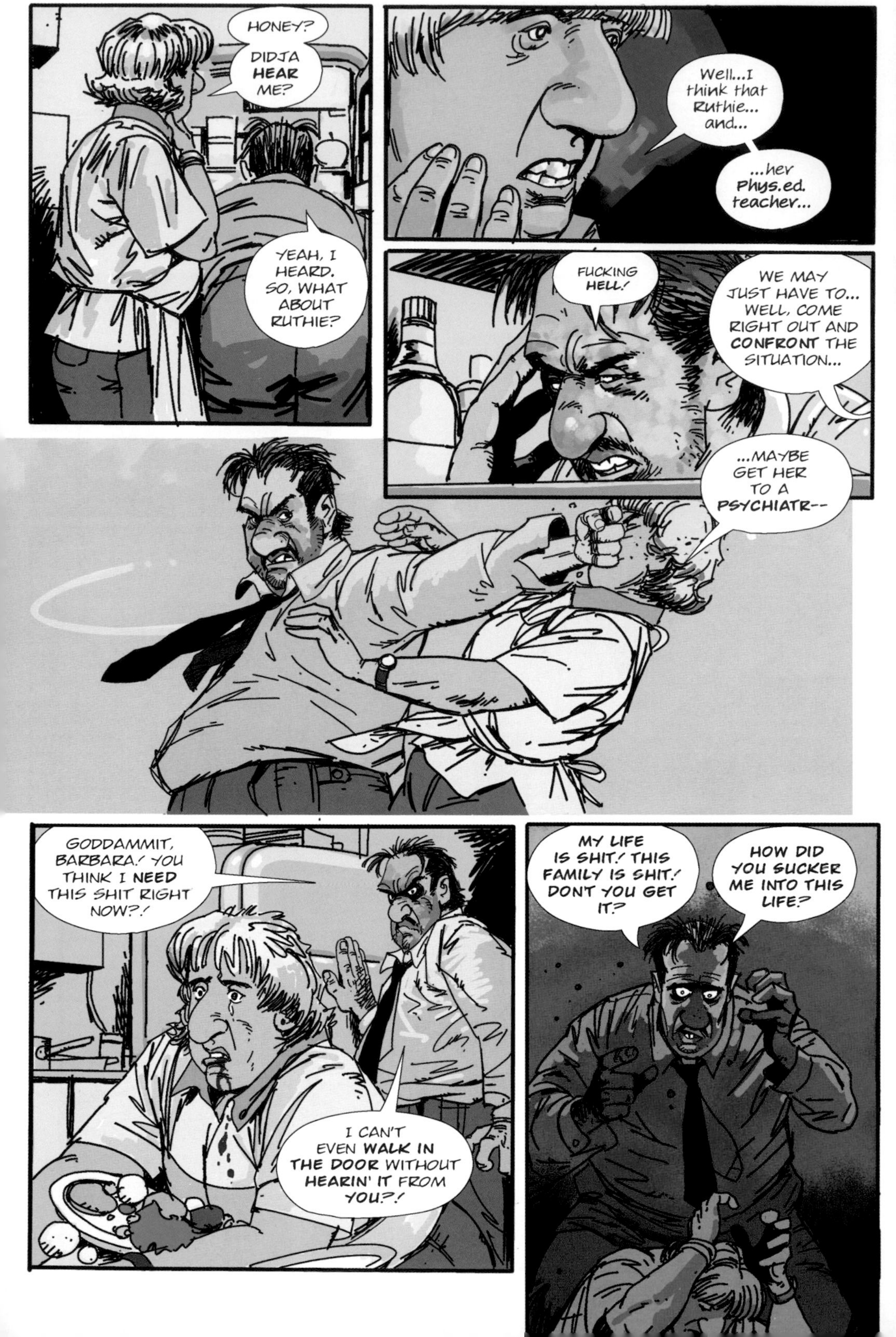
HONEY?
DIDJA HEAR ME?
YEAH, I HEARD. SO, WHAT ABOUT RUTHIE?
Well...I think that Ruthie... and...
...her Phys.ed. teacher...
FUCKING HELL!
WE MAY JUST HAVE TO... WELL, COME RIGHT OUT AND CONFRONT THE SITUATION...
...MAYBE GET HER TO A PSYCHIATR--
GODDAMMIT, BARBARA! YOU THINK I NEED THIS SHIT RIGHT NOW?!
I CAN'T EVEN WALK IN THE DOOR WITHOUT HEARIN' IT FROM YOU?!
MY LIFE IS SHIT! THIS FAMILY IS SHIT! DON'T YOU GET IT?
HOW DID YOU SUCKER ME INTO THIS LIFE?

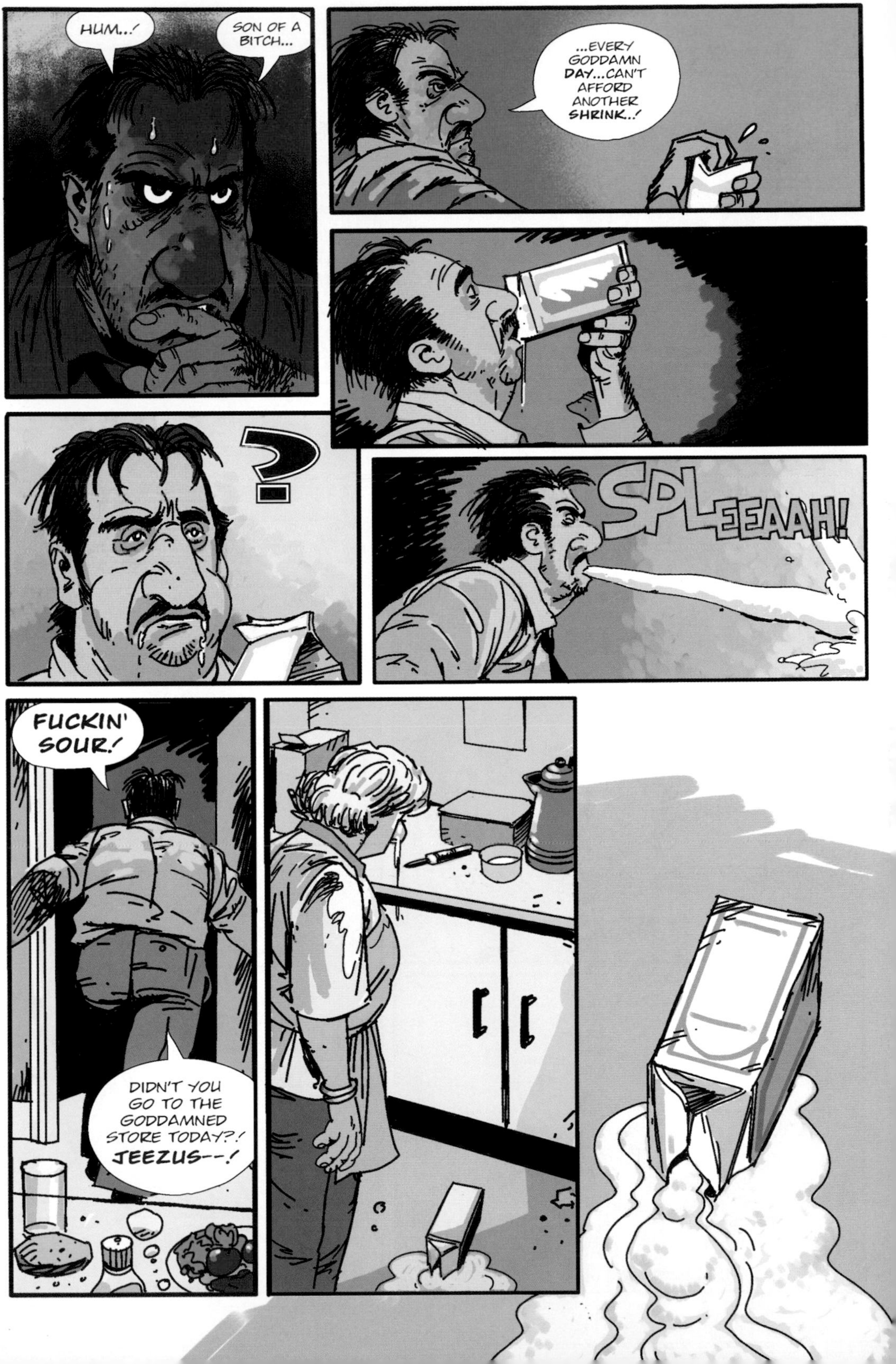
HUM...!
SON OF A BITCH...
...EVERY GODDAMN DAY...CAN'T AFFORD ANOTHER SHRINK..!
?
SPLEEAAH!
FUCKIN' SOUR!
DIDN'T YOU GO TO THE GODDAMNED STORE TODAY?! JEEZUS--!

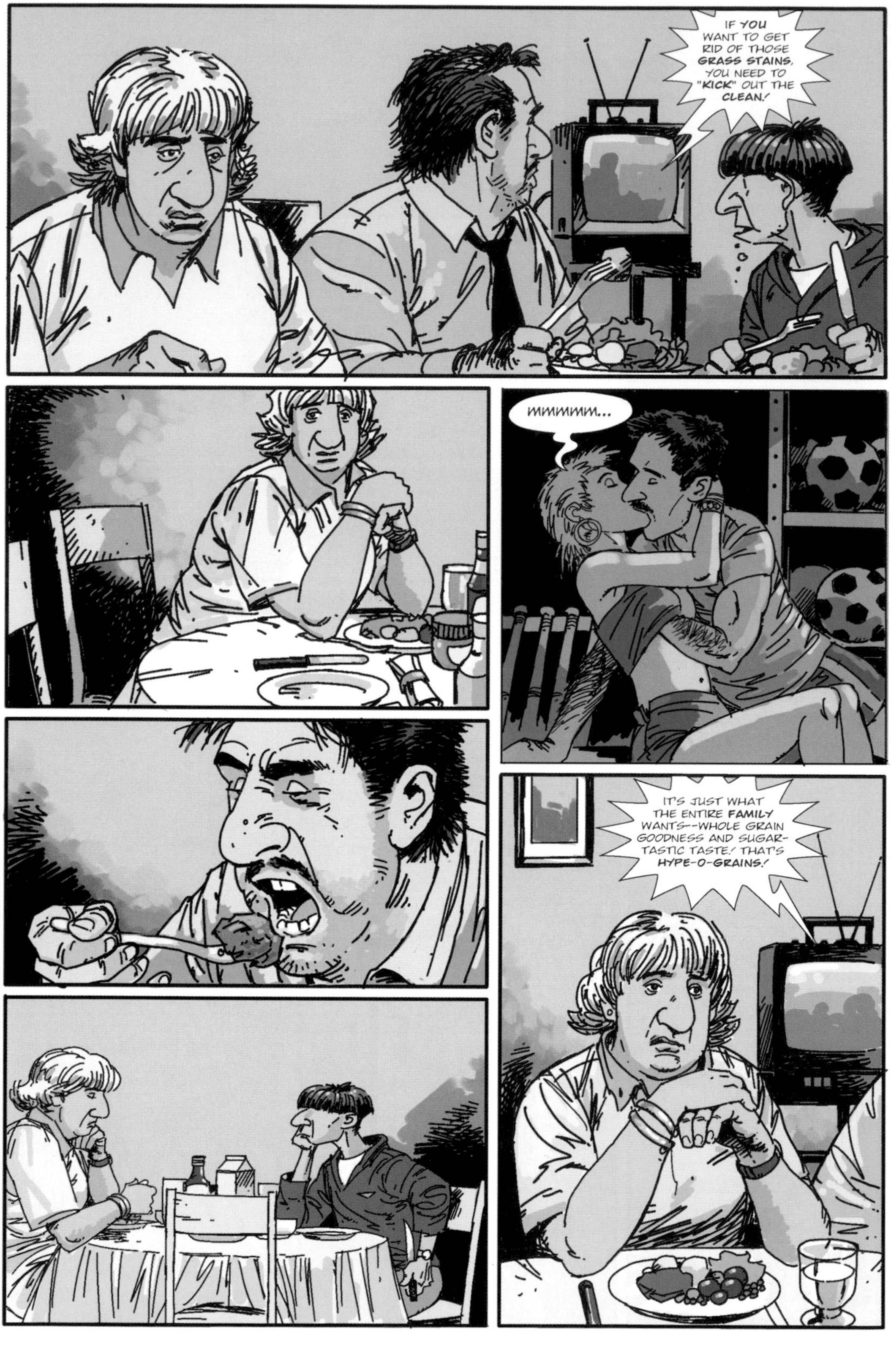
IF YOU WANT TO GET RID OF THOSE GRASS STAINS, YOU NEED TO "KICK" OUT THE CLEAN!
MMMMMM...
IT'S JUST WHAT THE ENTIRE FAMILY WANTS--WHOLE GRAIN GOODNESS AND SUGAR-TASTIC TASTE! THAT'S HYPE-O-GRAINS!

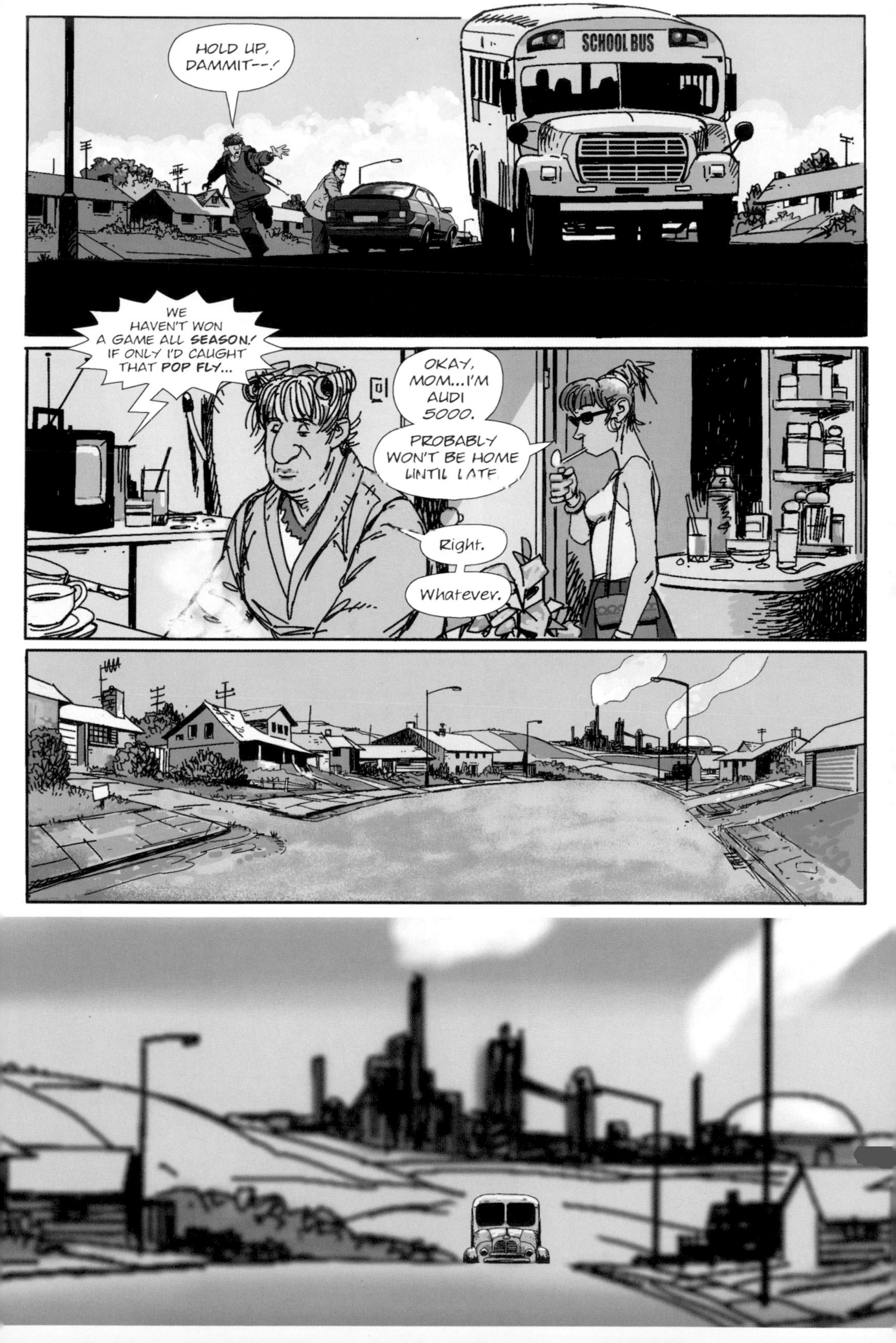

HOLD UP, DAMMIT--!
SCHOOL BUS
WE HAVEN'T WON A GAME ALL **SEASON**! IF ONLY I'D CAUGHT THAT **POP FLY**...
OKAY, MOM...I'M AUDI 5000.
PROBABLY WON'T BE HOME UNTIL LATE.
Right.
Whatever.

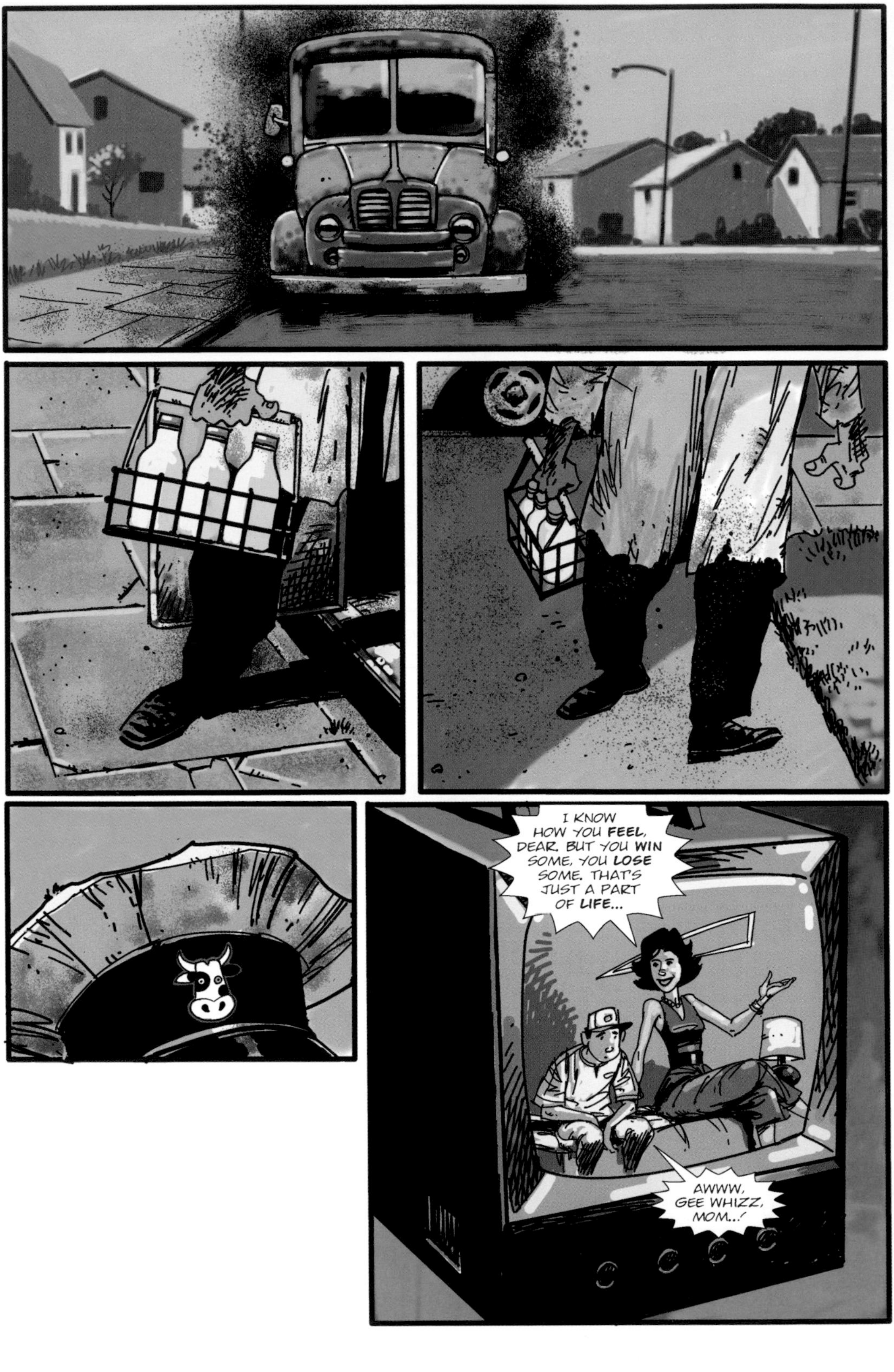
I KNOW HOW YOU **FEEL**, DEAR. BUT YOU **WIN** SOME, YOU **LOSE** SOME. THAT'S JUST A PART OF **LIFE**...
AWWW, GEE WHIZZ, MOM..!

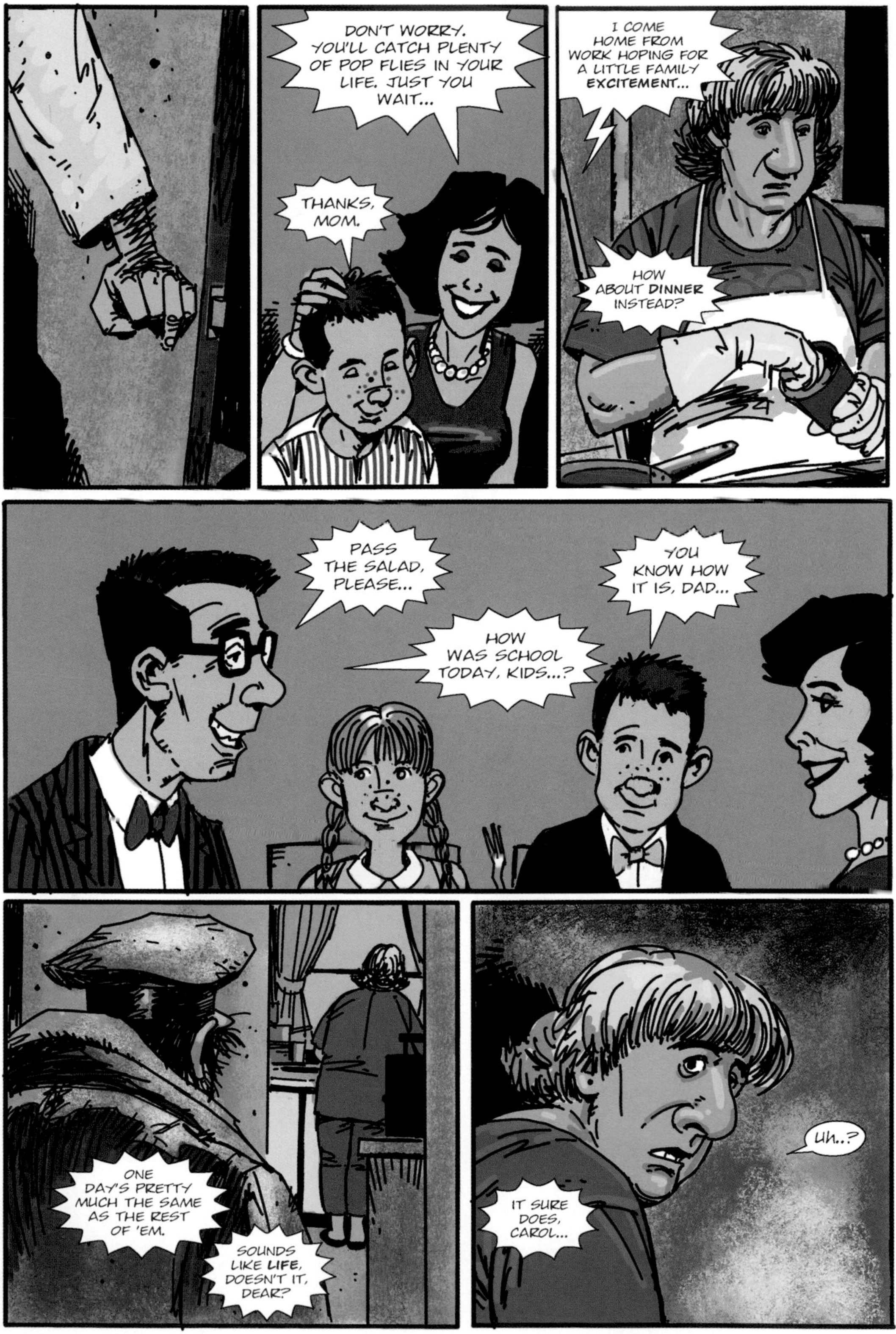
DON'T WORRY. YOU'LL CATCH PLENTY OF POP FLIES IN YOUR LIFE. JUST YOU WAIT...
THANKS, MOM.
I COME HOME FROM WORK HOPING FOR A LITTLE FAMILY **EXCITEMENT**...
HOW ABOUT **DINNER** INSTEAD?
PASS THE SALAD, PLEASE...
HOW WAS SCHOOL TODAY, KIDS...?
YOU KNOW HOW IT IS, DAD...
ONE DAY'S PRETTY MUCH THE SAME AS THE REST OF 'EM.
SOUNDS LIKE **LIFE**, DOESN'T IT, DEAR?
UH..?
IT SURE DOES, CAROL...

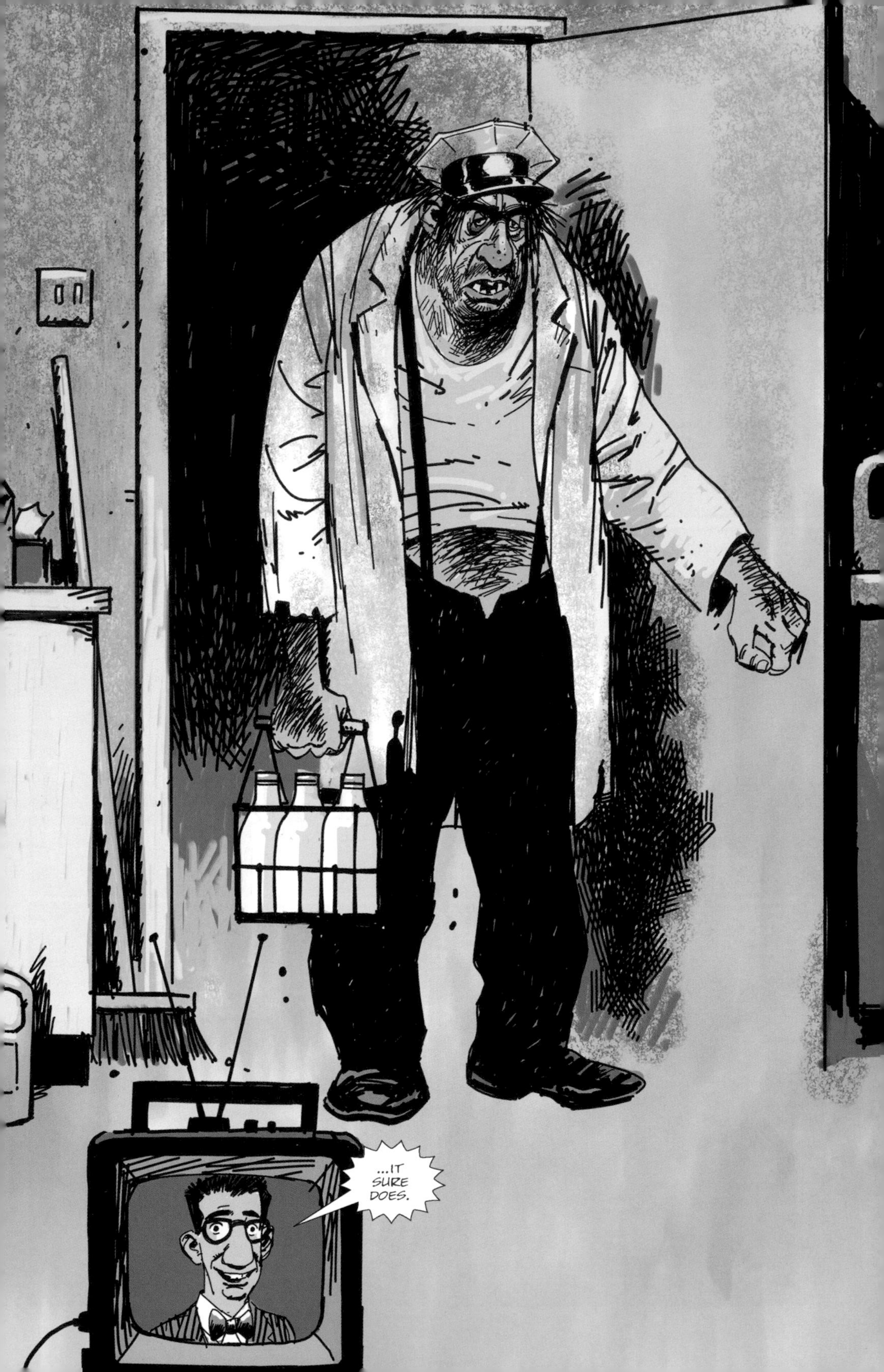
...IT SURE DOES.

CHAPTER 2

"DEEPER, HARDER, FASTER"

THE DARK SIDE OF THE AMERICAN DREAM

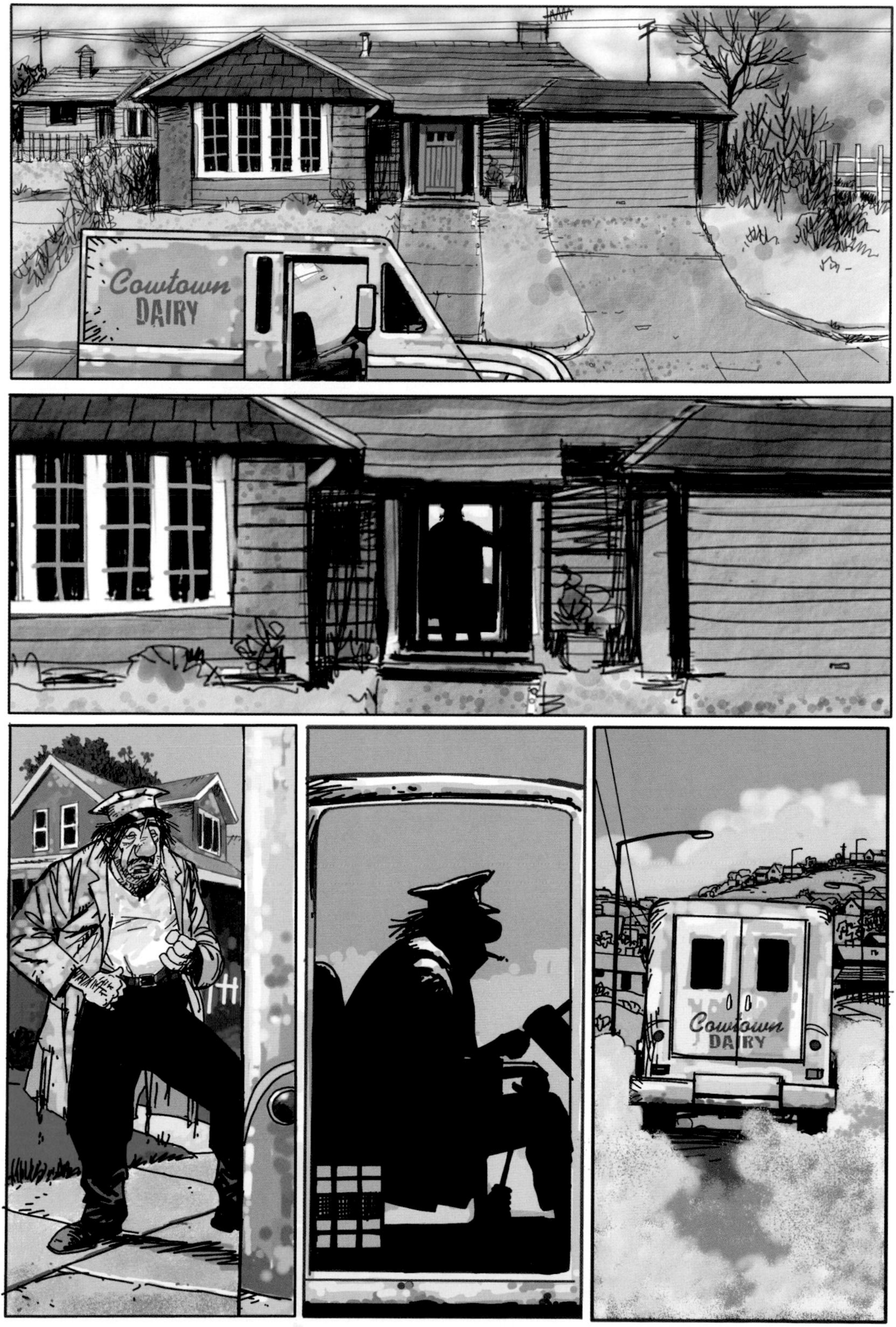
Cowtown
DAIRY
Cowtown
DAIRY

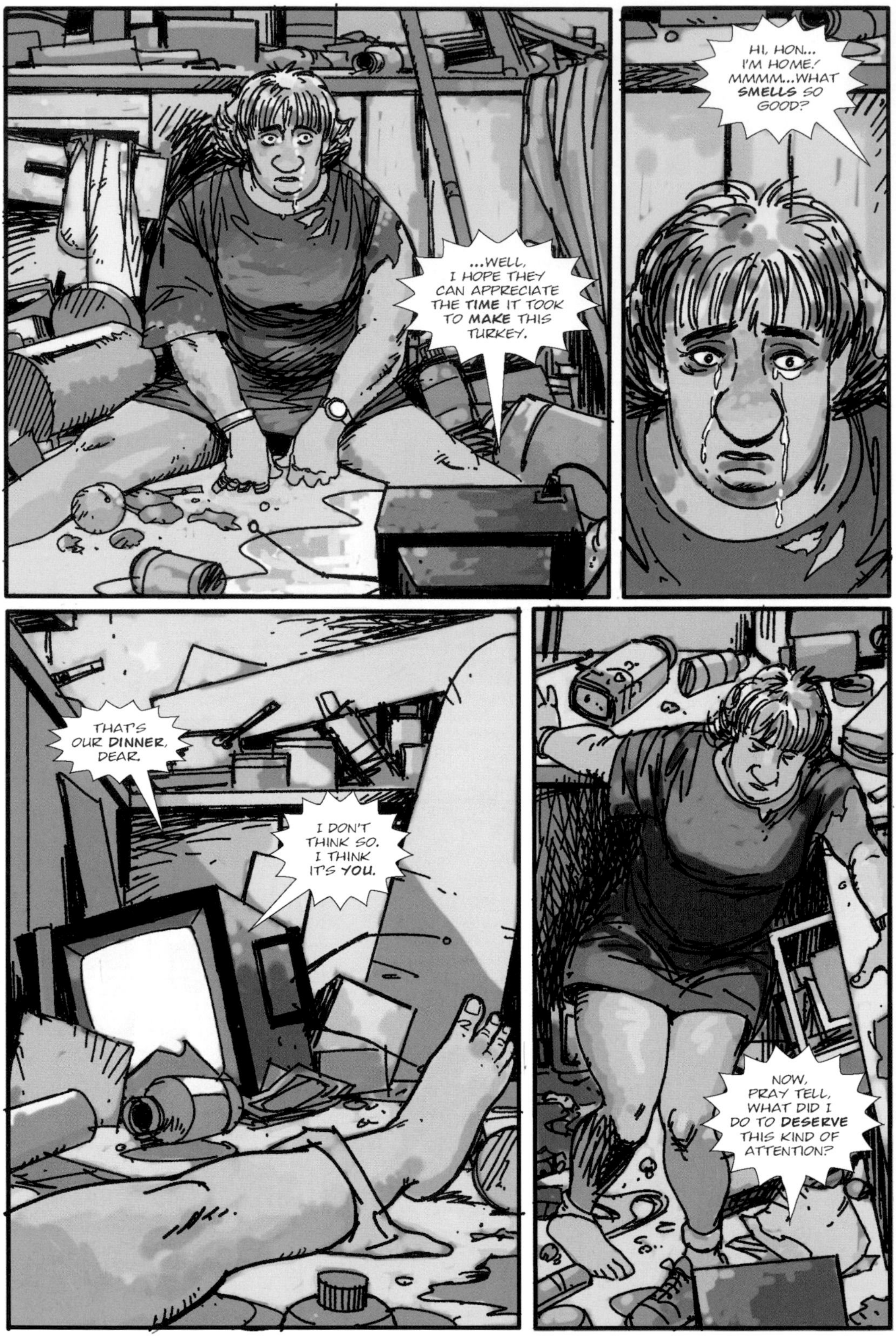
...WELL, I HOPE THEY CAN APPRECIATE THE TIME IT TOOK TO MAKE THIS TURKEY.
HI, HON... I'M HOME! MMMM...WHAT SMELLS SO GOOD?
THAT'S OUR DINNER, DEAR.
I DON'T THINK SO. I THINK IT'S YOU.
NOW, PRAY TELL, WHAT DID I DO TO DESERVE THIS KIND OF ATTENTION?

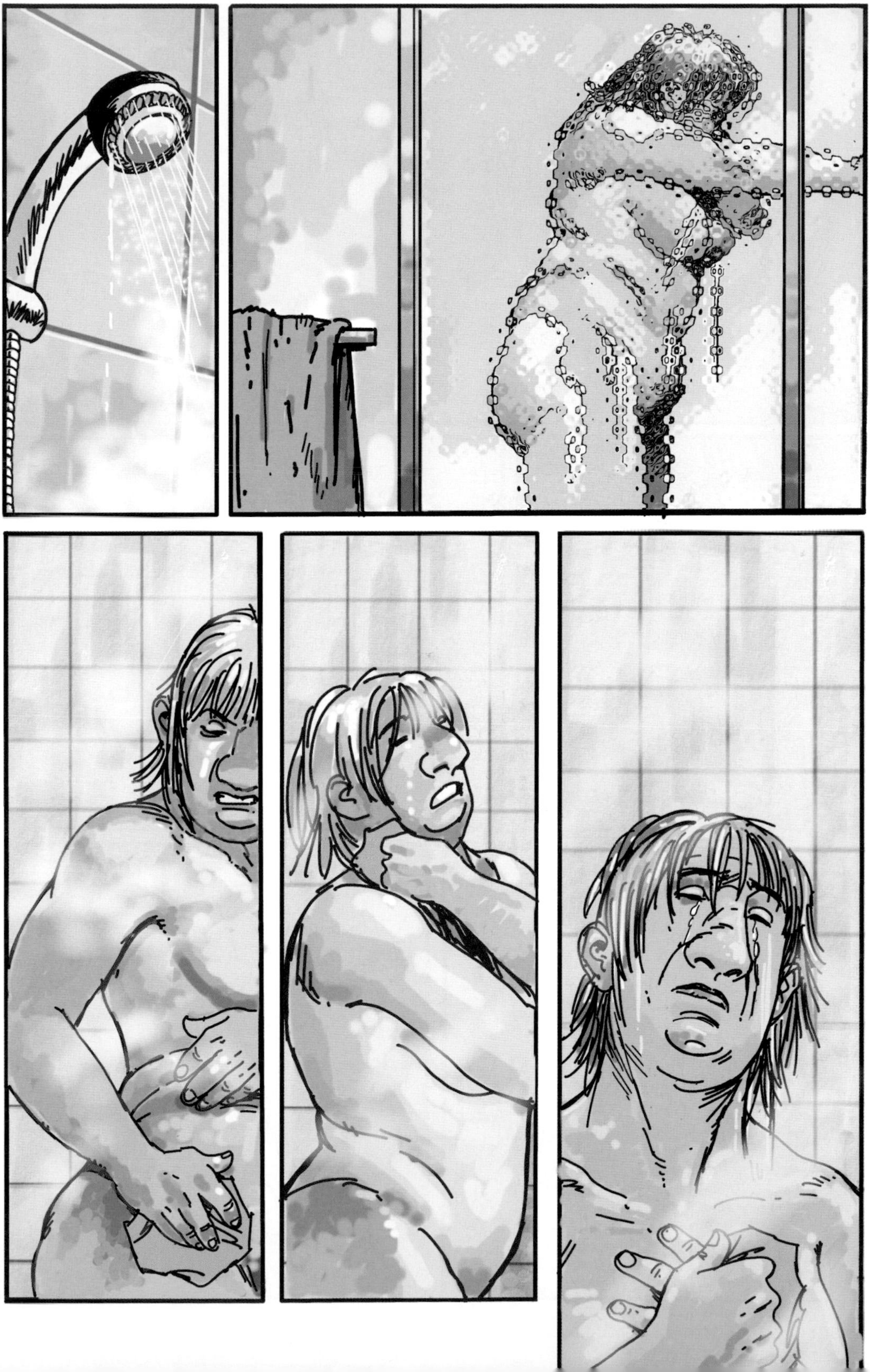

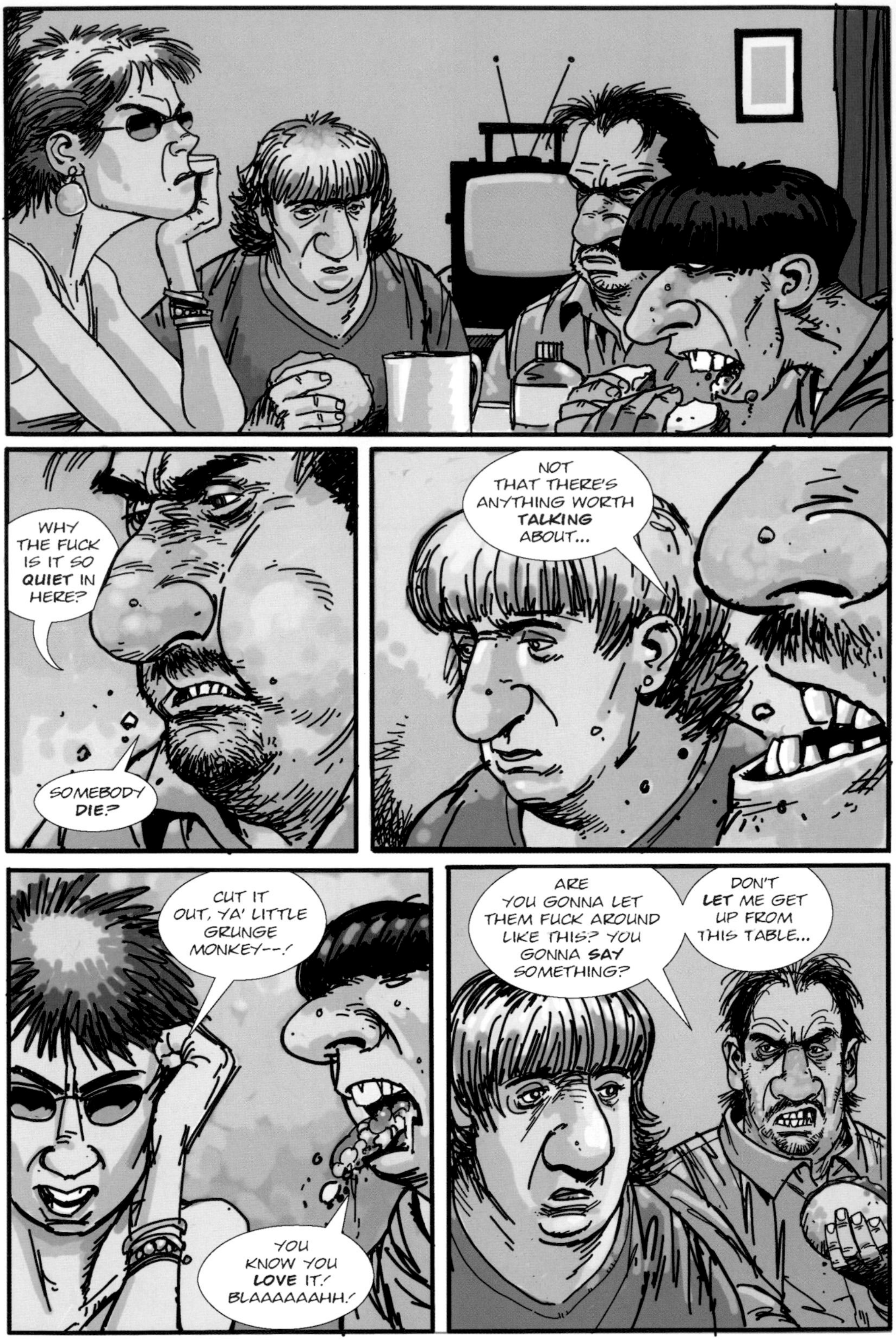

WHY THE FUCK IS IT SO **QUIET** IN HERE?
SOMEBODY **DIE**?
NOT THAT THERE'S ANYTHING WORTH **TALKING** ABOUT...
CUT IT OUT, YA' LITTLE GRUNGE MONKEY--!
YOU KNOW YOU **LOVE** IT! BLAAAAAAHH!
ARE YOU GONNA LET THEM FUCK AROUND LIKE THIS? YOU GONNA **SAY** SOMETHING?
DON'T **LET** ME GET UP FROM THIS TABLE...

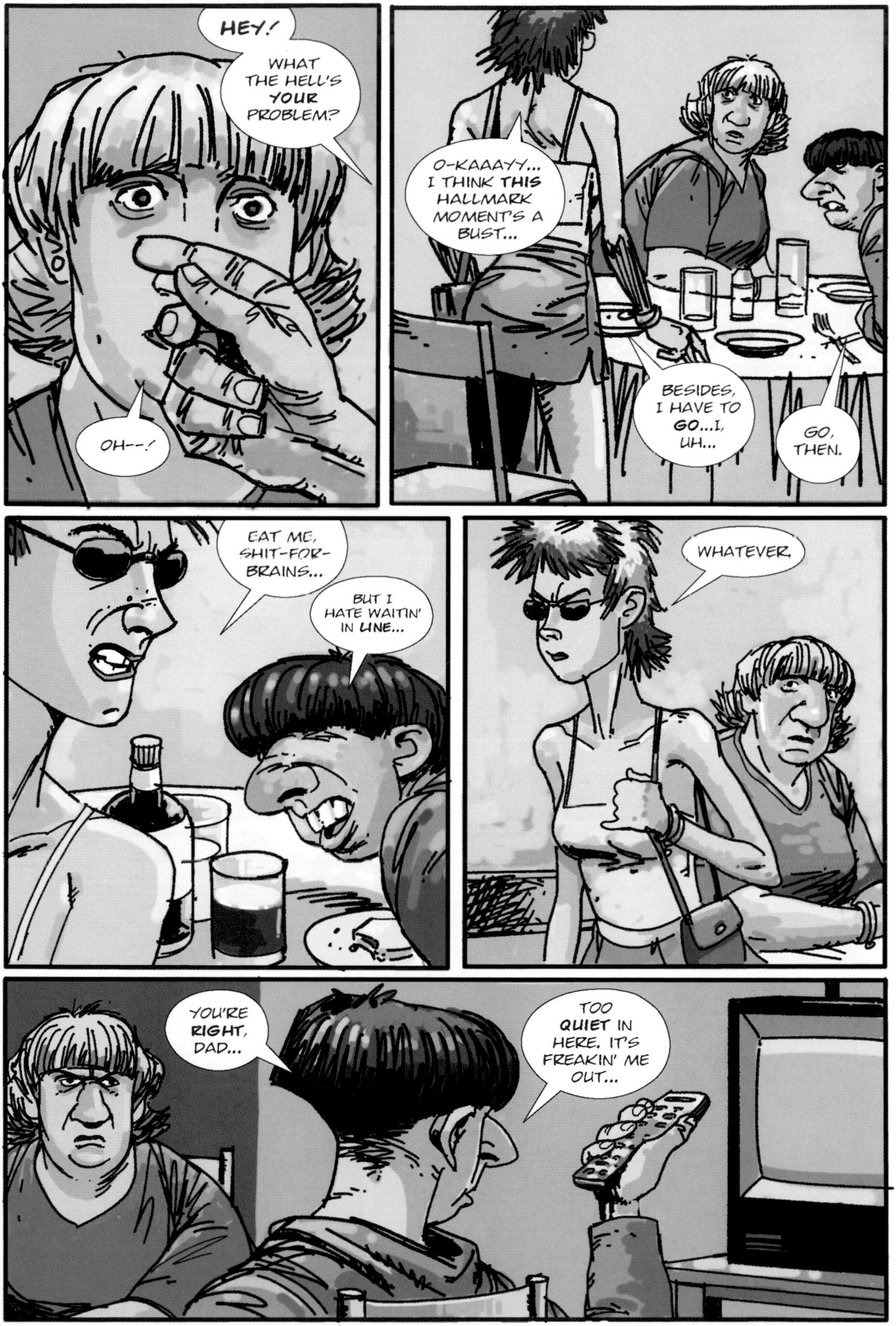
HEY!
WHAT THE HELL'S YOUR PROBLEM?
OH--!
O-KAAAYY... I THINK THIS HALLMARK MOMENT'S A BUST...
BESIDES, I HAVE TO GO...I, UH...
GO, THEN.
EAT ME, SHIT-FOR-BRAINS...
BUT I HATE WAITIN' IN LINE...
WHATEVER.
YOU'RE RIGHT, DAD...
TOO QUIET IN HERE. IT'S FREAKIN' ME OUT...

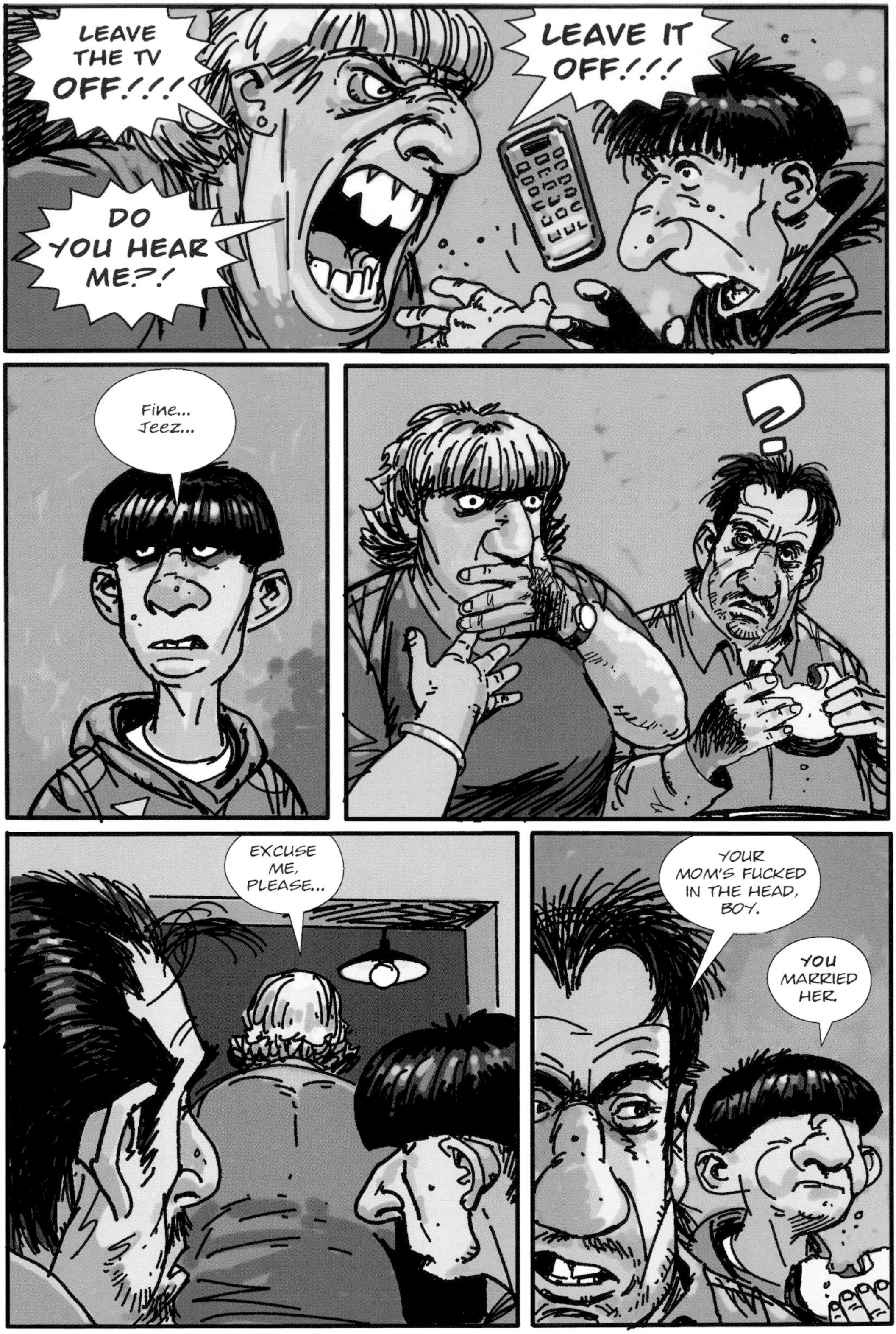
LEAVE THE TV OFF!!!!
LEAVE IT OFF!!!!
DO YOU HEAR ME?!
Fine... Jeez...
?
EXCUSE ME, PLEASE...
YOUR MOM'S FUCKED IN THE HEAD, BOY.
YOU MARRIED HER.

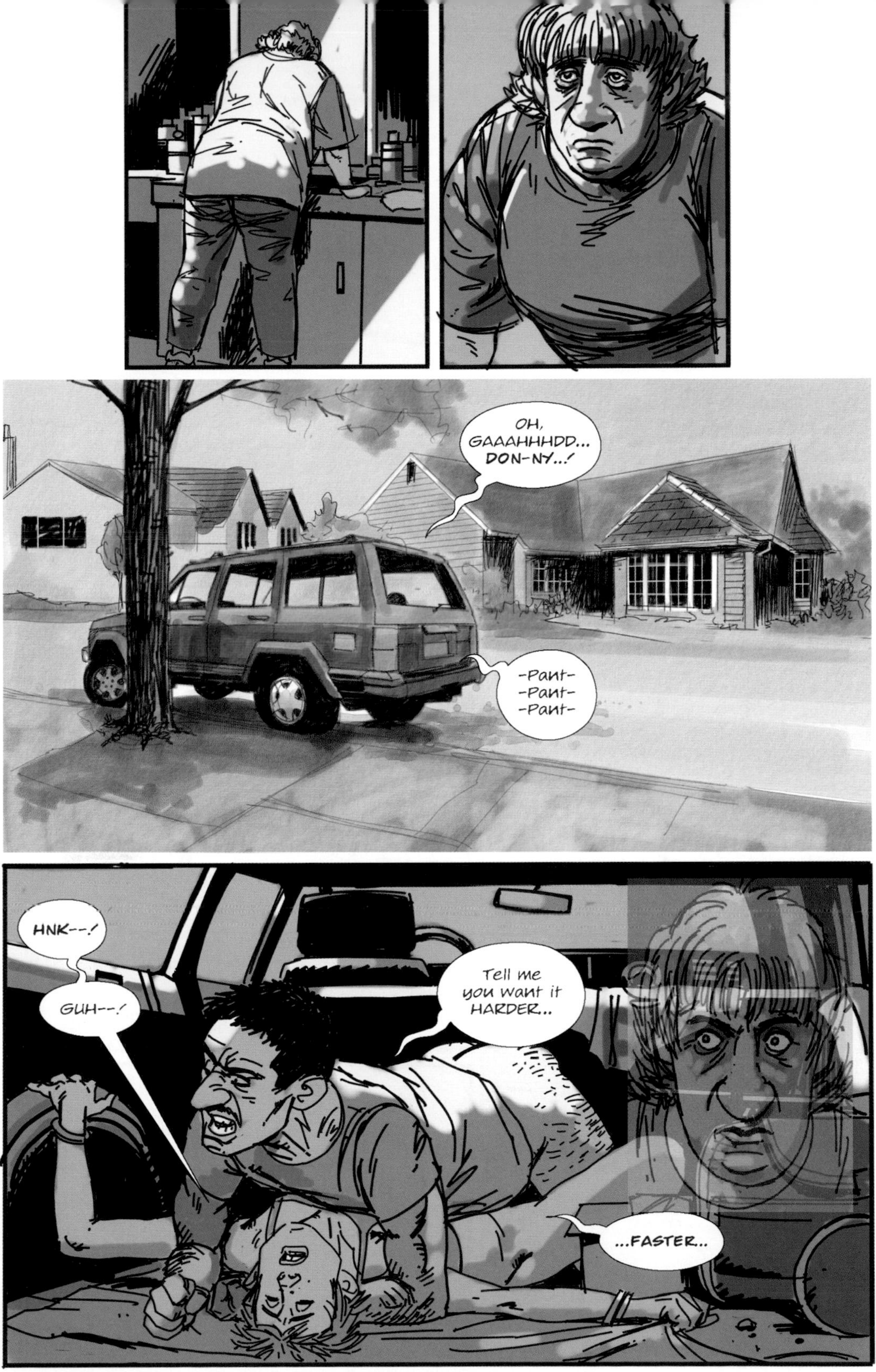
OH, GAAAHHHDD... DON-NY...!
-Pant- -Pant- -Pant-
HNK--!
GUH--!
Tell me you want it HARDER...
...FASTER...

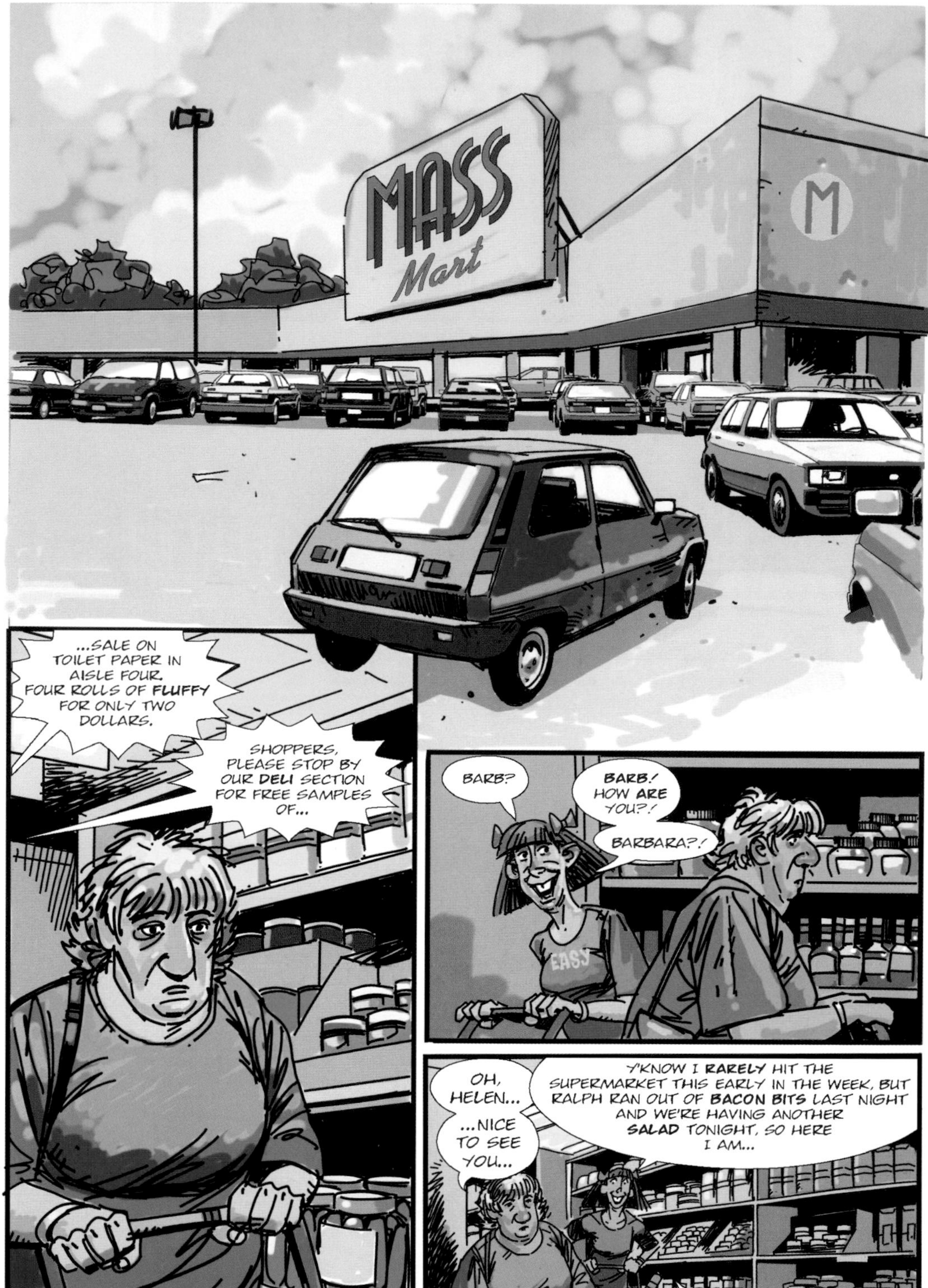
MASS
Mart
M
...SALE ON TOILET PAPER IN AISLE FOUR. FOUR ROLLS OF **FLUFFY** FOR ONLY TWO DOLLARS.
SHOPPERS, PLEASE STOP BY OUR **DELI** SECTION FOR FREE SAMPLES OF...
BARB?
BARB! HOW **ARE** YOU?!
BARBARA?!
EASY
OH, HELEN...
...NICE TO SEE YOU...
Y'KNOW I **RARELY** HIT THE SUPERMARKET THIS EARLY IN THE WEEK, BUT RALPH RAN OUT OF **BACON BITS** LAST NIGHT AND WE'RE HAVING ANOTHER **SALAD** TONIGHT, SO HERE I AM...
YOU KNOW **RALPH**...HE NEEDS HIS ROUGHAGE...

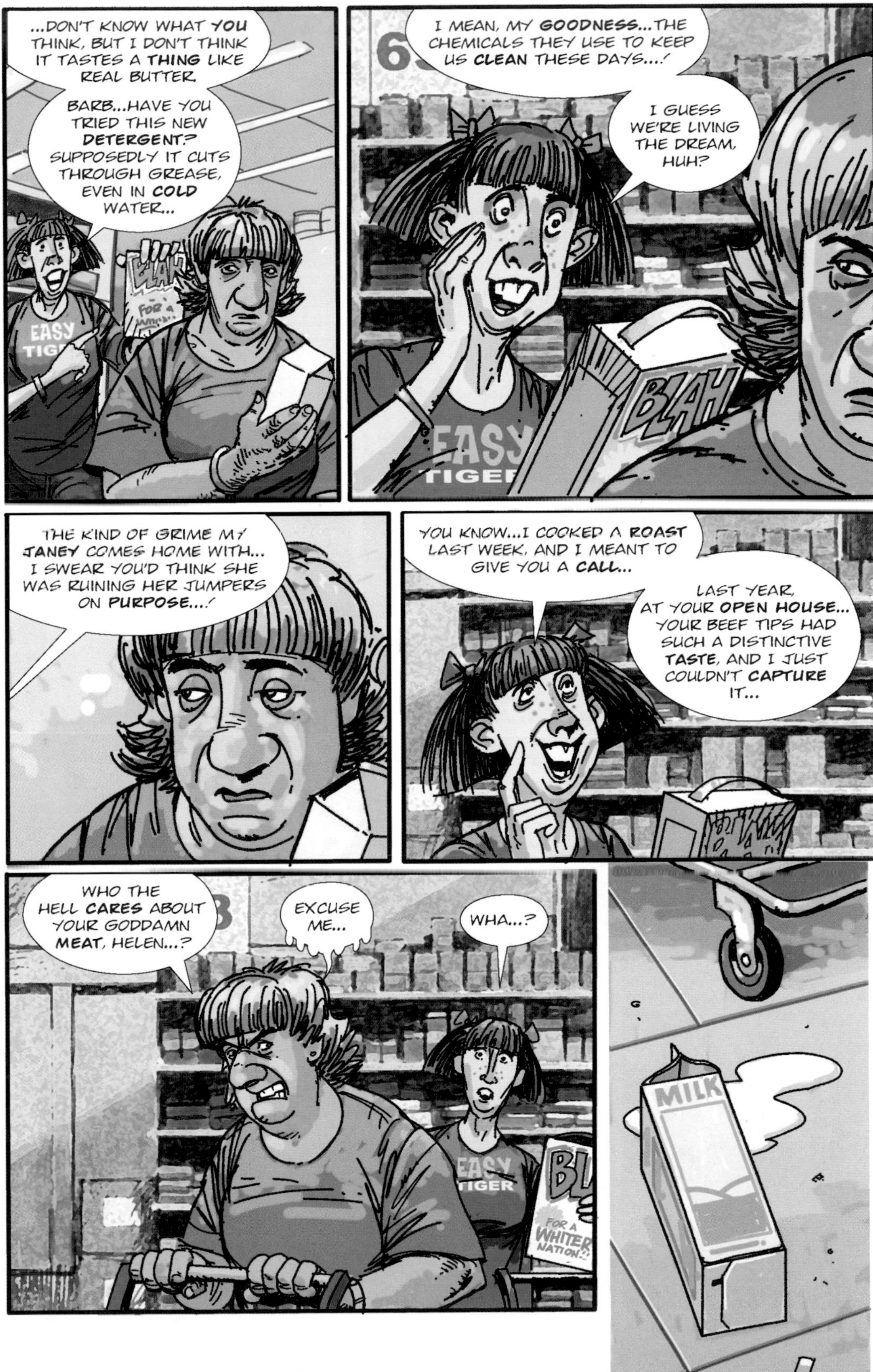
...DON'T KNOW WHAT YOU THINK, BUT I DON'T THINK IT TASTES A THING LIKE REAL BUTTER.
BARB...HAVE YOU TRIED THIS NEW DETERGENT? SUPPOSEDLY IT CUTS THROUGH GREASE, EVEN IN COLD WATER...
EASY TIGER
I MEAN, MY GOODNESS...THE CHEMICALS THEY USE TO KEEP US CLEAN THESE DAYS...!
I GUESS WE'RE LIVING THE DREAM, HUH?
BLAH
THE KIND OF GRIME MY JANEY COMES HOME WITH... I SWEAR YOU'D THINK SHE WAS RUINING HER JUMPERS ON PURPOSE...!
YOU KNOW...I COOKED A ROAST LAST WEEK, AND I MEANT TO GIVE YOU A CALL...
LAST YEAR, AT YOUR OPEN HOUSE... YOUR BEEF TIPS HAD SUCH A DISTINCTIVE TASTE, AND I JUST COULDN'T CAPTURE IT...
WHO THE HELL CARES ABOUT YOUR GODDAMN MEAT, HELEN...?
EXCUSE ME...
WHA...?
EASY TIGER
BLAH FOR A WHITER NATION!!
MILK

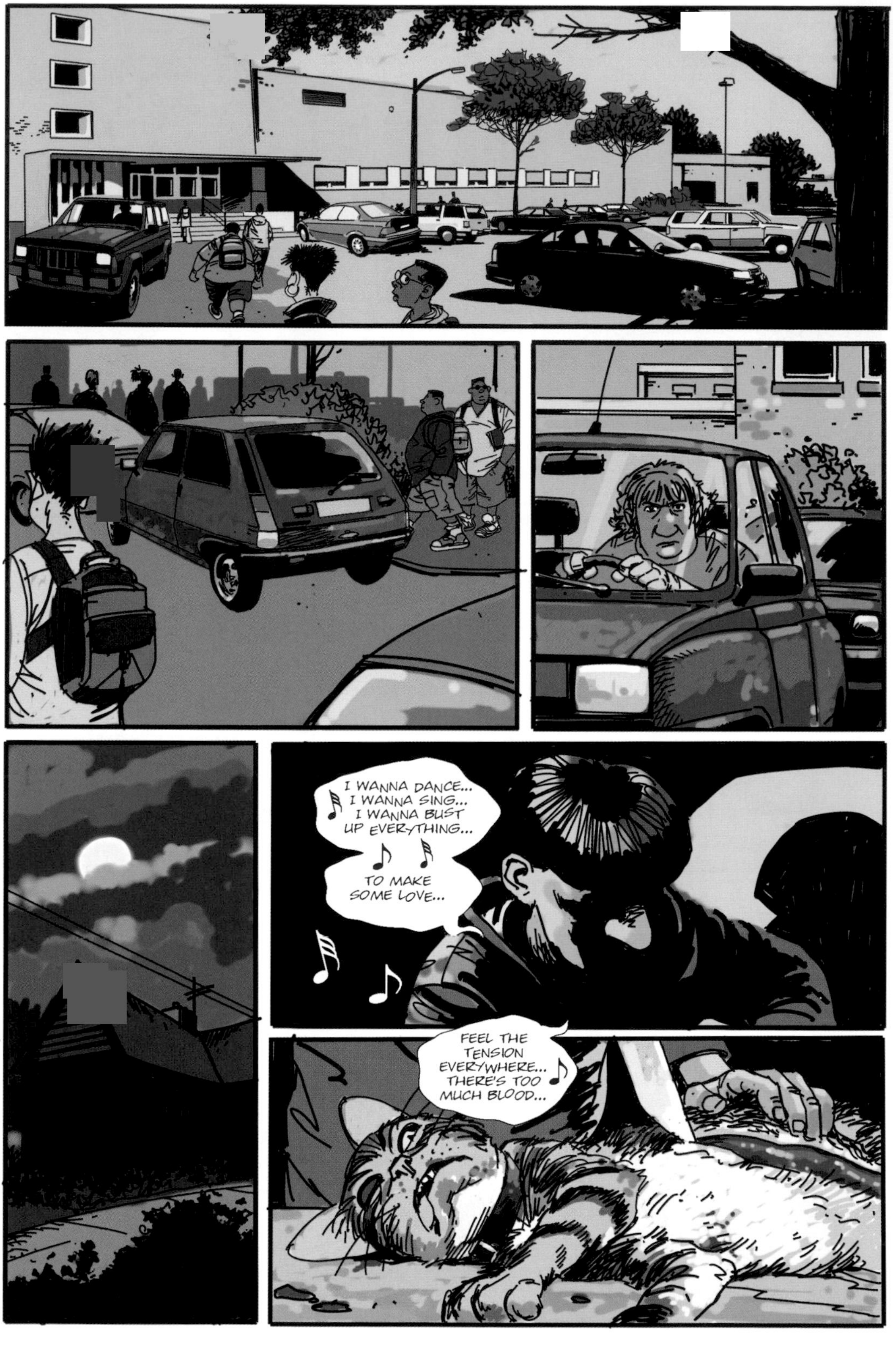
I WANNA DANCE... I WANNA SING... I WANNA BUST UP EVERYTHING...
TO MAKE SOME LOVE...
FEEL THE TENSION EVERYWHERE... THERE'S TOO MUCH BLOOD...

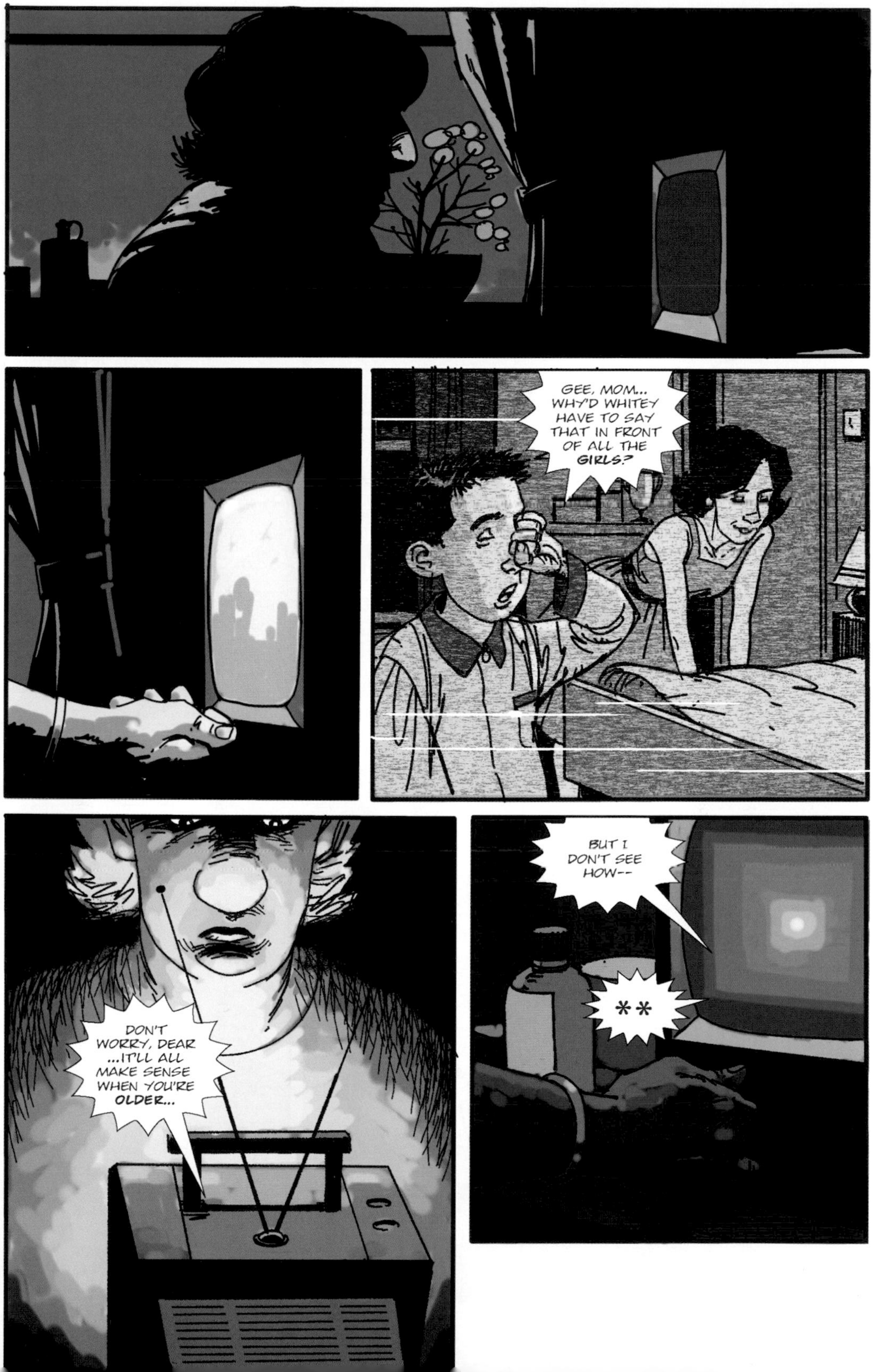
GEE, MOM... WHY'D WHITEY HAVE TO SAY THAT IN FRONT OF ALL THE GIRLS?
DON'T WORRY, DEAR ...IT'LL ALL MAKE SENSE WHEN YOU'RE OLDER...
BUT I DON'T SEE HOW--
**

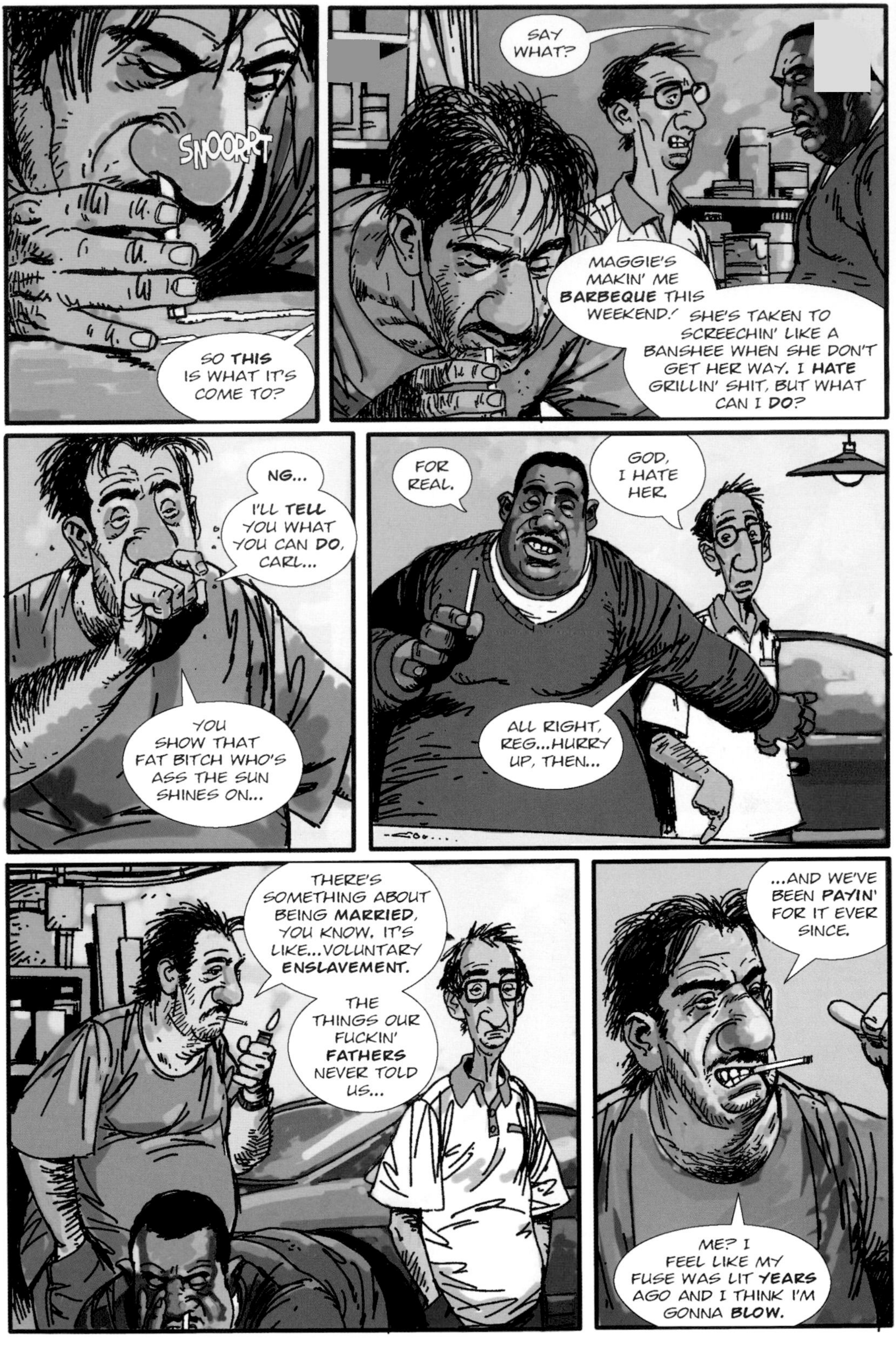
SNOORRT
SO THIS IS WHAT IT'S COME TO?
SAY WHAT?
MAGGIE'S MAKIN' ME BARBEQUE THIS WEEKEND!
SHE'S TAKEN TO SCREECHIN' LIKE A BANSHEE WHEN SHE DON'T GET HER WAY. I HATE GRILLIN' SHIT, BUT WHAT CAN I DO?
NG...
I'LL TELL YOU WHAT YOU CAN DO, CARL...
YOU SHOW THAT FAT BITCH WHO'S ASS THE SUN SHINES ON...
FOR REAL.
GOD, I HATE HER.
ALL RIGHT, REG...HURRY UP, THEN...
THERE'S SOMETHING ABOUT BEING MARRIED, YOU KNOW. IT'S LIKE...VOLUNTARY ENSLAVEMENT.
THE THINGS OUR FUCKIN' FATHERS NEVER TOLD US...
...AND WE'VE BEEN PAYIN' FOR IT EVER SINCE.
ME? I FEEL LIKE MY FUSE WAS LIT YEARS AGO AND I THINK I'M GONNA BLOW.

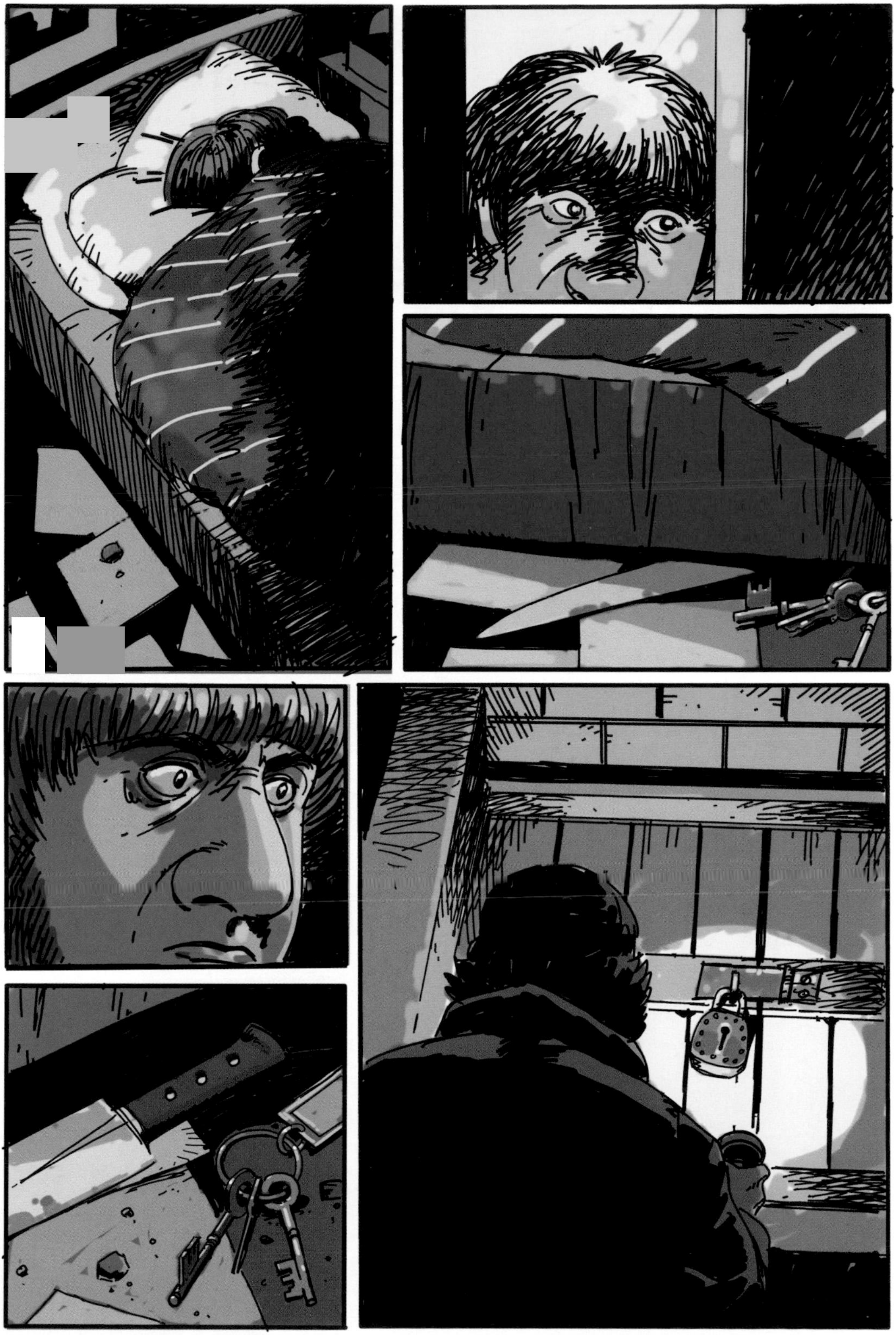

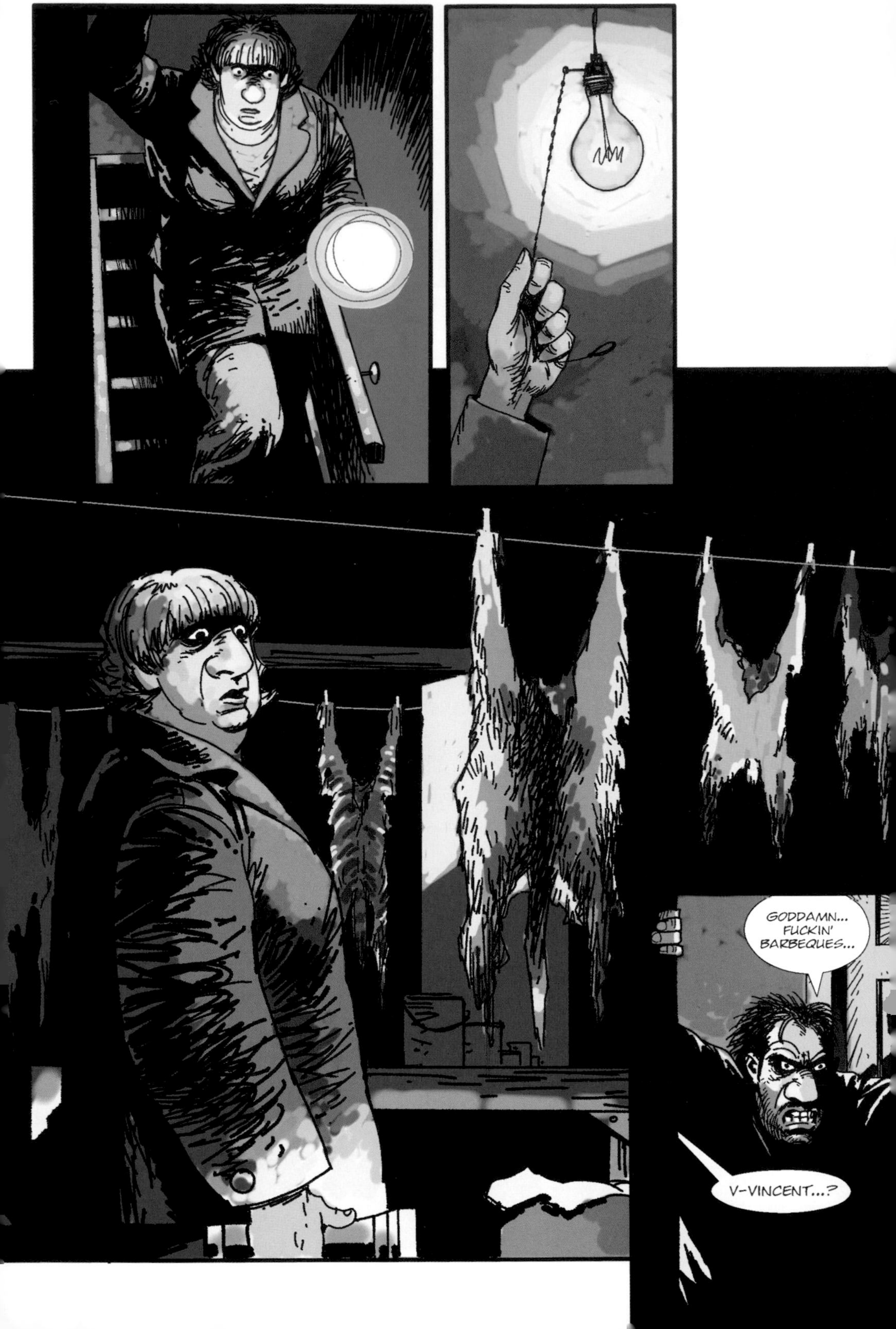
GODDAMN... FUCKIN' BARBEQUES...
V-VINCENT...?

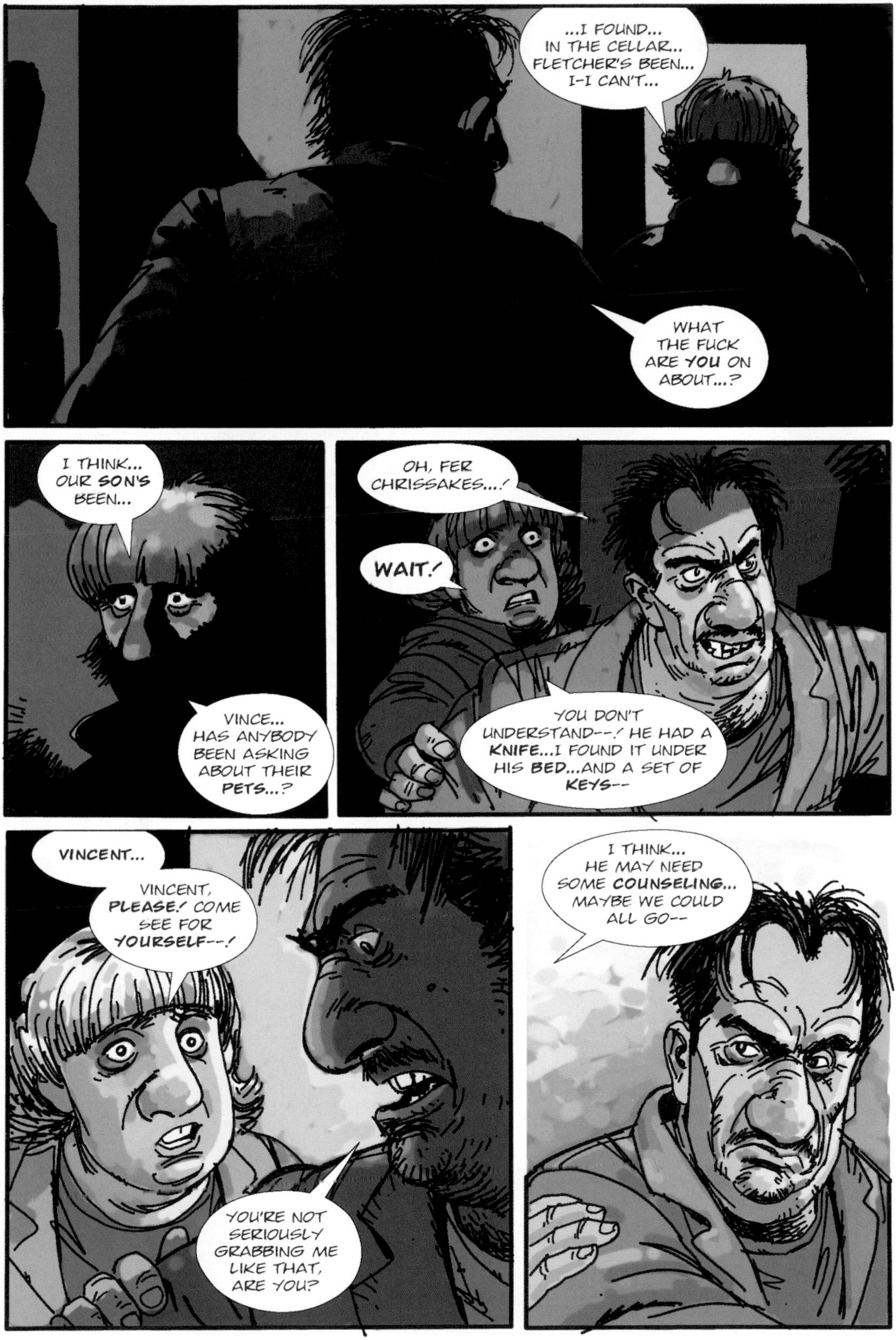
...I FOUND... IN THE CELLAR... FLETCHER'S BEEN... I-I CAN'T...
WHAT THE FUCK ARE **YOU** ON ABOUT...?
I THINK... OUR **SON'S** BEEN...
VINCE... HAS ANYBODY BEEN ASKING ABOUT THEIR **PETS**...?
OH, FER CHRISSAKES...!
WAIT!
YOU DON'T UNDERSTAND--! HE HAD A **KNIFE**...I FOUND IT UNDER HIS **BED**...AND A SET OF **KEYS**--
VINCENT...
VINCENT, **PLEASE!** COME SEE FOR **YOURSELF**--!
YOU'RE NOT SERIOUSLY GRABBING ME LIKE THAT, ARE YOU?
I THINK... HE MAY NEED SOME **COUNSELING**... MAYBE WE COULD ALL GO--

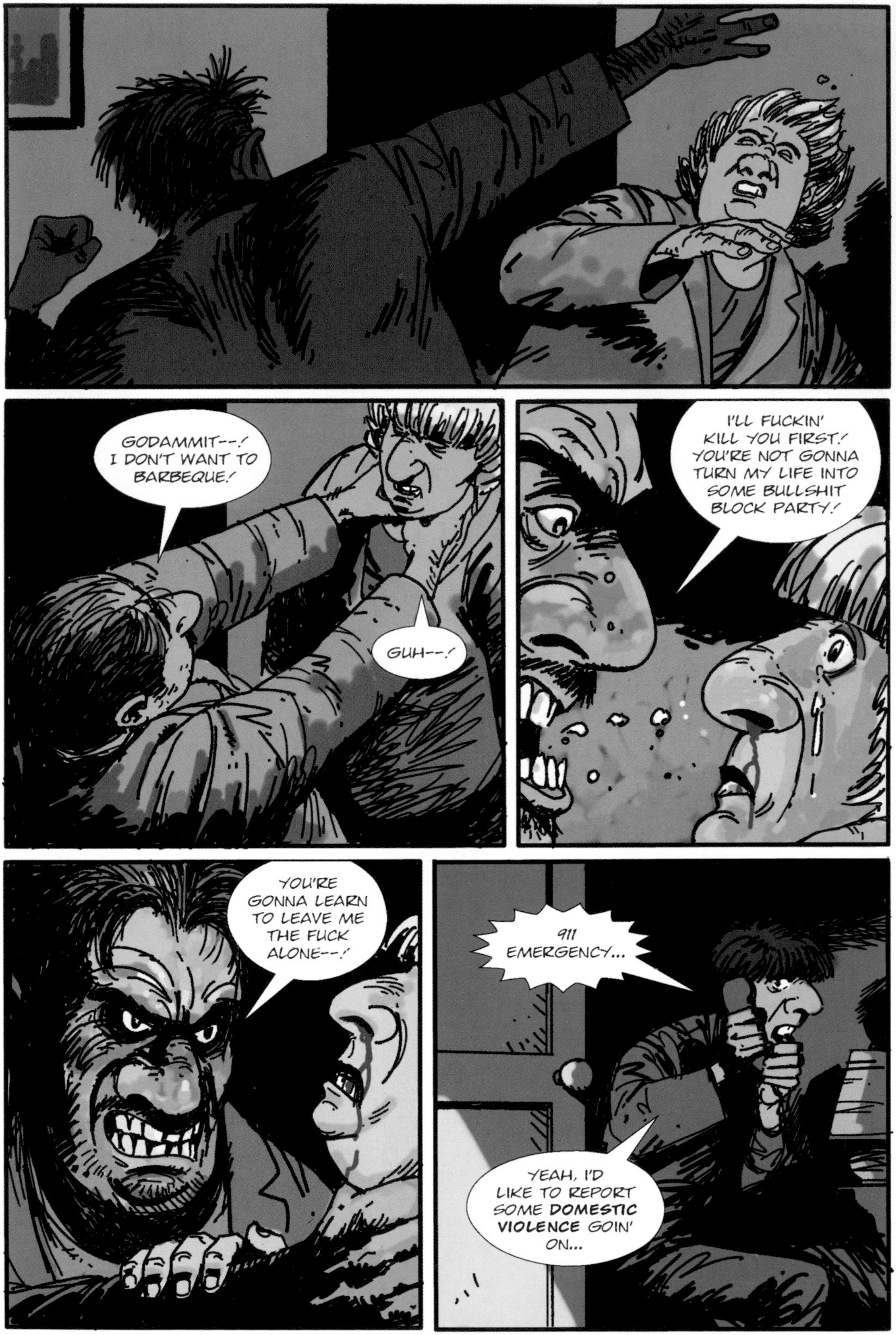
GODAMMIT--! I DON'T WANT TO BARBEQUE!
GUH--!
I'LL FUCKIN' KILL YOU FIRST! YOU'RE NOT GONNA TURN MY LIFE INTO SOME BULLSHIT BLOCK PARTY!
YOU'RE GONNA LEARN TO LEAVE ME THE FUCK ALONE--!
911 EMERGENCY...
YEAH, I'D LIKE TO REPORT SOME **DOMESTIC VIOLENCE** GOIN' ON...

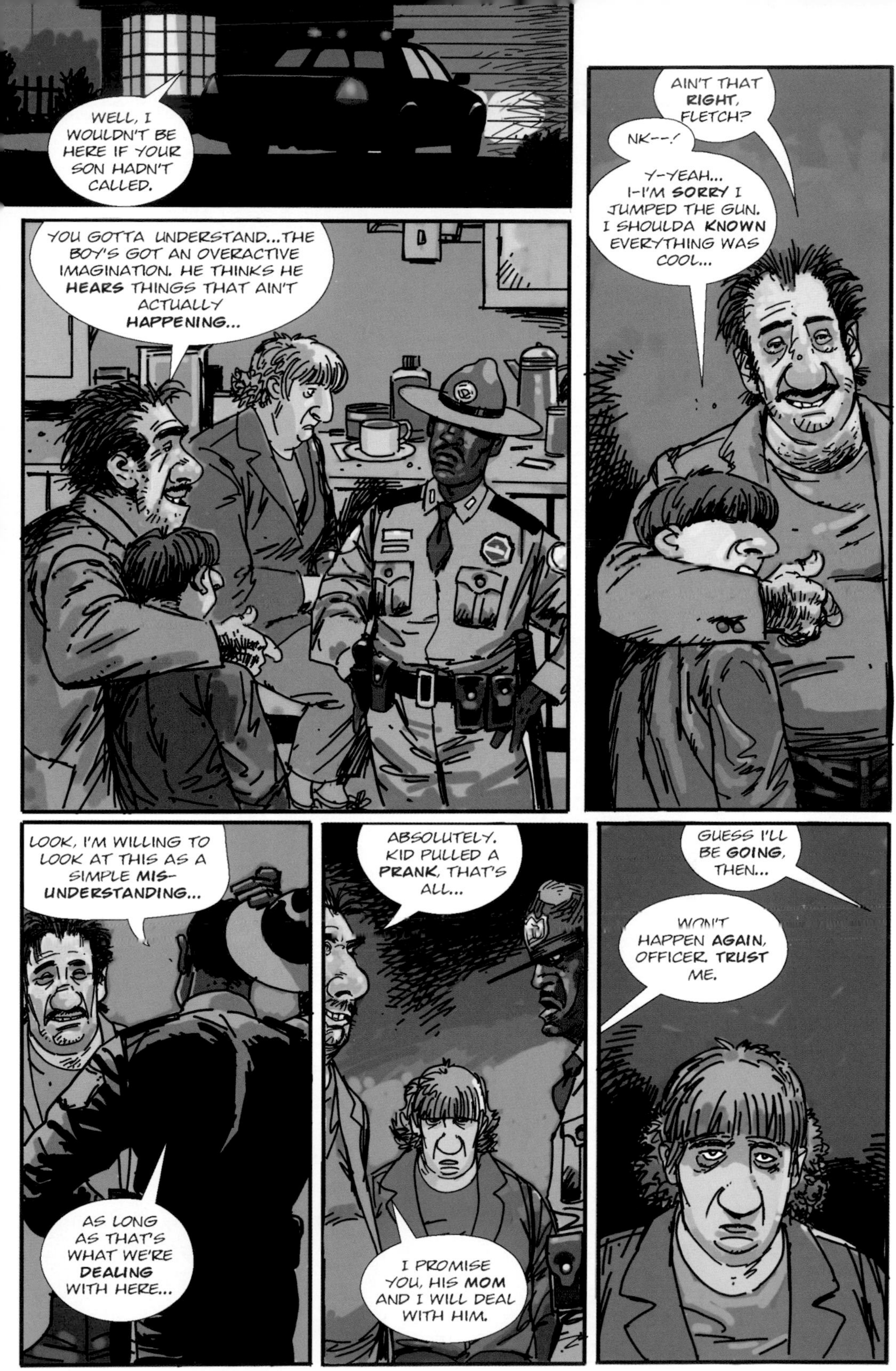
WELL, I WOULDN'T BE HERE IF YOUR SON HADN'T CALLED.
AIN'T THAT **RIGHT**, FLETCH?
NK--!
Y-YEAH... I-I'M **SORRY** I JUMPED THE GUN. I SHOULDA **KNOWN** EVERYTHING WAS COOL...
YOU GOTTA UNDERSTAND...THE BOY'S GOT AN OVERACTIVE IMAGINATION. HE THINKS HE **HEARS** THINGS THAT AIN'T ACTUALLY **HAPPENING...**
LOOK, I'M WILLING TO LOOK AT THIS AS A SIMPLE **MIS-UNDERSTANDING...**
AS LONG AS THAT'S WHAT WE'RE **DEALING** WITH HERE...
ABSOLUTELY. KID PULLED A **PRANK**, THAT'S ALL...
I PROMISE YOU, HIS **MOM** AND I WILL DEAL WITH HIM.
GUESS I'LL BE **GOING**, THEN...
WON'T HAPPEN **AGAIN**, OFFICER. **TRUST** ME.

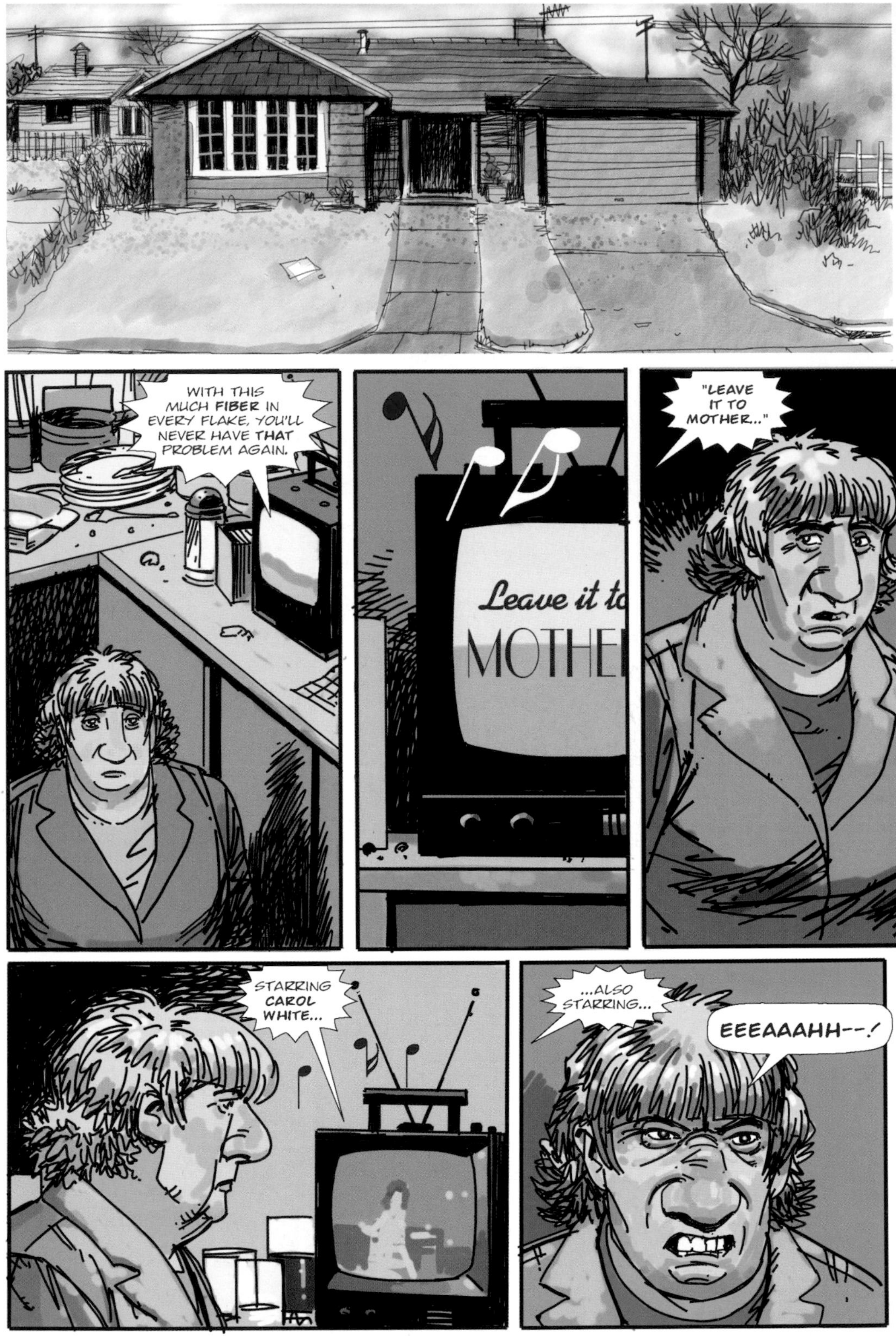
WITH THIS MUCH FIBER IN EVERY FLAKE, YOU'LL NEVER HAVE THAT PROBLEM AGAIN.
Leave it to
MOTHE
"LEAVE IT TO MOTHER..."
STARRING CAROL WHITE...
...ALSO STARRING...
EEEAAAHH--!

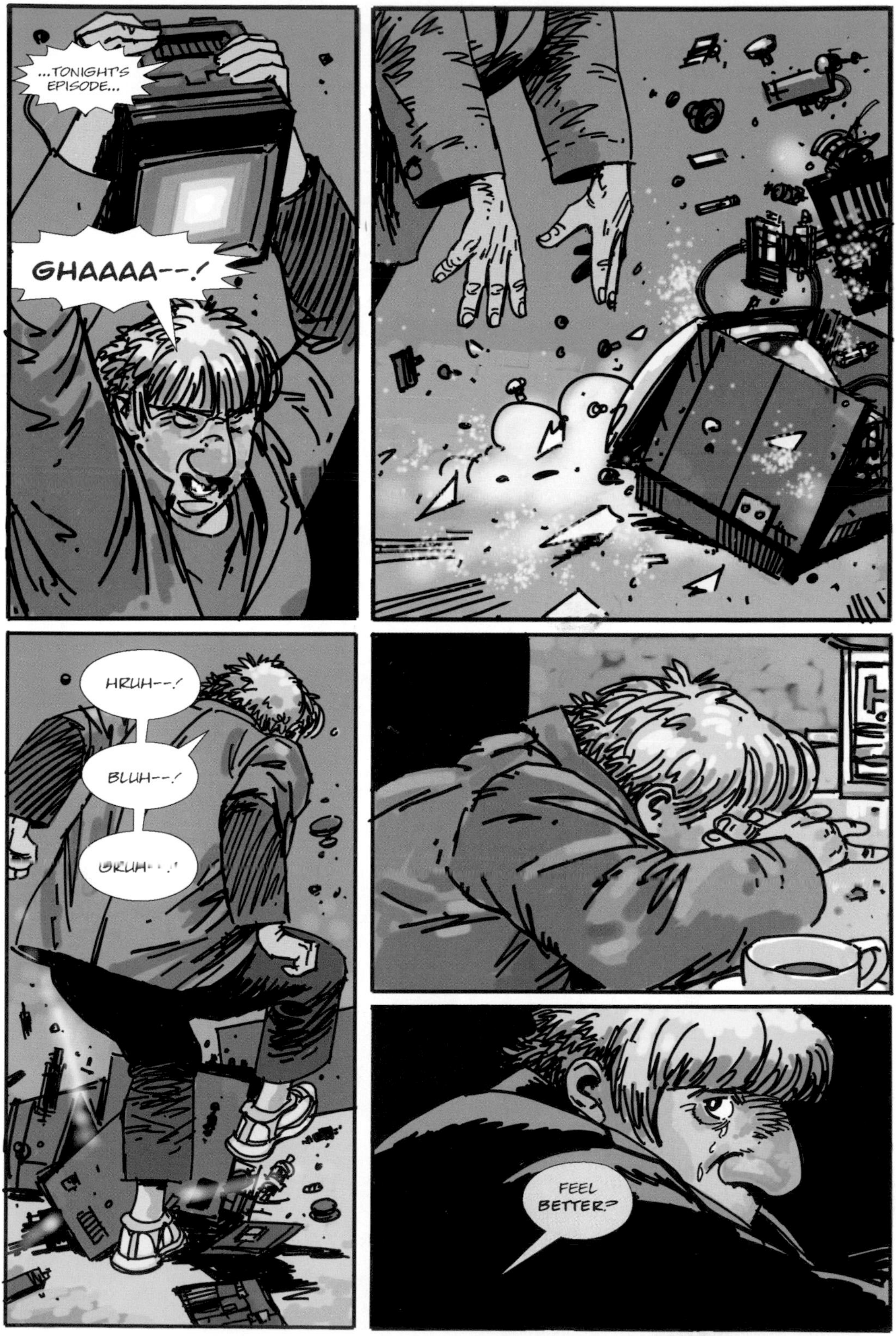
...TONIGHT'S EPISODE...
GHAAAA--!
HRUH--!
BLUH--!
GRUH--!
FEEL BETTER?

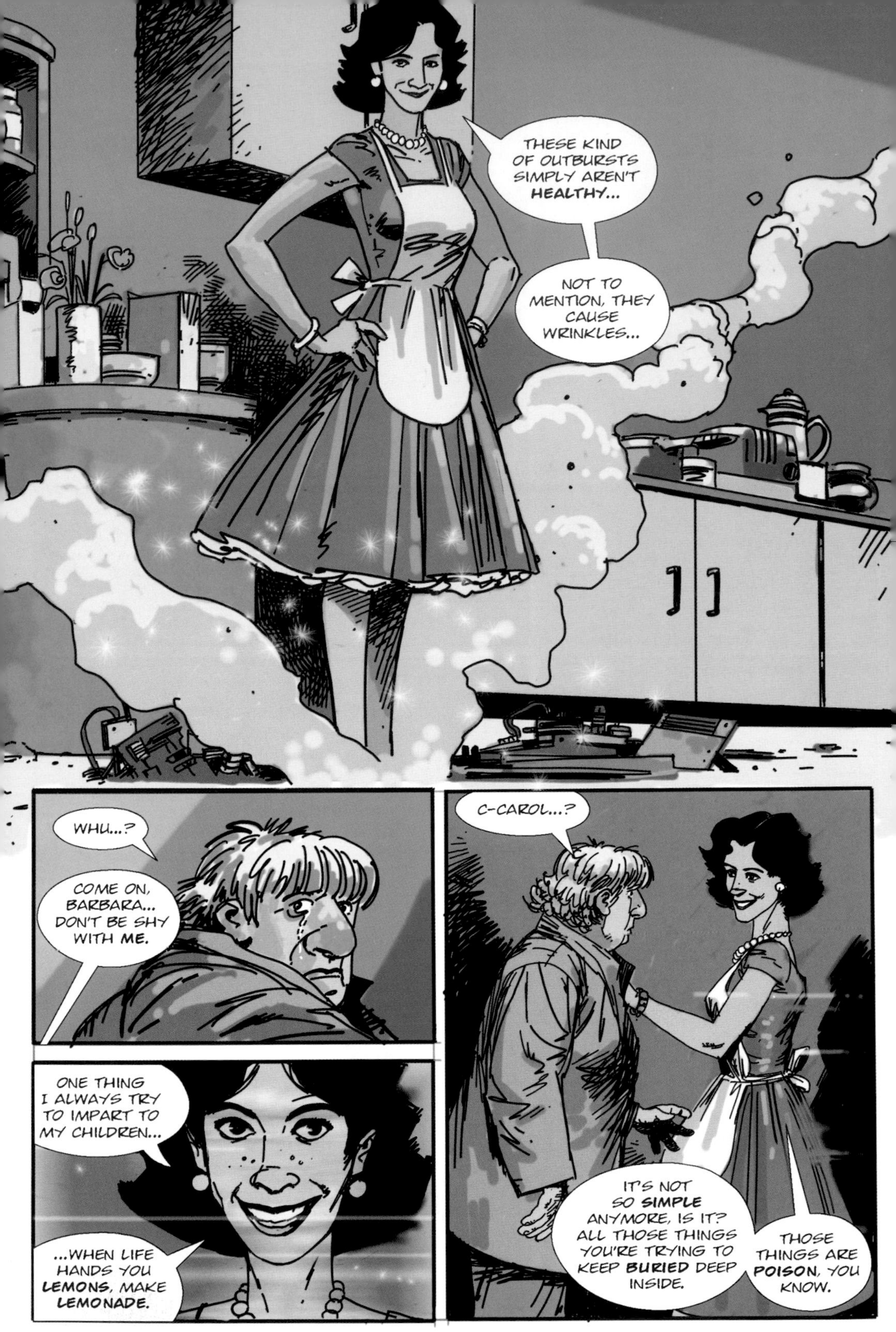
THESE KIND OF OUTBURSTS SIMPLY AREN'T **HEALTHY...**
NOT TO MENTION, THEY CAUSE WRINKLES...
WHU...?
COME ON, BARBARA... DON'T BE SHY WITH **ME.**
ONE THING I ALWAYS TRY TO IMPART TO MY CHILDREN...
...WHEN LIFE HANDS YOU **LEMONS**, MAKE **LEMONADE.**
C-CAROL...?
IT'S NOT SO **SIMPLE** ANYMORE, IS IT? ALL THOSE THINGS YOU'RE TRYING TO KEEP **BURIED** DEEP INSIDE.
THOSE THINGS ARE **POISON**, YOU KNOW.

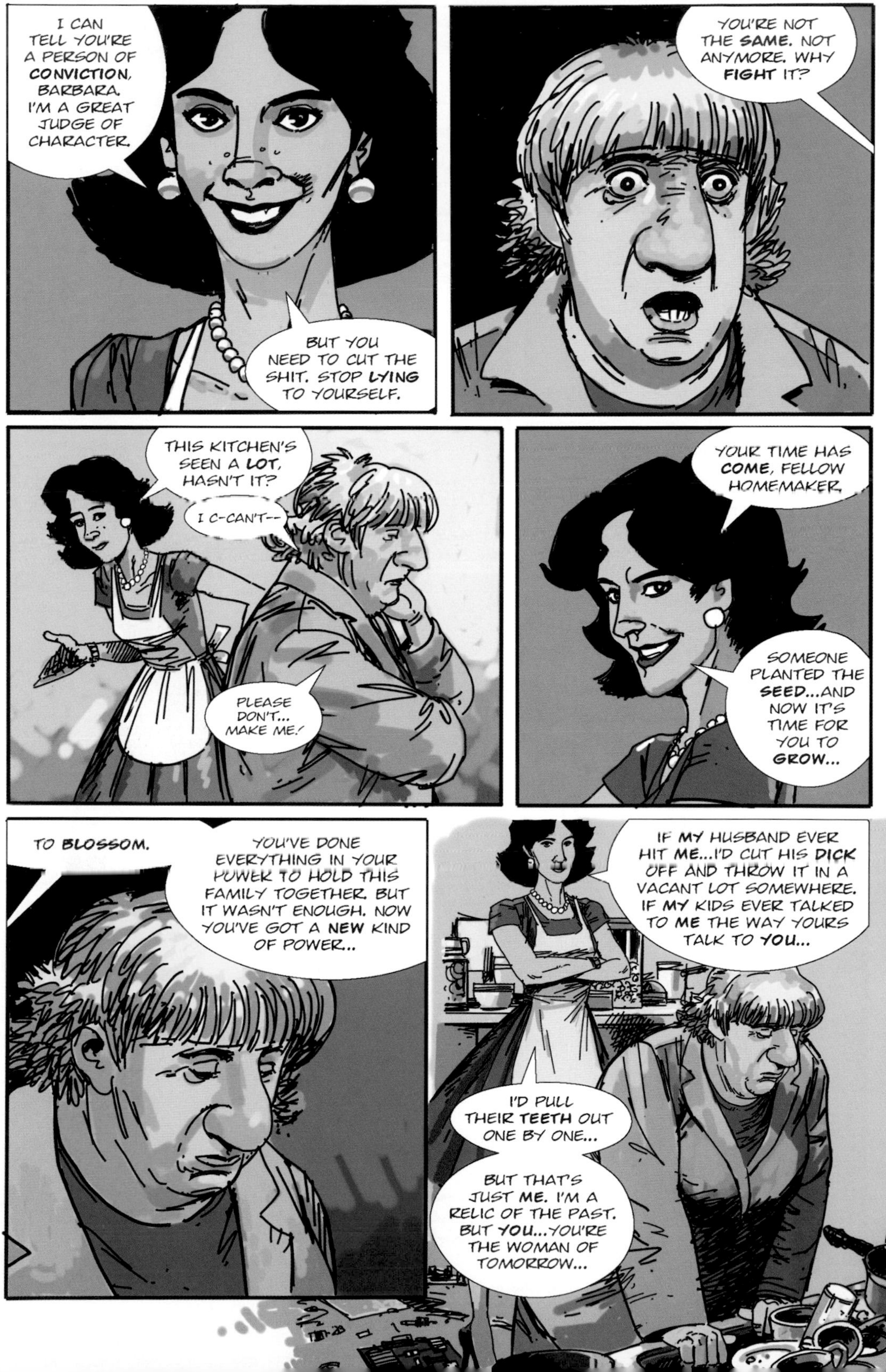
I CAN TELL YOU'RE A PERSON OF **CONVICTION**, BARBARA. I'M A GREAT JUDGE OF CHARACTER.
BUT YOU NEED TO CUT THE SHIT. STOP **LYING** TO YOURSELF.
YOU'RE NOT THE **SAME**. NOT ANYMORE. WHY **FIGHT** IT?
THIS KITCHEN'S SEEN A **LOT**, HASN'T IT?
I C-CAN'T--
PLEASE DON'T... MAKE ME!
YOUR TIME HAS **COME**, FELLOW HOMEMAKER.
SOMEONE PLANTED THE **SEED**...AND NOW IT'S TIME FOR YOU TO **GROW**...
TO **BLOSSOM**.
YOU'VE DONE EVERYTHING IN YOUR POWER TO HOLD THIS FAMILY TOGETHER. BUT IT WASN'T ENOUGH. NOW YOU'VE GOT A **NEW** KIND OF POWER...
IF **MY** HUSBAND EVER HIT **ME**...I'D CUT HIS **DICK** OFF AND THROW IT IN A VACANT LOT SOMEWHERE. IF **MY** KIDS EVER TALKED TO **ME** THE WAY YOURS TALK TO **YOU**...
I'D PULL THEIR **TEETH** OUT ONE BY ONE...
BUT THAT'S JUST **ME**. I'M A RELIC OF THE PAST. BUT **YOU**...YOU'RE THE WOMAN OF TOMORROW...

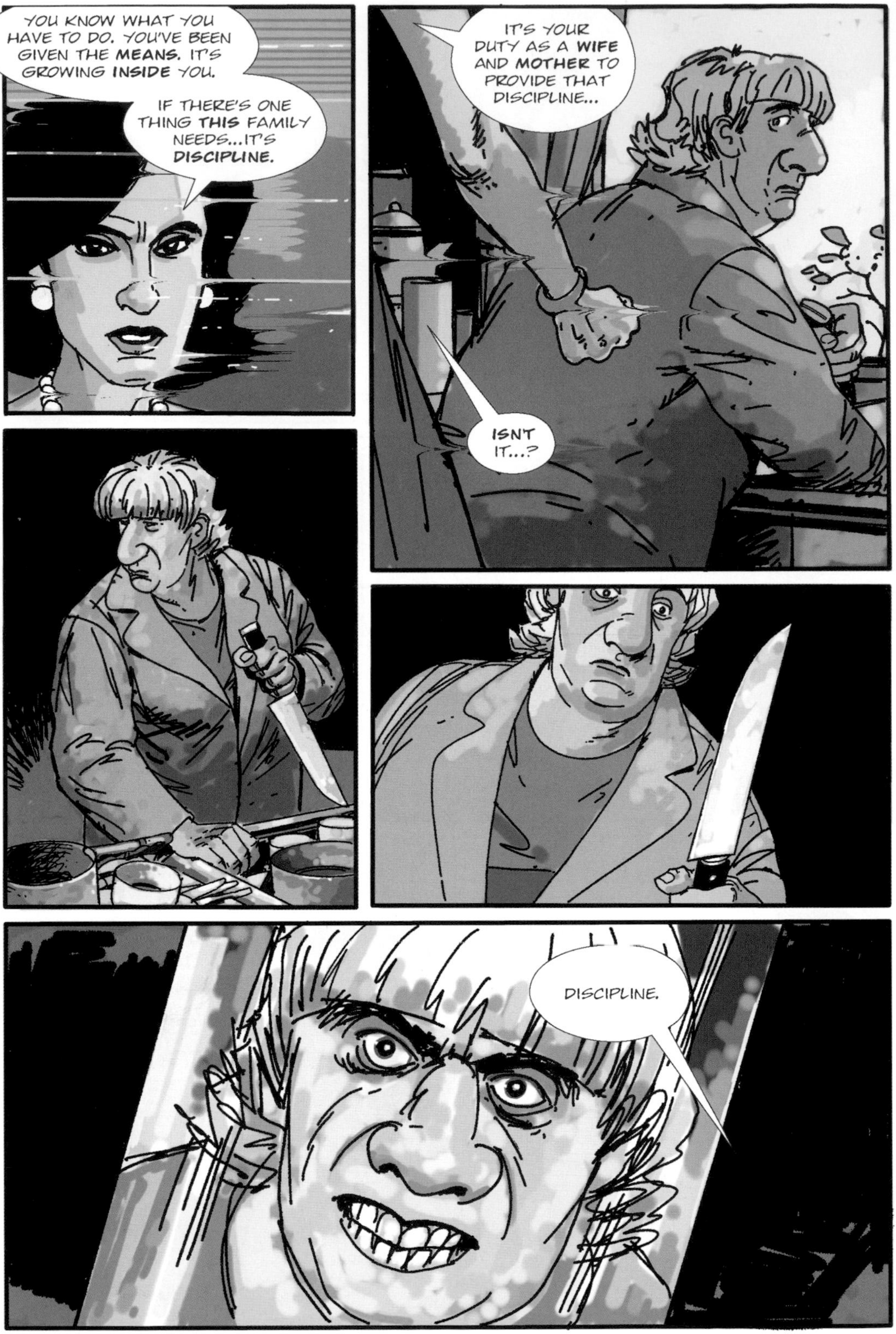
YOU KNOW WHAT YOU HAVE TO DO. YOU'VE BEEN GIVEN THE **MEANS.** IT'S GROWING **INSIDE** YOU.
IF THERE'S ONE THING **THIS** FAMILY NEEDS...IT'S **DISCIPLINE.**
IT'S YOUR DUTY AS A **WIFE** AND **MOTHER** TO PROVIDE THAT DISCIPLINE...
ISN'T IT...?
DISCIPLINE.

CHAPTER 3

"WHAT I'D DO FOR MY FAMILY"

21ˢᵀ CENTURY HOMEMAKER

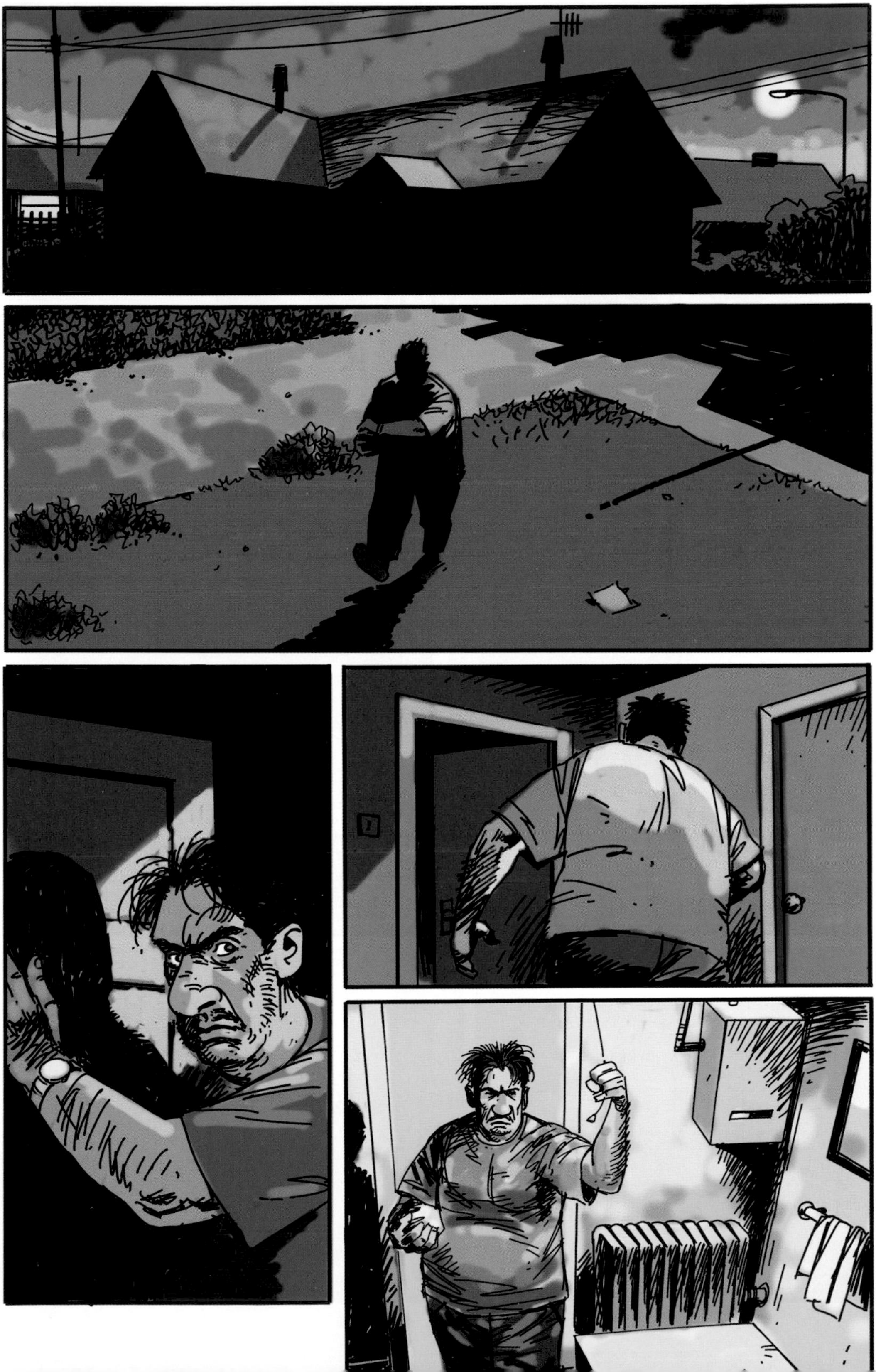

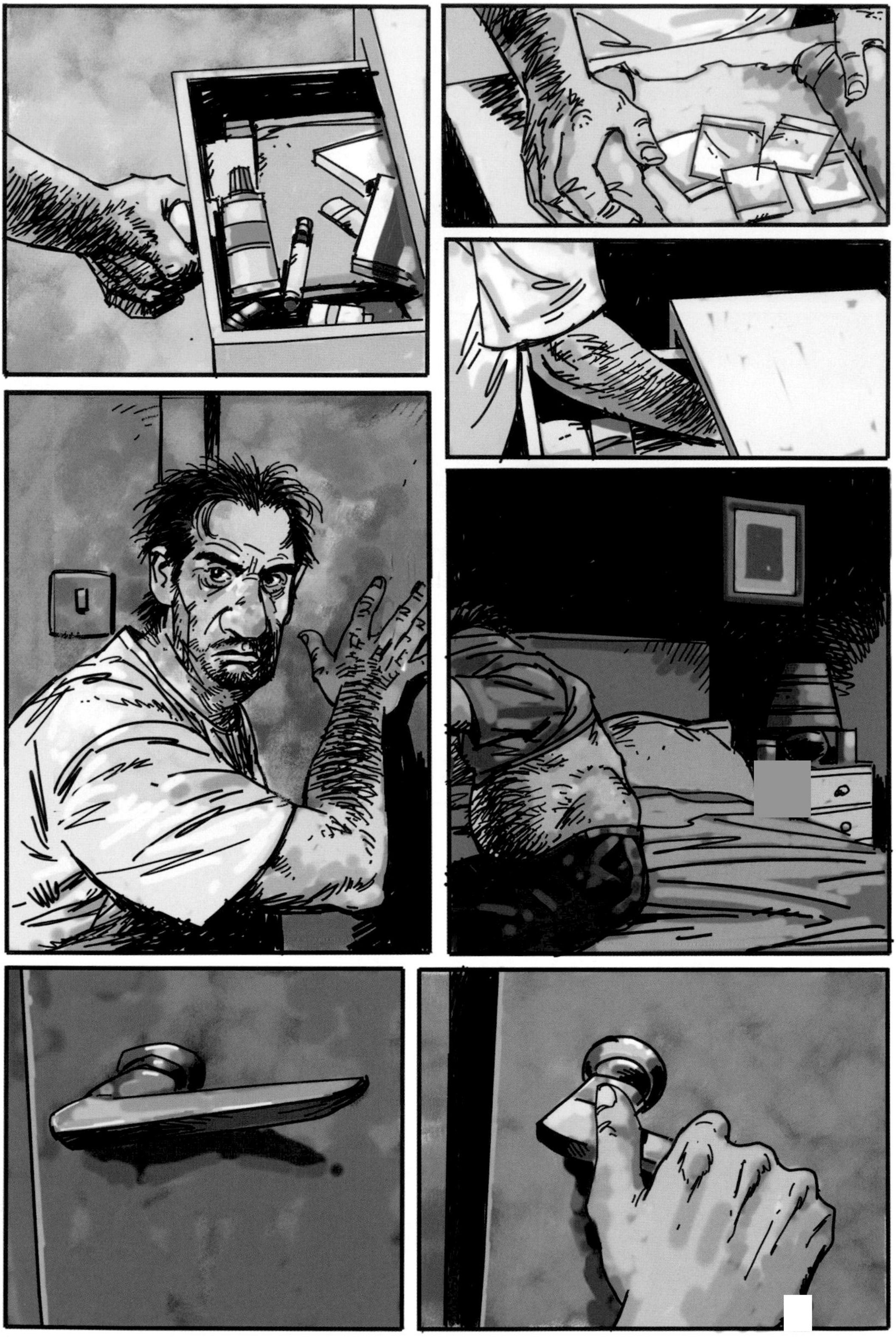

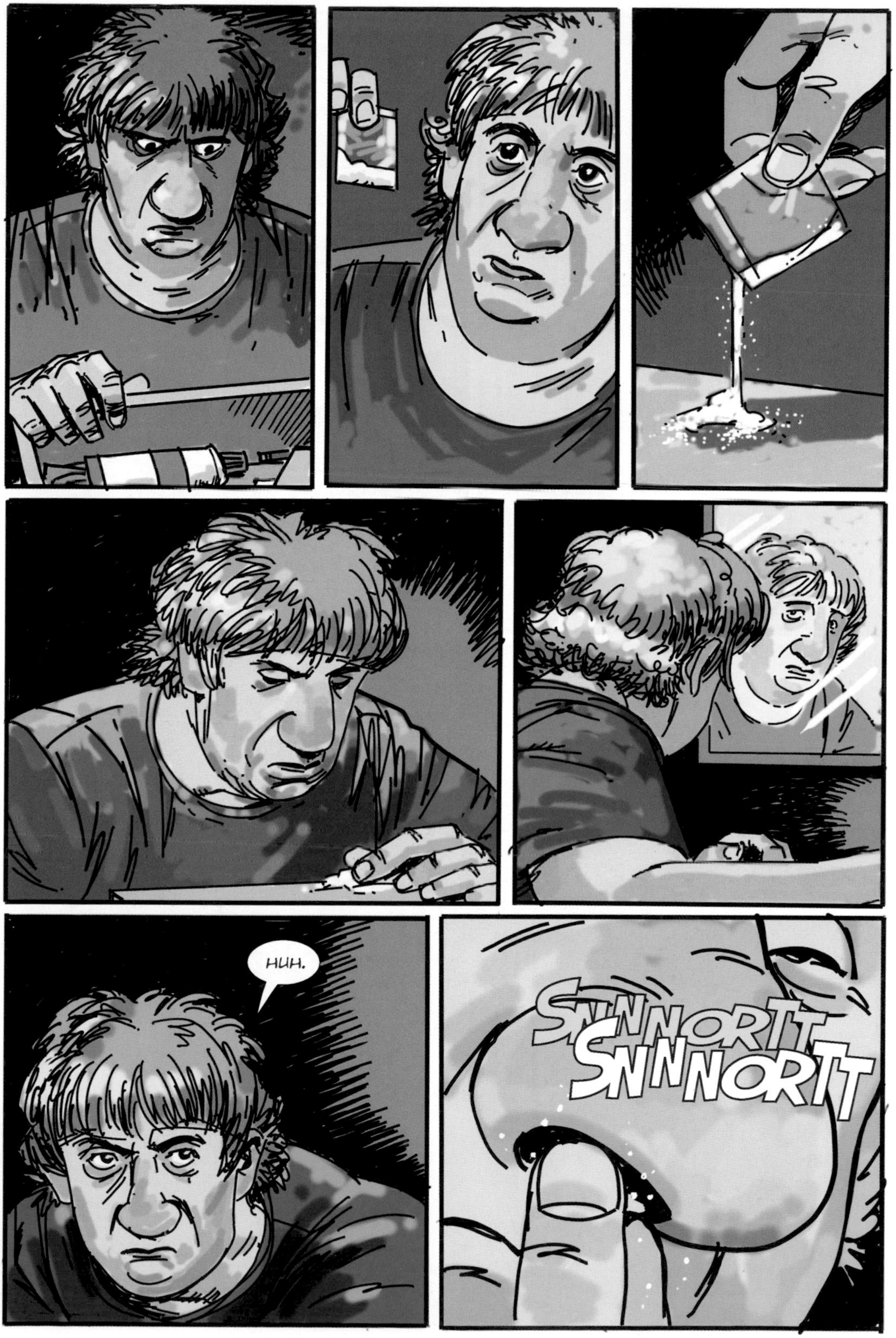
HUH.
SNNNORTT
SNNNORTT

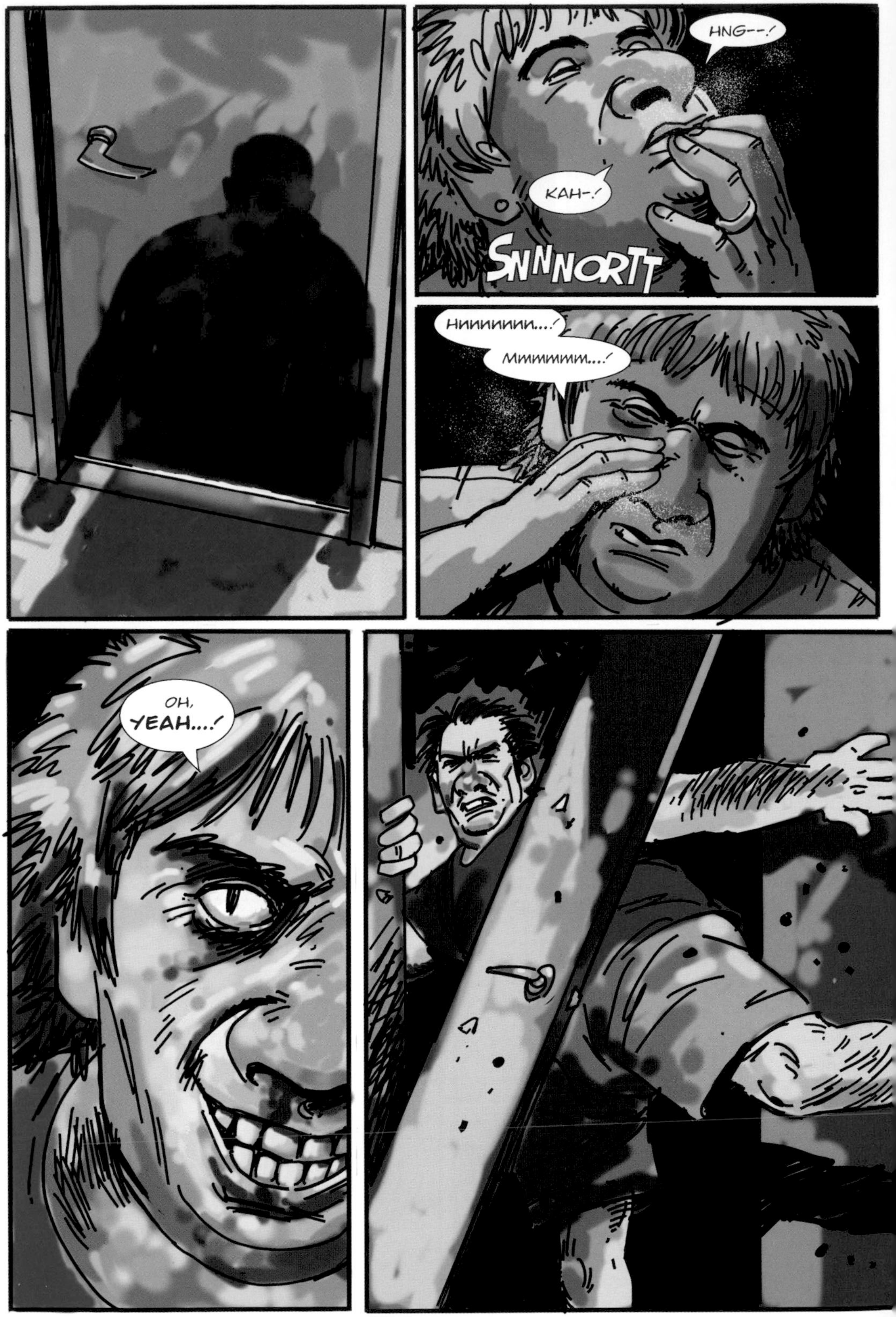
HNG--!
KAH-!
SNNNORTT
Hnnnnnnn...!
Mmmmmm...!
OH, YEAH...!

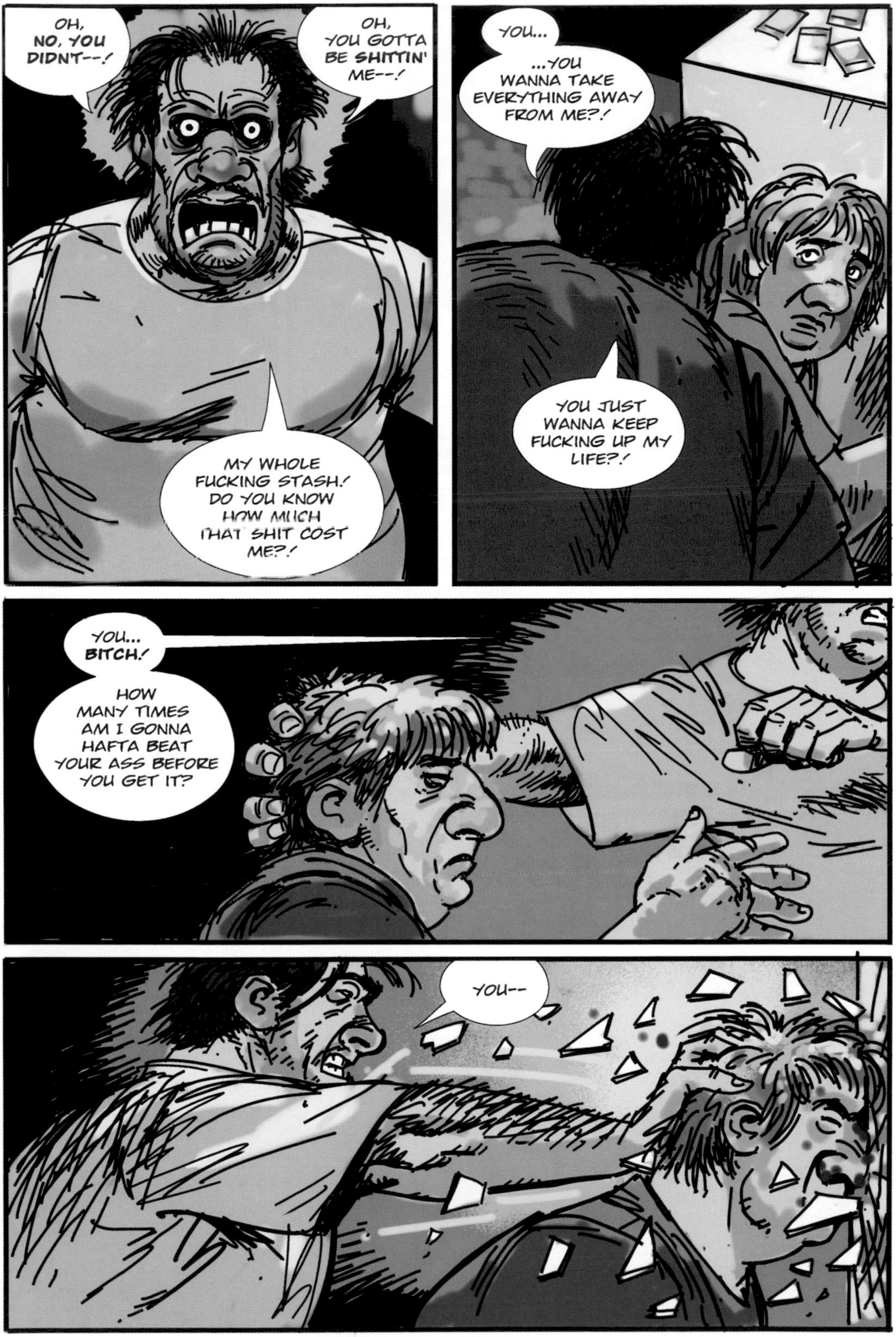
OH, NO, YOU DIDN'T--!
OH, YOU GOTTA BE SHITTIN' ME--!
MY WHOLE FUCKING STASH! DO YOU KNOW HOW MUCH THAT SHIT COST ME?!
YOU...
...YOU WANNA TAKE EVERYTHING AWAY FROM ME?!
YOU JUST WANNA KEEP FUCKING UP MY LIFE?!
YOU... BITCH!
HOW MANY TIMES AM I GONNA HAFTA BEAT YOUR ASS BEFORE YOU GET IT?
YOU--

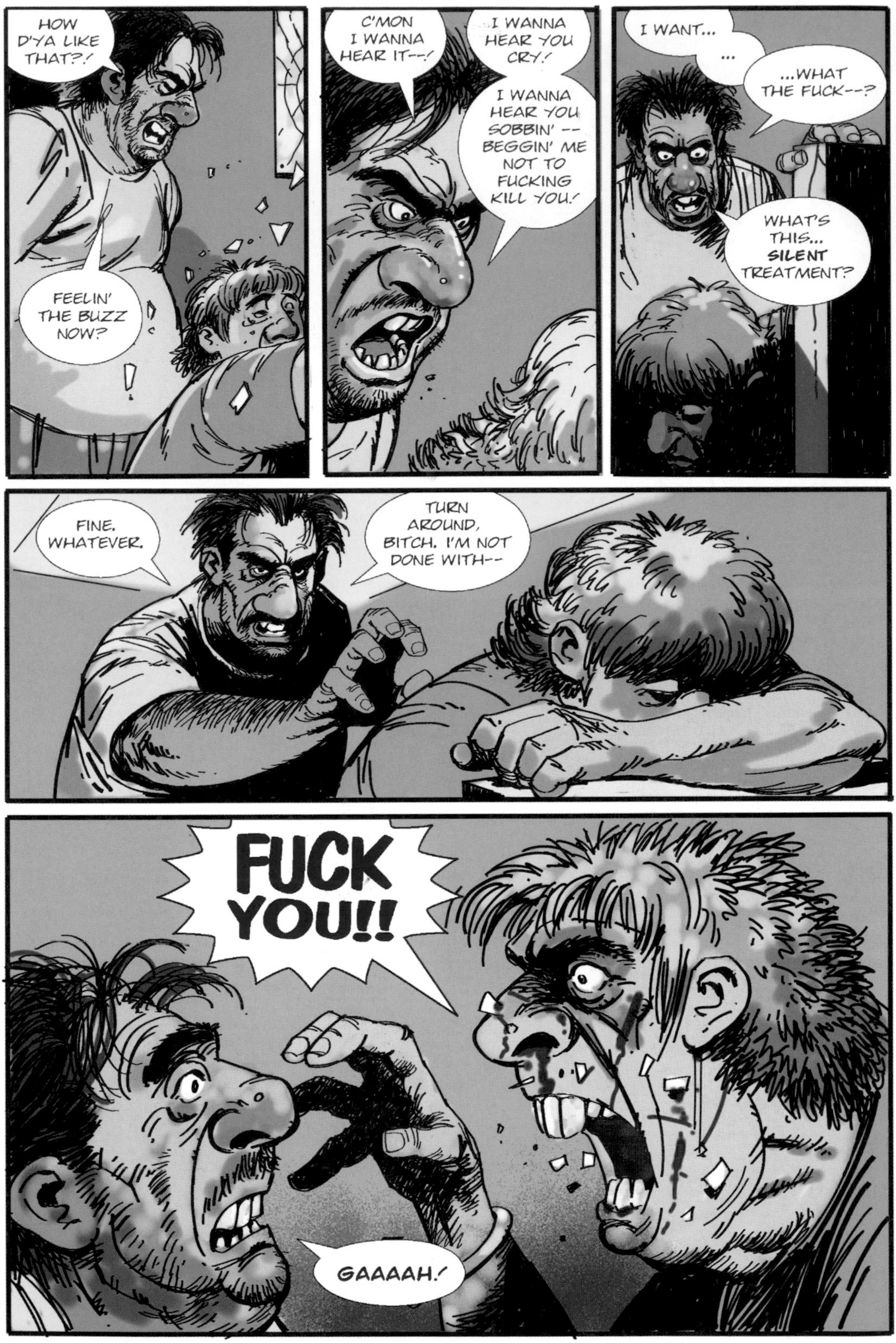
HOW D'YA LIKE THAT?!
FEELIN' THE BUZZ NOW?
C'MON I WANNA HEAR IT--!
I WANNA HEAR YOU CRY!
I WANNA HEAR YOU SOBBIN' -- BEGGIN' ME NOT TO FUCKING KILL YOU!
I WANT...
...
...WHAT THE FUCK--?
WHAT'S THIS... **SILENT** TREATMENT?
FINE. WHATEVER.
TURN AROUND, BITCH. I'M NOT DONE WITH--
FUCK YOU!!
GAAAAH!

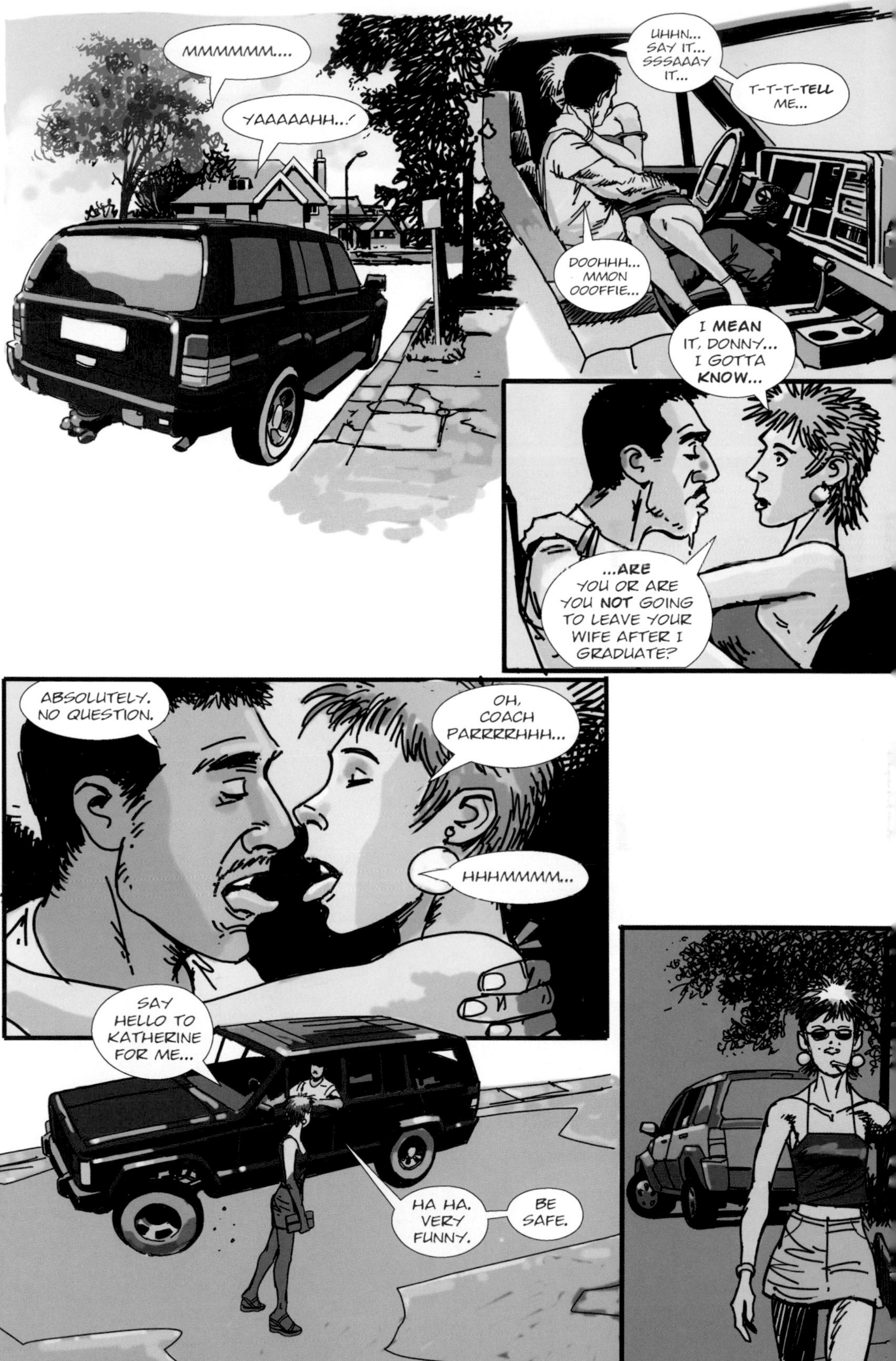
MMMMMM....
YAAAAAHH...!
UHHN... SAY IT... SSSAAAY IT...
T-T-T-**TELL** ME...
DOOHHH... MMON OOOFFIE...
I **MEAN** IT, DONNY... I GOTTA **KNOW**...
...**ARE** YOU OR ARE YOU **NOT** GOING TO LEAVE YOUR WIFE AFTER I GRADUATE?
ABSOLUTELY. NO QUESTION.
OH, COACH PARRRRHHH...
HHHMMMM...
SAY HELLO TO KATHERINE FOR ME...
HA HA. VERY FUNNY.
BE SAFE.

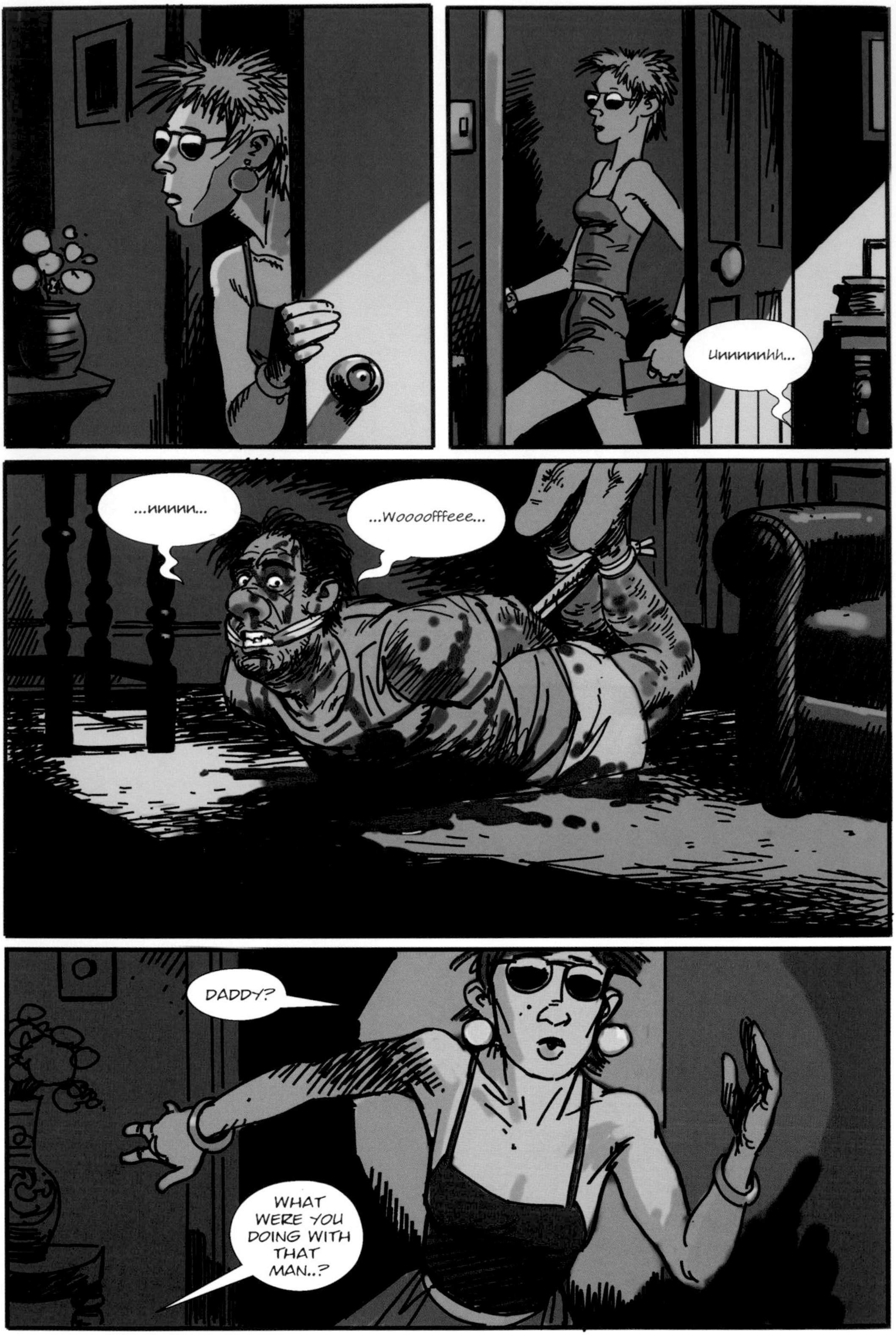
Unnnnnhh...
...nnnnn...
...Wooooffeee...
DADDY?
WHAT WERE YOU DOING WITH THAT MAN..?

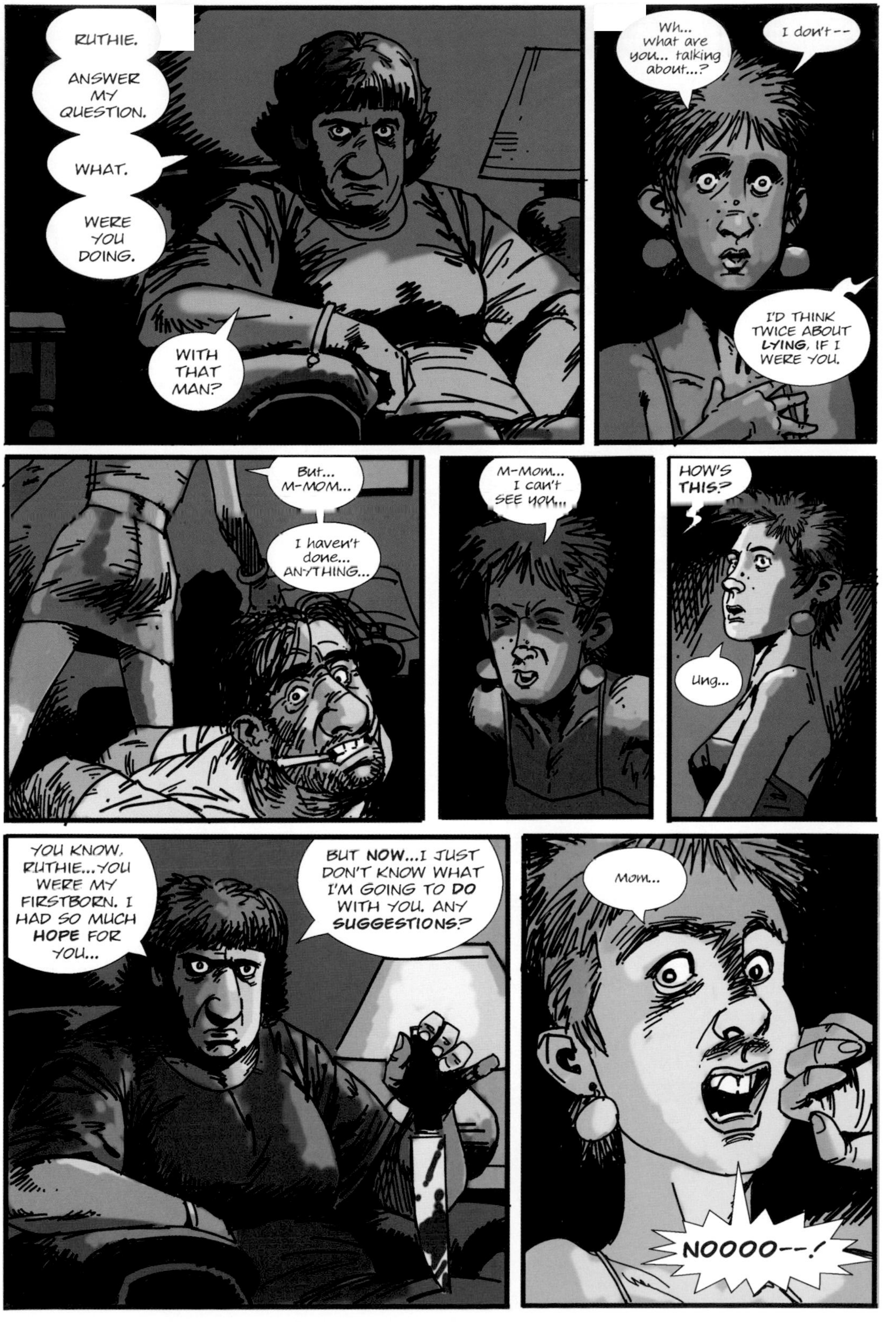
RUTHIE.
ANSWER MY QUESTION.
WHAT.
WERE YOU DOING.
WITH THAT MAN?
Wh... what are you... talking about...?
I don't --
I'D THINK TWICE ABOUT **LYING**, IF I WERE YOU.
But... M-MOM...
I haven't done... ANYTHING...
M-Mom... I can't see you...
HOW'S **THIS**?
Ung...
YOU KNOW, RUTHIE...YOU WERE MY FIRSTBORN. I HAD SO MUCH **HOPE** FOR YOU...
BUT **NOW**...I JUST DON'T KNOW WHAT I'M GOING TO **DO** WITH YOU. ANY **SUGGESTIONS**?
Mom...
NOOOO--!

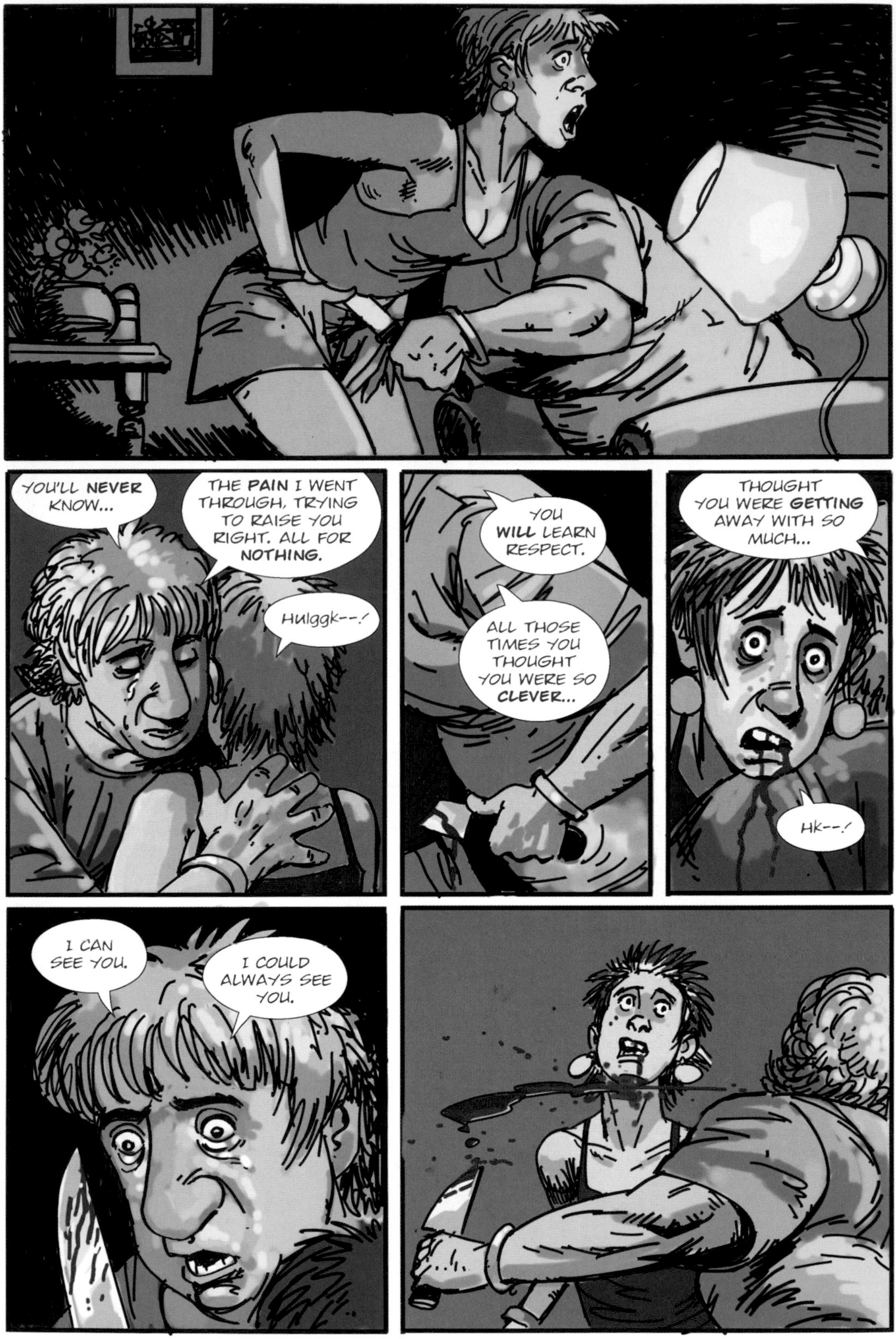

YOU'LL **NEVER** KNOW...
THE **PAIN** I WENT THROUGH, TRYING TO RAISE YOU RIGHT. ALL FOR **NOTHING.**
Hulggk--!
YOU **WILL** LEARN RESPECT.
ALL THOSE TIMES YOU THOUGHT YOU WERE SO **CLEVER...**
THOUGHT YOU WERE **GETTING** AWAY WITH SO MUCH...
HK--!
I CAN SEE YOU.
I COULD ALWAYS SEE YOU.

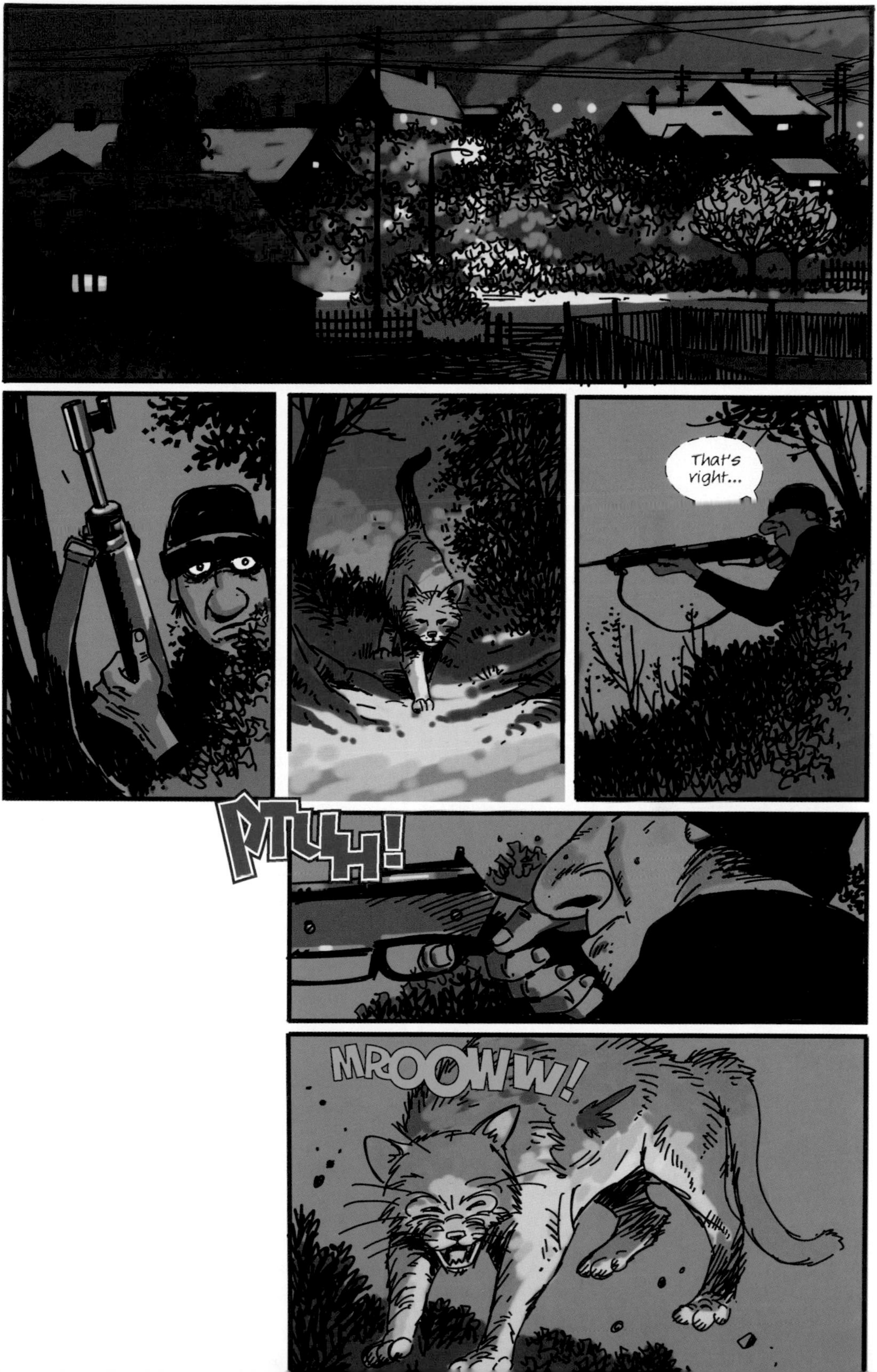
That's right...
PTUH!
MROOWW!

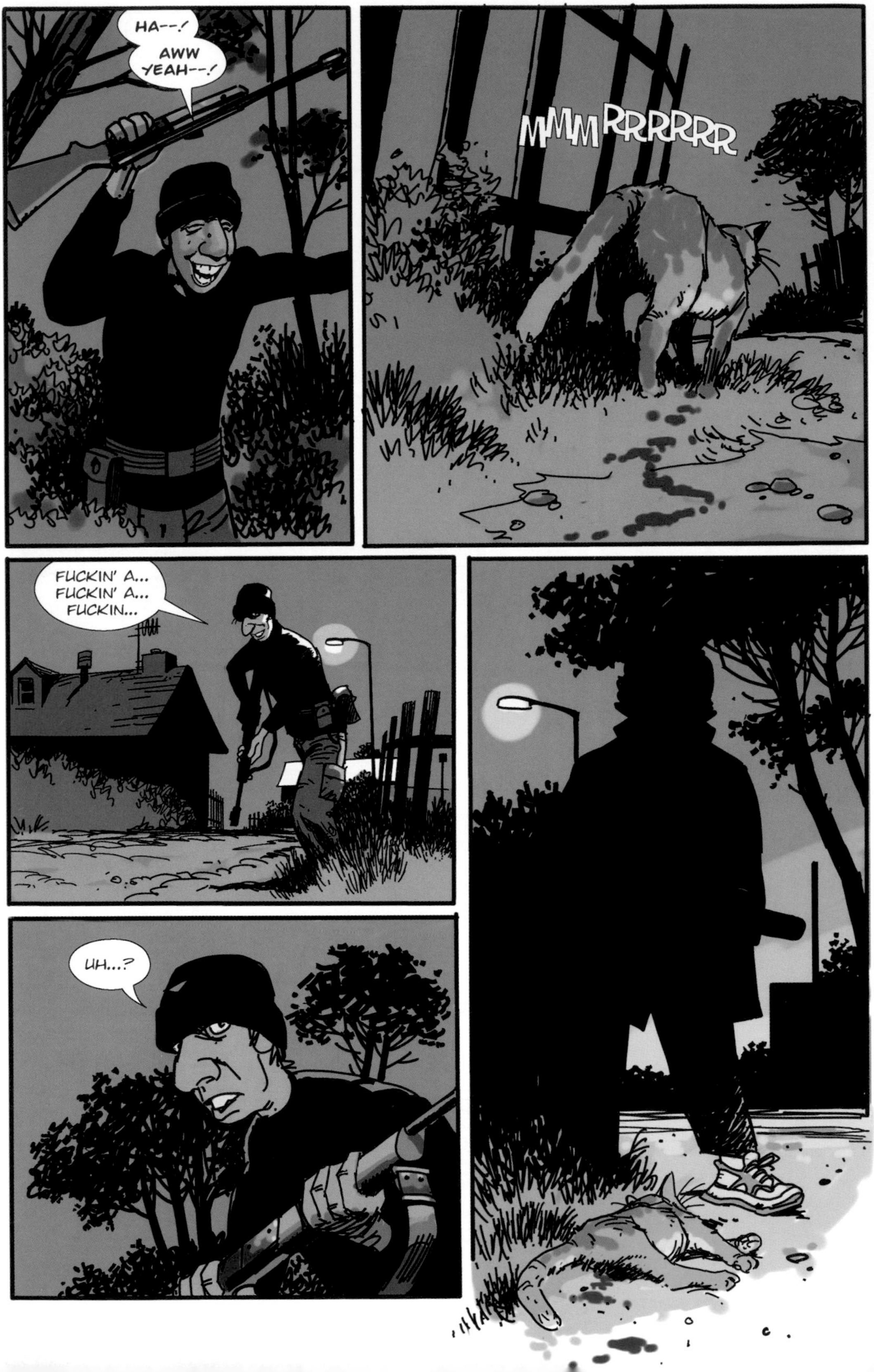
HA--!
AWW YEAH--!
MMMRRRRRRR
FUCKIN' A... FUCKIN' A... FUCKIN...
UH...?

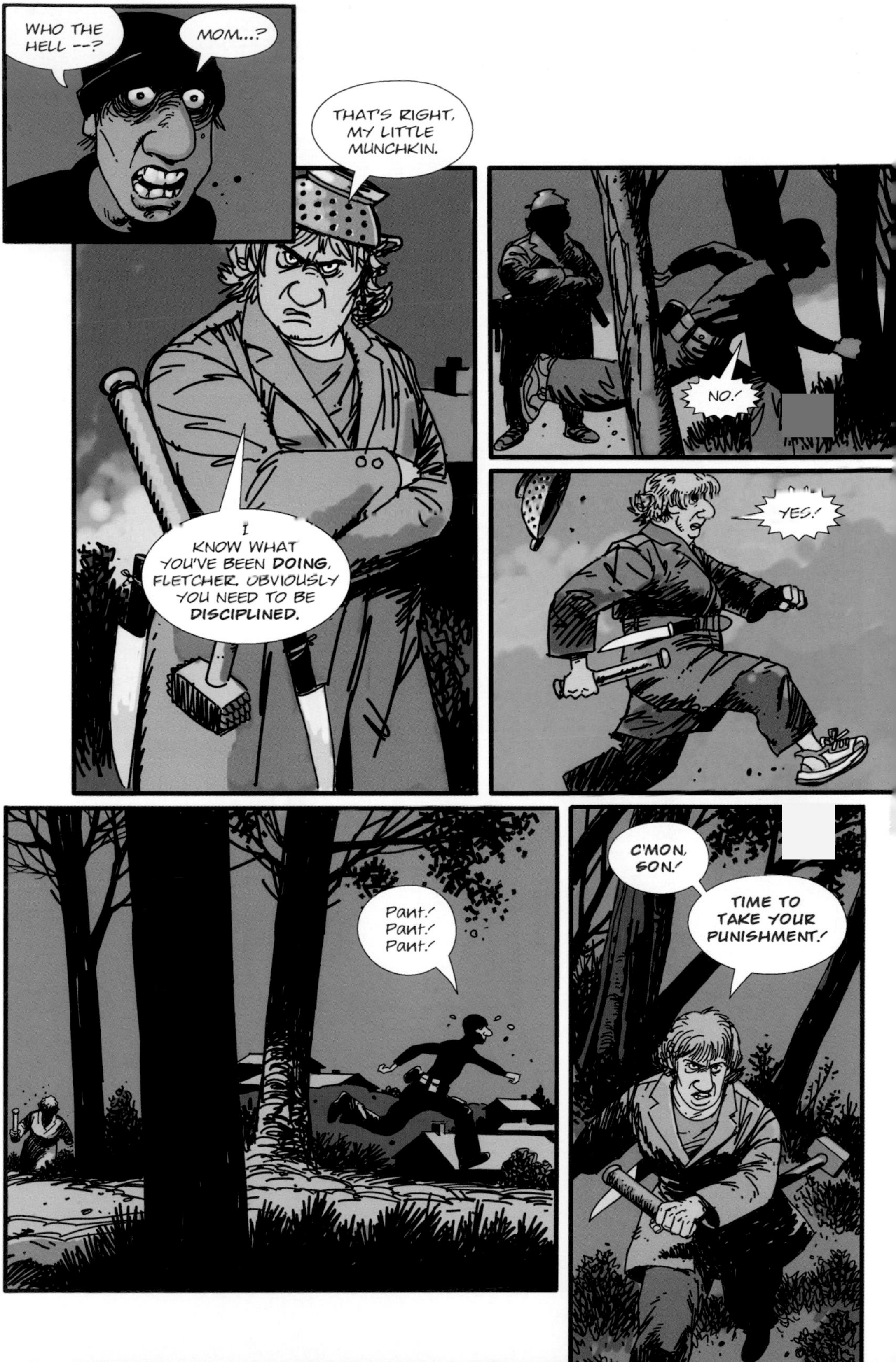
WHO THE HELL --?
MOM...?
THAT'S RIGHT, MY LITTLE MUNCHKIN.
I KNOW WHAT YOU'VE BEEN DOING, FLETCHER. OBVIOUSLY YOU NEED TO BE DISCIPLINED.
NO!
YES!
Pant! Pant! Pant!
C'MON, SON!
TIME TO TAKE YOUR PUNISHMENT!

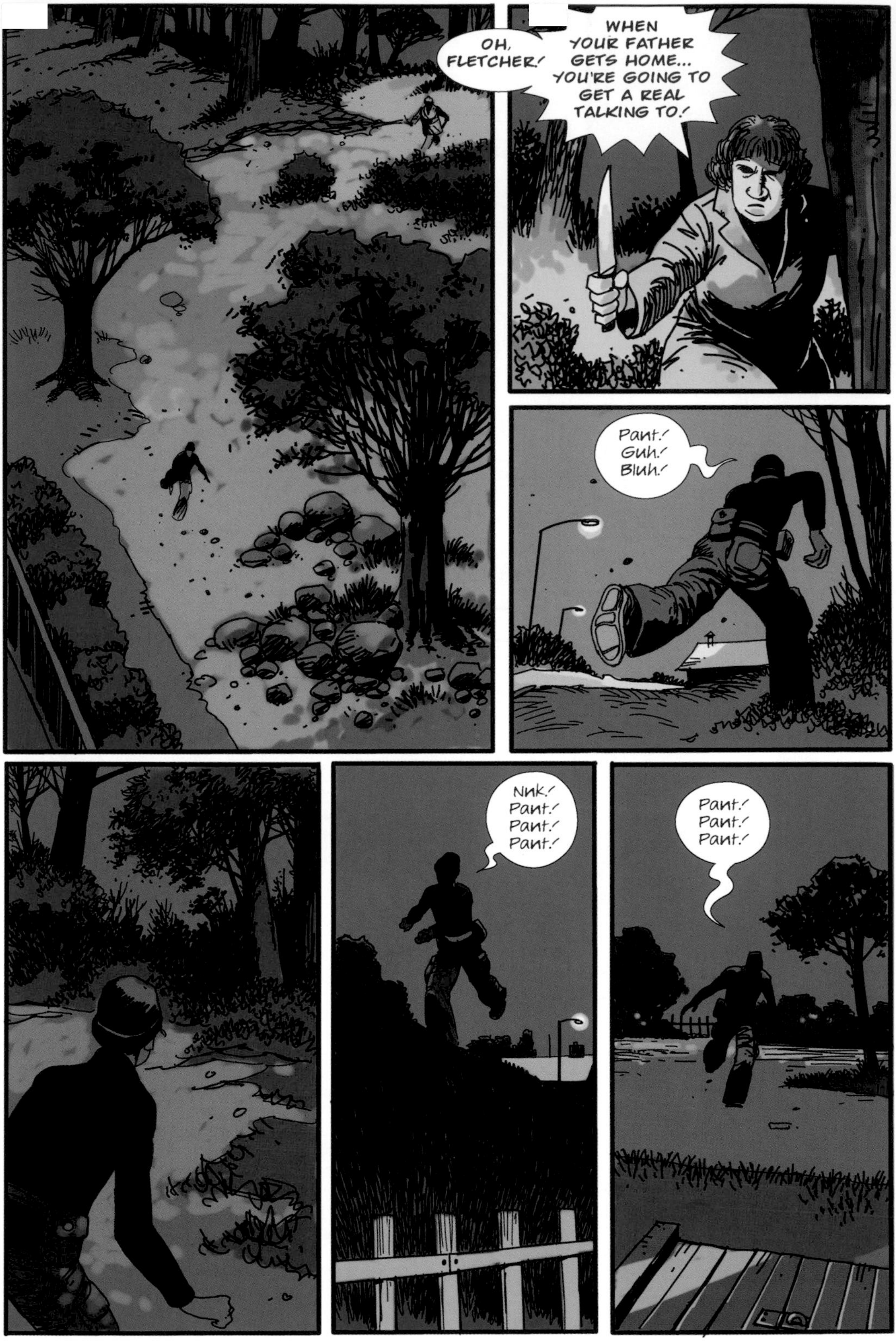
OH, FLETCHER!
WHEN YOUR FATHER GETS HOME... YOU'RE GOING TO GET A REAL TALKING TO!
Pant! Guh! Bluh!
Nnk! Pant! Pant! Pant!
Pant! Pant! Pant!

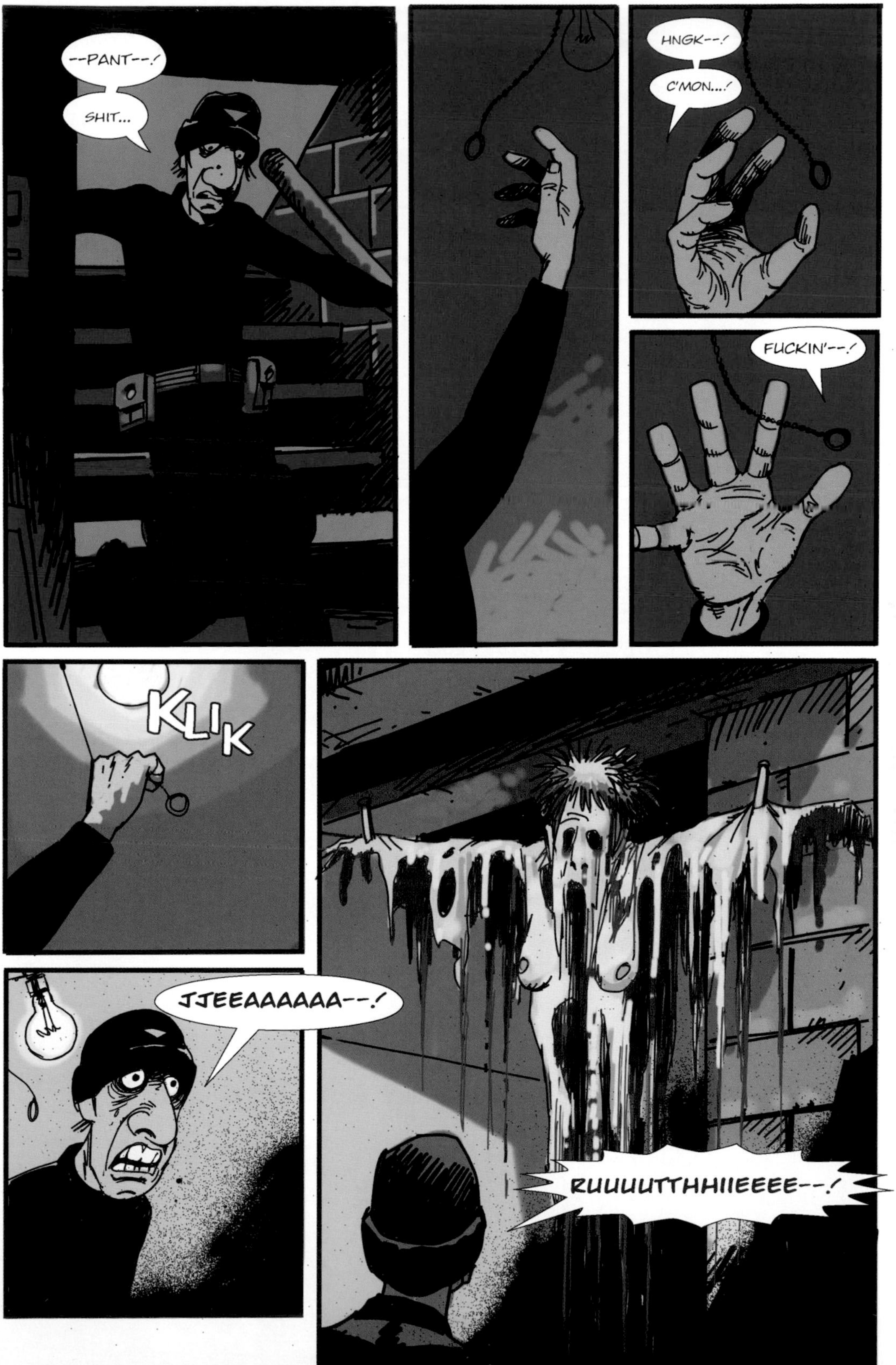
--PANT--!
SHIT...
HNGK--!
C'MON...!
FUCKIN'--!
KLIK
JJEEAAAAAA--!
RUUUUTTHHIIEEEE--!

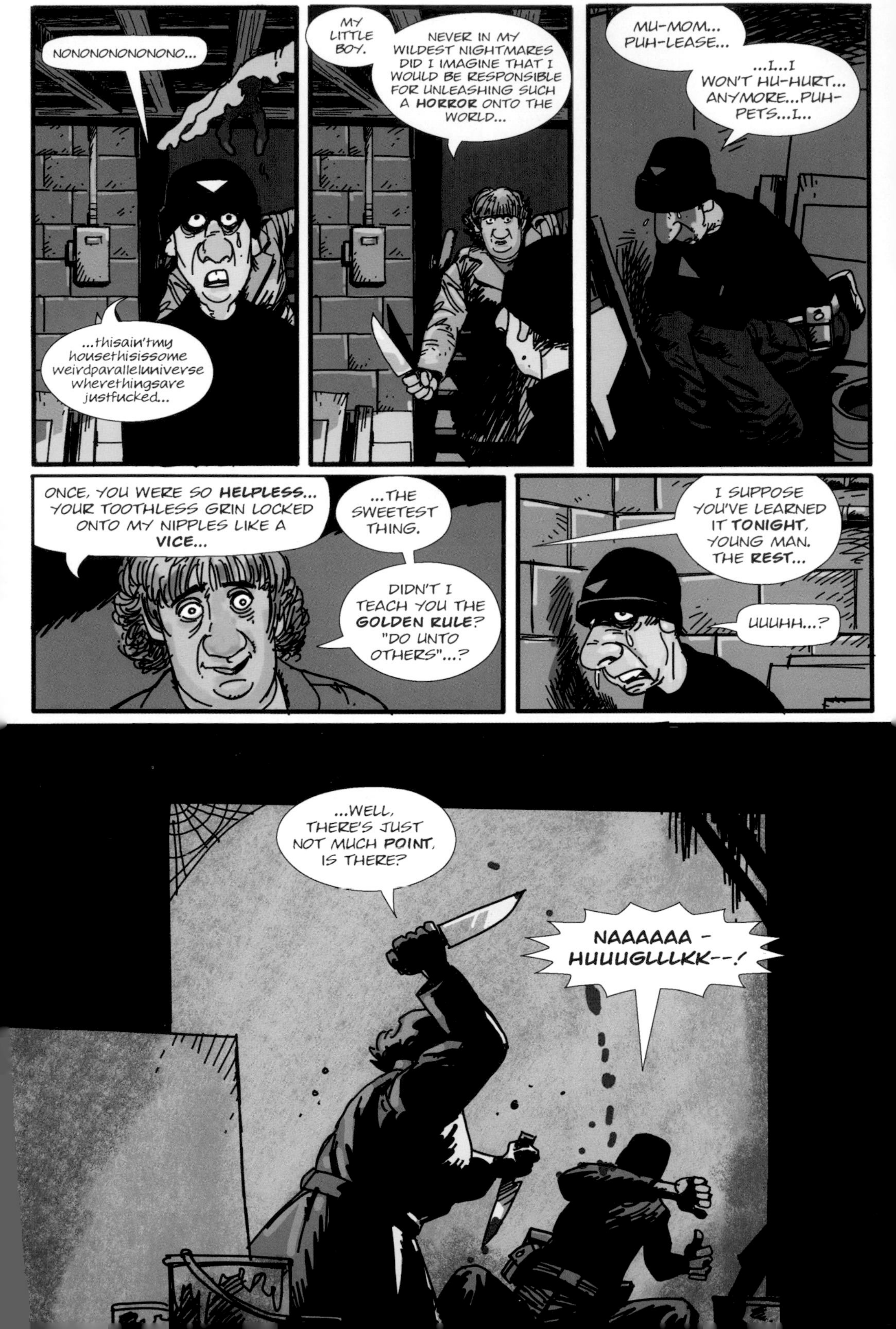
NONONONONONONO...
...thisain'tmy housethisissome weirdparalleluniverse wherethingsare justfucked...
MY LITTLE BOY.
NEVER IN MY WILDEST NIGHTMARES DID I IMAGINE THAT I WOULD BE RESPONSIBLE FOR UNLEASHING SUCH A HORROR ONTO THE WORLD...
MU-MOM... PUH-LEASE...
...I...I WON'T HU-HURT... ANYMORE...PUH-PETS...I...
ONCE, YOU WERE SO HELPLESS... YOUR TOOTHLESS GRIN LOCKED ONTO MY NIPPLES LIKE A VICE...
...THE SWEETEST THING.
DIDN'T I TEACH YOU THE GOLDEN RULE? "DO UNTO OTHERS"...?
I SUPPOSE YOU'VE LEARNED IT TONIGHT, YOUNG MAN. THE REST...
UUUHH...?
...WELL, THERE'S JUST NOT MUCH POINT, IS THERE?
NAAAAAA - HUUUGLLLKK--!

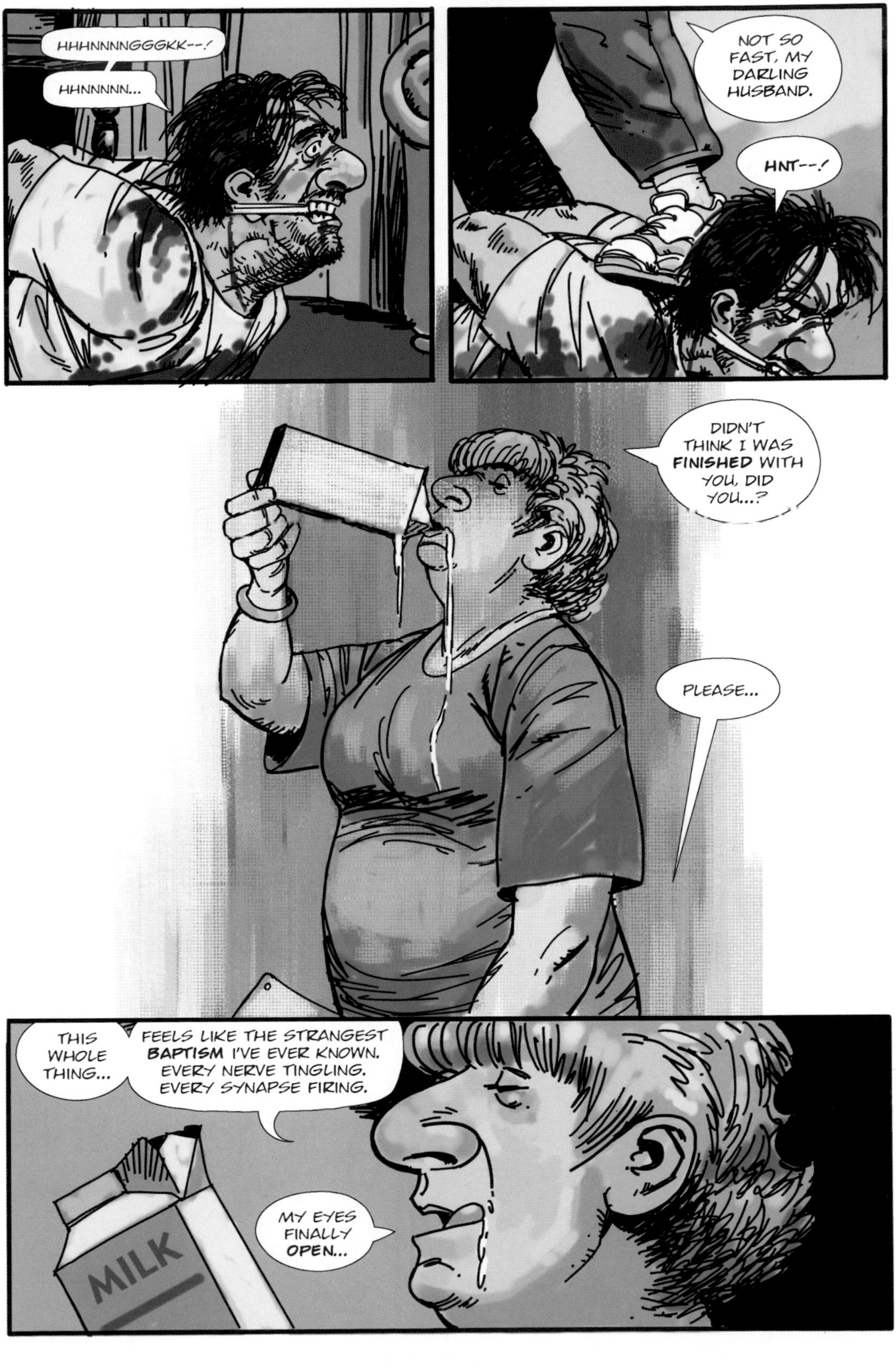
HHHHNNNNGGGKK--!
HHHNNNNN...
NOT SO FAST, MY DARLING HUSBAND.
HNT--!
DIDN'T THINK I WAS **FINISHED** WITH YOU, DID YOU...?
PLEASE...
THIS WHOLE THING...
FEELS LIKE THE STRANGEST **BAPTISM** I'VE EVER KNOWN. EVERY NERVE TINGLING. EVERY SYNAPSE FIRING.
MY EYES FINALLY **OPEN**...
MILK

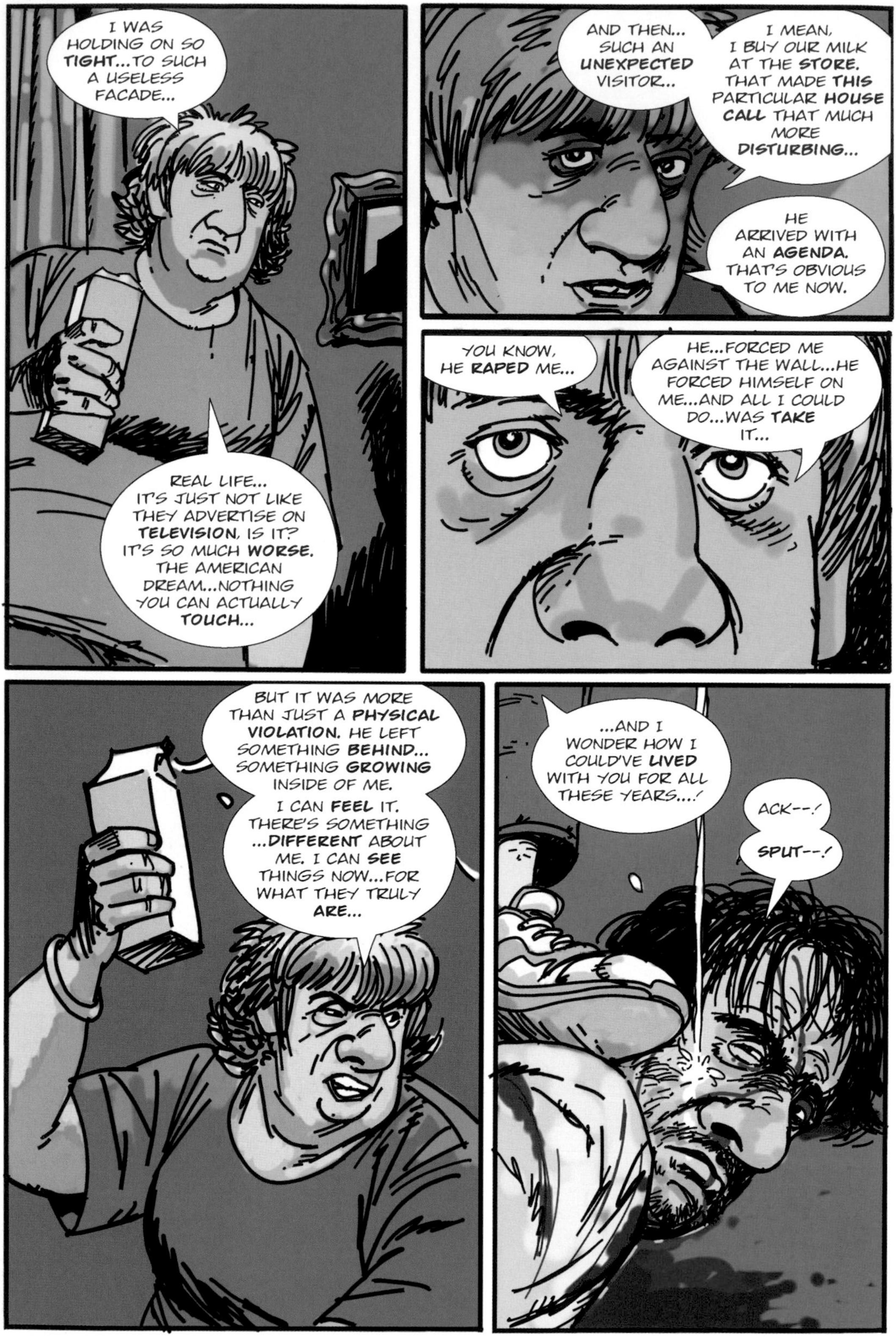
I WAS HOLDING ON SO TIGHT...TO SUCH A USELESS FACADE...
REAL LIFE... IT'S JUST NOT LIKE THEY ADVERTISE ON TELEVISION, IS IT? IT'S SO MUCH WORSE. THE AMERICAN DREAM...NOTHING YOU CAN ACTUALLY TOUCH...
AND THEN... SUCH AN UNEXPECTED VISITOR...
I MEAN, I BUY OUR MILK AT THE STORE. THAT MADE THIS PARTICULAR HOUSE CALL THAT MUCH MORE DISTURBING...
HE ARRIVED WITH AN AGENDA. THAT'S OBVIOUS TO ME NOW.
YOU KNOW, HE RAPED ME...
HE...FORCED ME AGAINST THE WALL...HE FORCED HIMSELF ON ME...AND ALL I COULD DO...WAS TAKE IT...
BUT IT WAS MORE THAN JUST A PHYSICAL VIOLATION. HE LEFT SOMETHING BEHIND... SOMETHING GROWING INSIDE OF ME.
I CAN FEEL IT. THERE'S SOMETHING ...DIFFERENT ABOUT ME. I CAN SEE THINGS NOW...FOR WHAT THEY TRULY ARE...
...AND I WONDER HOW I COULD'VE LIVED WITH YOU FOR ALL THESE YEARS...!
ACK--!
SPUT--!

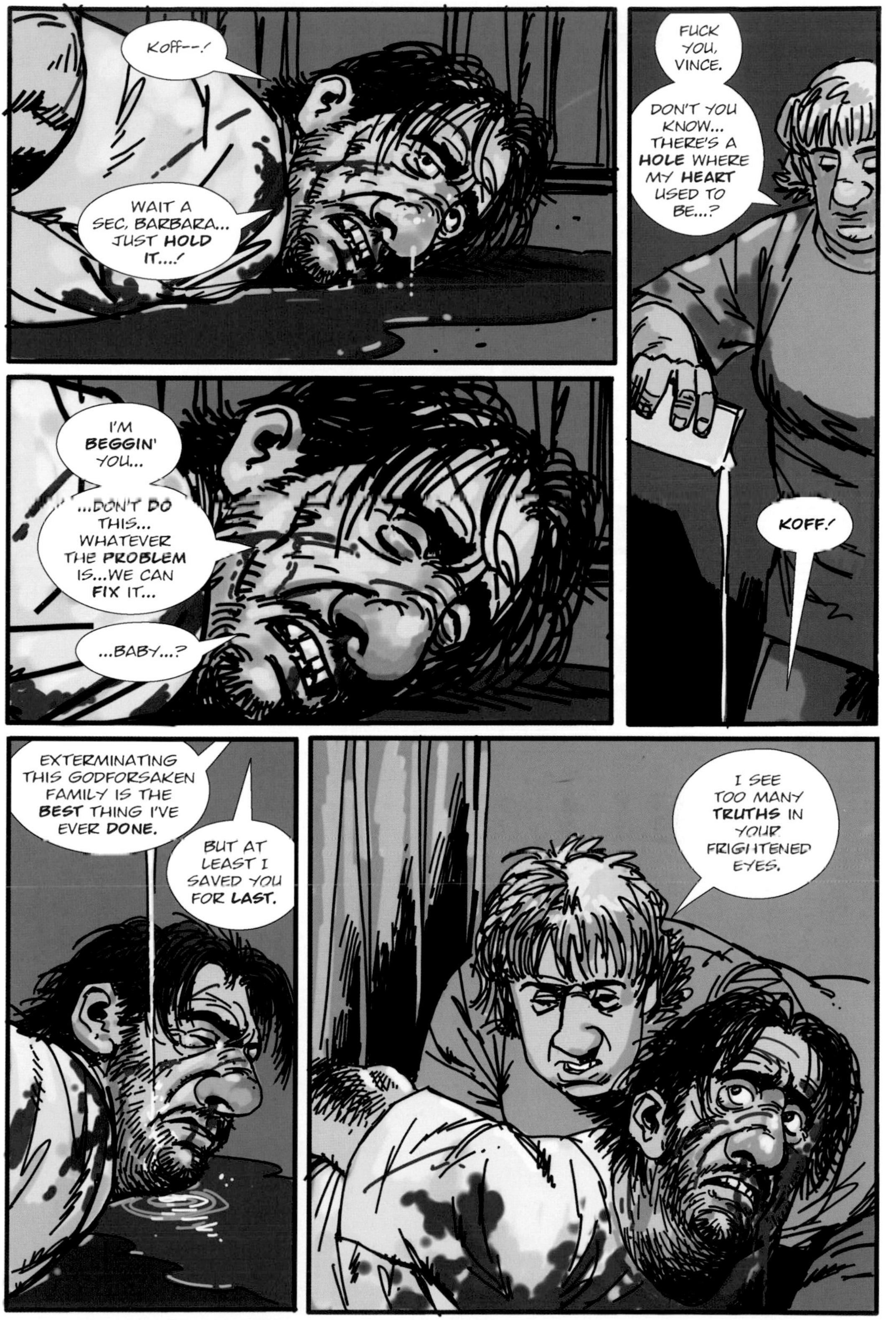
Koff--!
WAIT A SEC, BARBARA... JUST **HOLD** IT....!
FUCK YOU, VINCE.
DON'T YOU KNOW... THERE'S A **HOLE** WHERE MY **HEART** USED TO BE...?
I'M **BEGGIN'** YOU...
...DON'T **DO** THIS... WHATEVER THE **PROBLEM** IS...WE CAN **FIX** IT...
...BABY...?
KOFF!
EXTERMINATING THIS GODFORSAKEN FAMILY IS THE **BEST** THING I'VE EVER **DONE.**
BUT AT LEAST I SAVED YOU FOR **LAST.**
I SEE TOO MANY **TRUTHS** IN YOUR FRIGHTENED EYES.

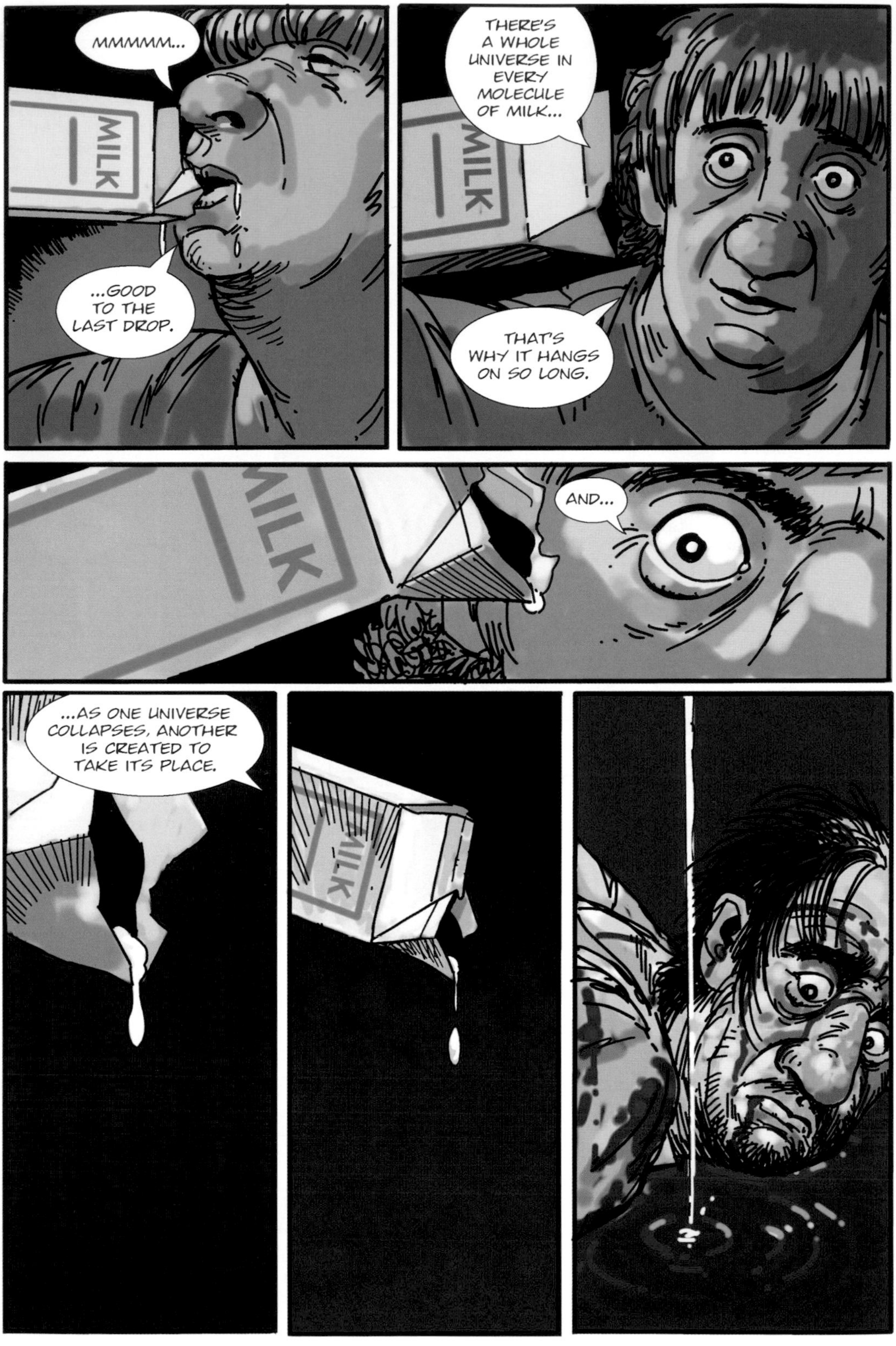
MMMMM...
...GOOD TO THE LAST DROP.
MILK
THERE'S A WHOLE UNIVERSE IN EVERY MOLECULE OF MILK...
THAT'S WHY IT HANGS ON SO LONG.
MILK
AND...
MILK
...AS ONE UNIVERSE COLLAPSES, ANOTHER IS CREATED TO TAKE ITS PLACE.
MILK

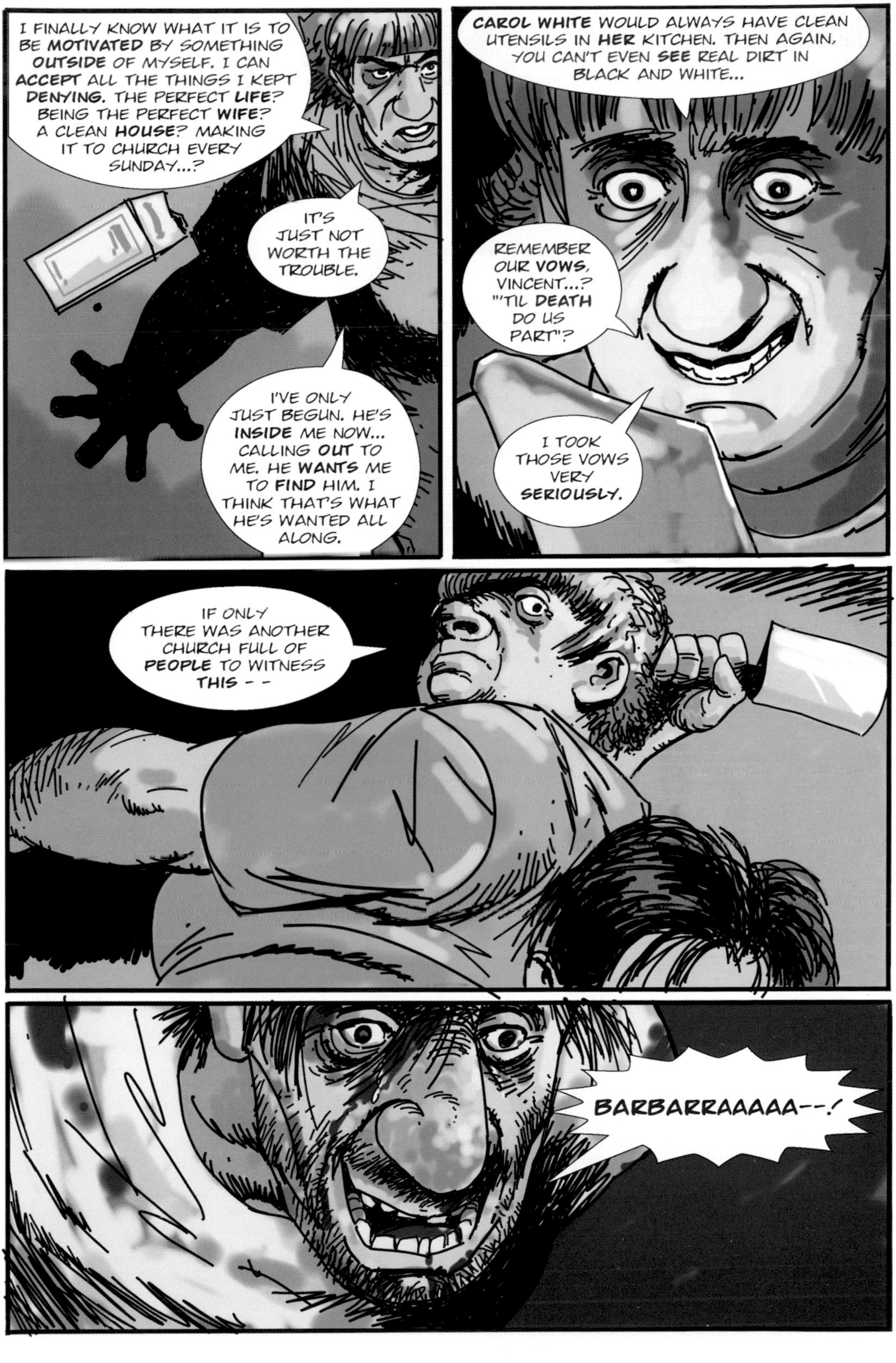
I FINALLY KNOW WHAT IT IS TO BE MOTIVATED BY SOMETHING OUTSIDE OF MYSELF. I CAN ACCEPT ALL THE THINGS I KEPT DENYING. THE PERFECT LIFE? BEING THE PERFECT WIFE? A CLEAN HOUSE? MAKING IT TO CHURCH EVERY SUNDAY...?
IT'S JUST NOT WORTH THE TROUBLE.
I'VE ONLY JUST BEGUN. HE'S INSIDE ME NOW... CALLING OUT TO ME. HE WANTS ME TO FIND HIM. I THINK THAT'S WHAT HE'S WANTED ALL ALONG.
CAROL WHITE WOULD ALWAYS HAVE CLEAN UTENSILS IN HER KITCHEN. THEN AGAIN, YOU CAN'T EVEN SEE REAL DIRT IN BLACK AND WHITE...
REMEMBER OUR VOWS, VINCENT...? "'TIL DEATH DO US PART"?
I TOOK THOSE VOWS VERY SERIOUSLY.
IF ONLY THERE WAS ANOTHER CHURCH FULL OF PEOPLE TO WITNESS THIS - -
BARBARRAAAAA--!

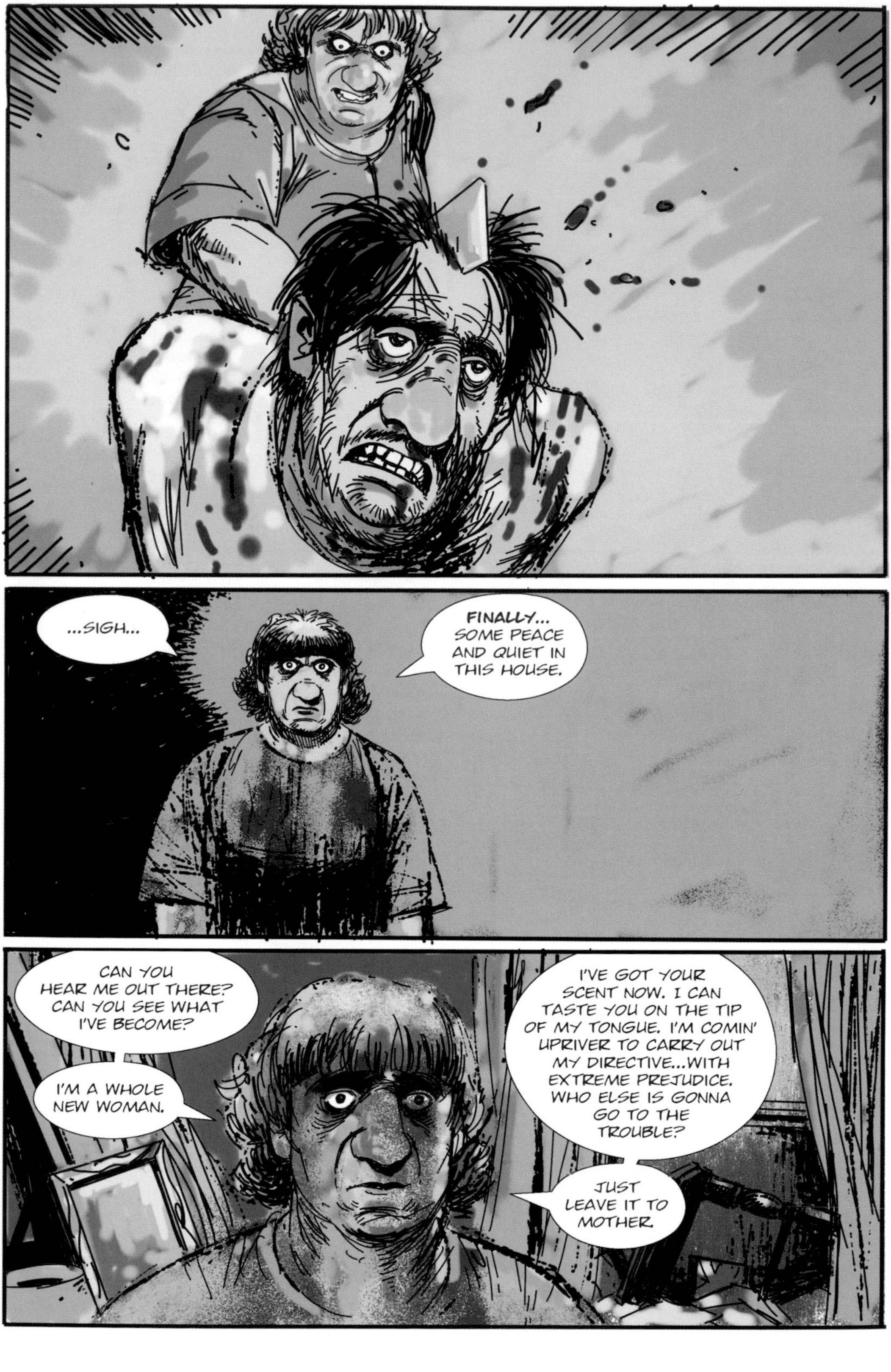
...SIGH...
FINALLY... SOME PEACE AND QUIET IN THIS HOUSE.
CAN YOU HEAR ME OUT THERE? CAN YOU SEE WHAT I'VE BECOME?
I'M A WHOLE NEW WOMAN.
I'VE GOT YOUR SCENT NOW. I CAN TASTE YOU ON THE TIP OF MY TONGUE. I'M COMIN' UPRIVER TO CARRY OUT MY DIRECTIVE...WITH EXTREME PREJUDICE. WHO ELSE IS GONNA GO TO THE TROUBLE?
JUST LEAVE IT TO MOTHER.

CHAPTER 4

"I TOUCH MYSELF"

SUBURBAN LAWNCARE GOES URBAN RENEWAL

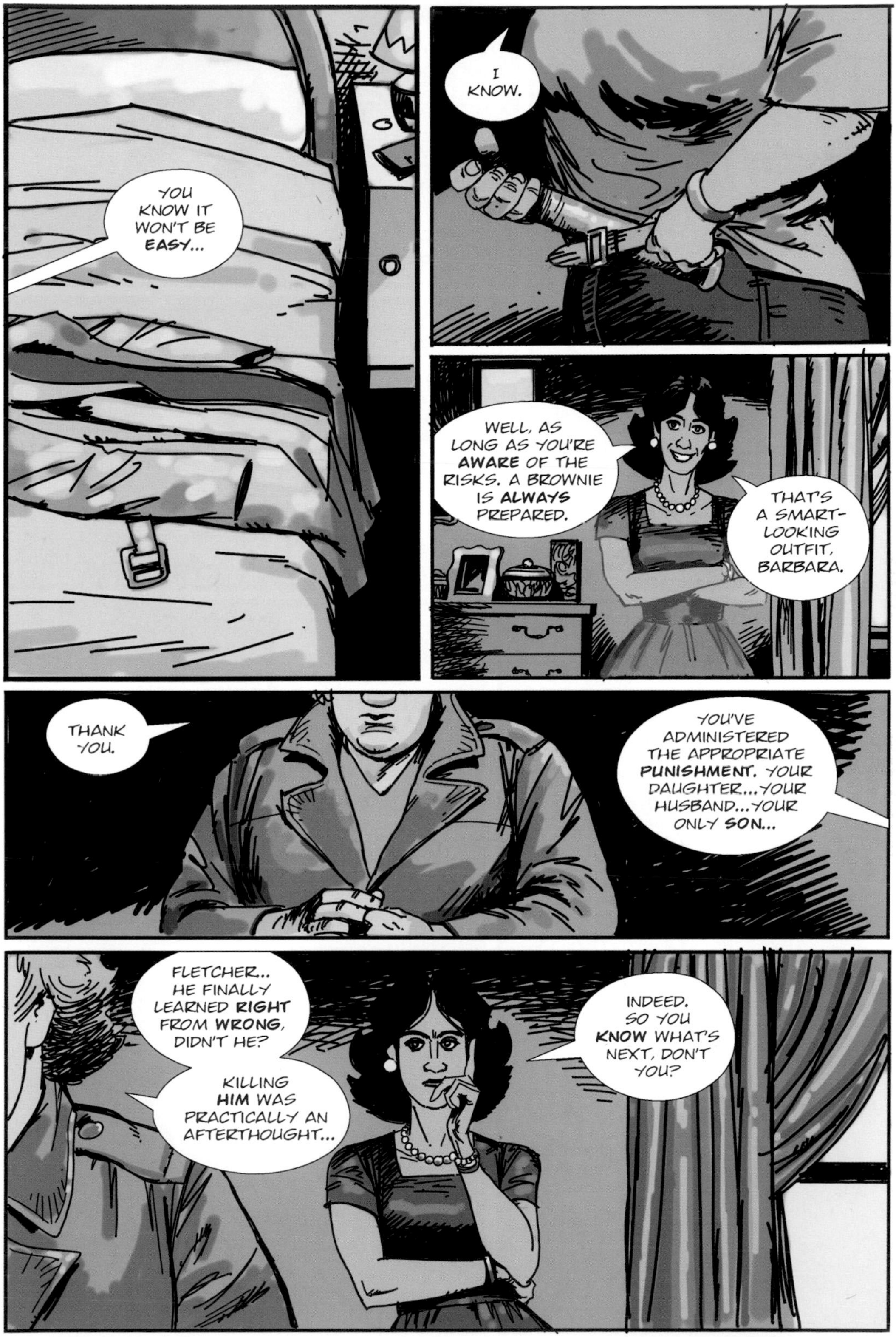
YOU KNOW IT WON'T BE EASY...
I KNOW.
WELL, AS LONG AS YOU'RE AWARE OF THE RISKS. A BROWNIE IS ALWAYS PREPARED.
THAT'S A SMART-LOOKING OUTFIT, BARBARA.
THANK YOU.
YOU'VE ADMINISTERED THE APPROPRIATE PUNISHMENT. YOUR DAUGHTER...YOUR HUSBAND...YOUR ONLY SON...
FLETCHER... HE FINALLY LEARNED RIGHT FROM WRONG, DIDN'T HE?
KILLING HIM WAS PRACTICALLY AN AFTERTHOUGHT...
INDEED. SO YOU KNOW WHAT'S NEXT, DON'T YOU?

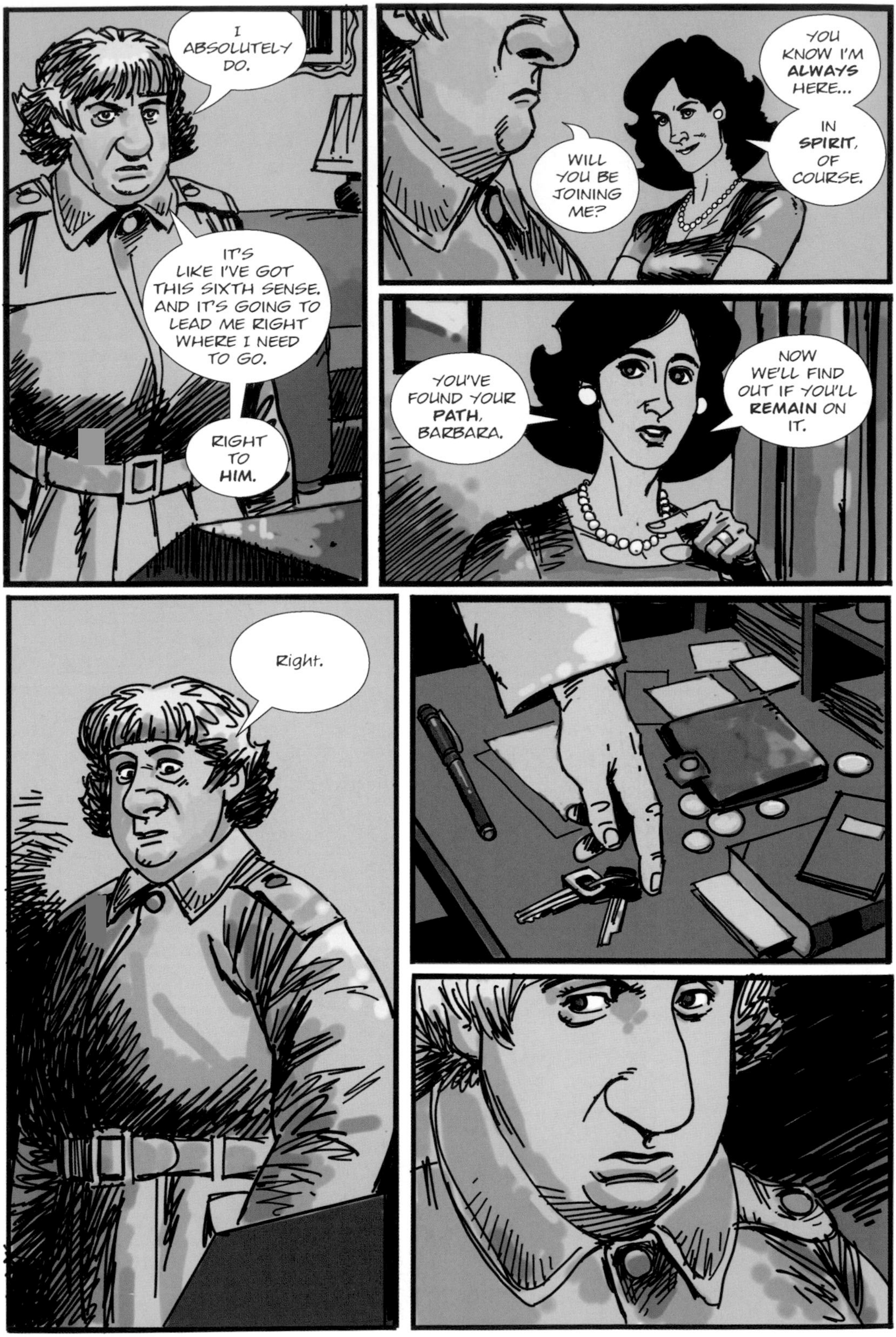
I ABSOLUTELY DO.
IT'S LIKE I'VE GOT THIS SIXTH SENSE. AND IT'S GOING TO LEAD ME RIGHT WHERE I NEED TO GO.
RIGHT TO **HIM.**
WILL YOU BE JOINING ME?
YOU KNOW I'M **ALWAYS** HERE...
IN **SPIRIT**, OF COURSE.
YOU'VE FOUND YOUR **PATH**, BARBARA.
NOW WE'LL FIND OUT IF YOU'LL **REMAIN** ON IT.
Right.

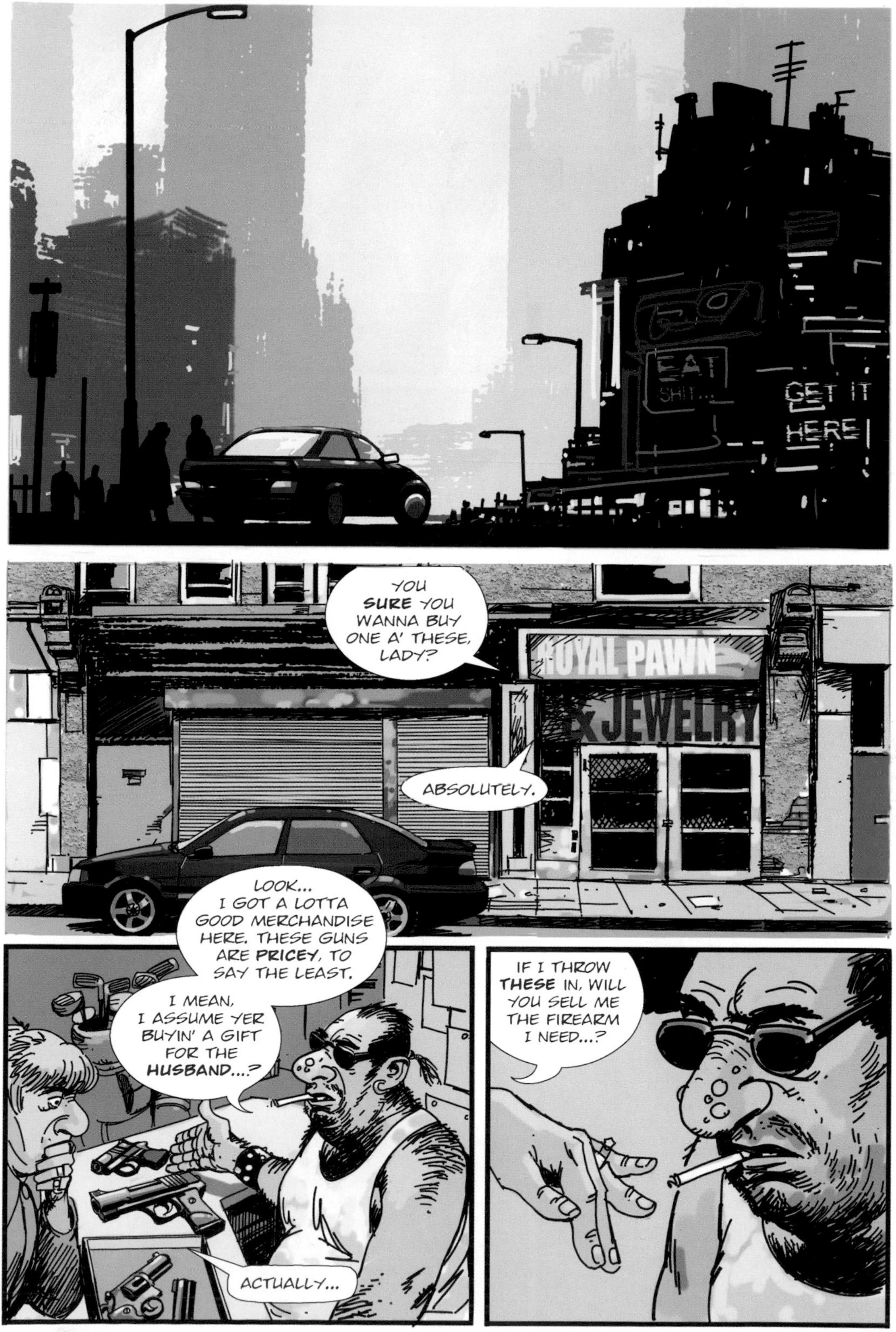
EAT SHIT...
GET IT HERE
YOU SURE YOU WANNA BUY ONE A' THESE, LADY?
ROYAL PAWN & JEWELRY
ABSOLUTELY.
LOOK... I GOT A LOTTA GOOD MERCHANDISE HERE. THESE GUNS ARE PRICEY, TO SAY THE LEAST.
I MEAN, I ASSUME YER BUYIN' A GIFT FOR THE HUSBAND...?
ACTUALLY...
IF I THROW THESE IN, WILL YOU SELL ME THE FIREARM I NEED...?

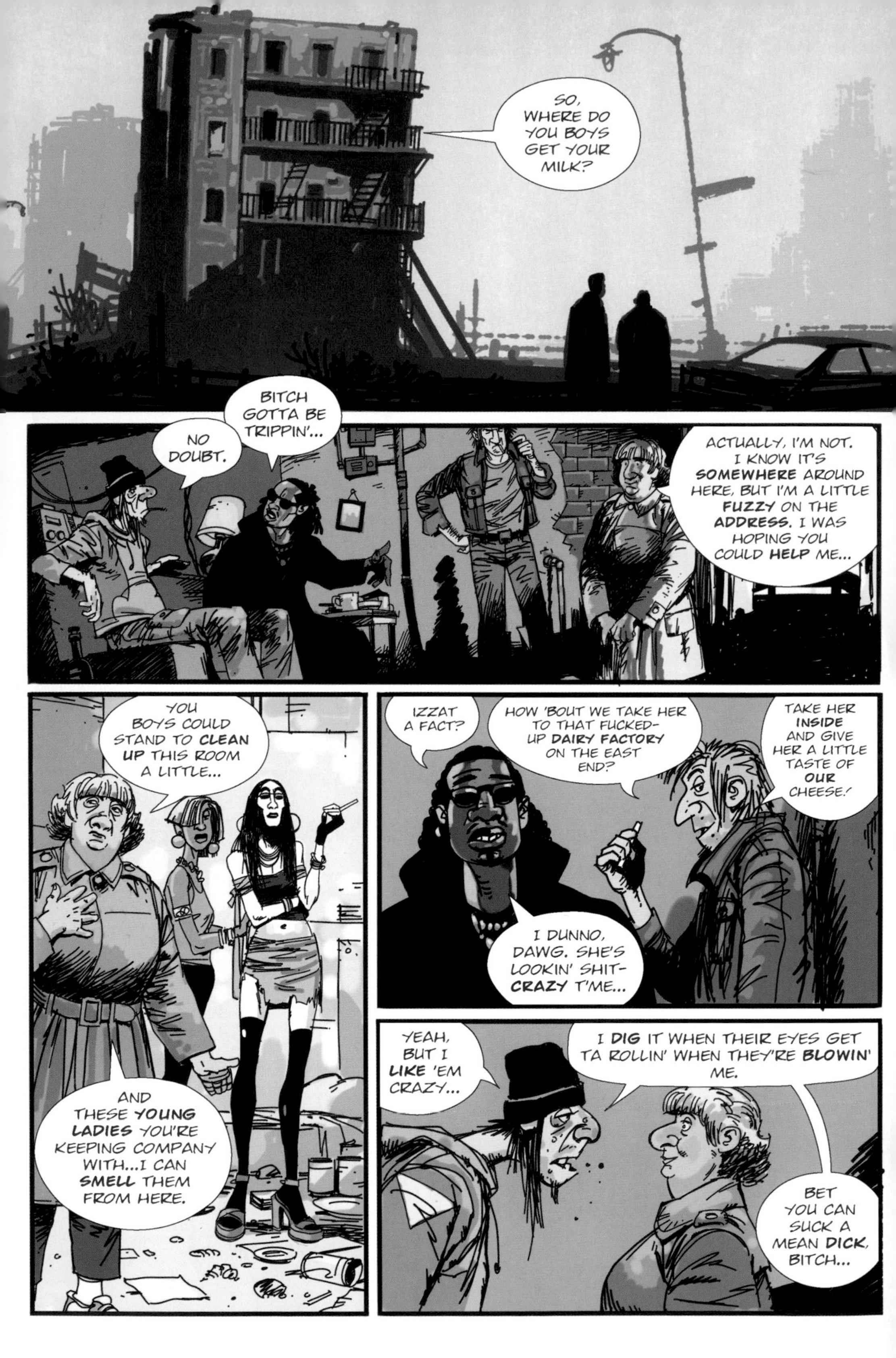
SO, WHERE DO YOU BOYS GET YOUR MILK?
NO DOUBT.
BITCH GOTTA BE TRIPPIN'...
ACTUALLY, I'M NOT. I KNOW IT'S **SOMEWHERE** AROUND HERE, BUT I'M A LITTLE **FUZZY** ON THE **ADDRESS.** I WAS HOPING YOU COULD **HELP** ME...
YOU BOYS COULD STAND TO **CLEAN UP** THIS ROOM A LITTLE...
AND THESE **YOUNG LADIES** YOU'RE KEEPING COMPANY WITH...I CAN **SMELL** THEM FROM HERE.
IZZAT A FACT?
HOW 'BOUT WE TAKE HER TO THAT FUCKED-UP **DAIRY FACTORY** ON THE EAST END?
TAKE HER **INSIDE** AND GIVE HER A LITTLE TASTE OF **OUR** CHEESE!
I DUNNO, DAWG. SHE'S LOOKIN' SHIT-**CRAZY** T'ME...
YEAH, BUT I **LIKE** 'EM CRAZY...
I **DIG** IT WHEN THEIR EYES GET TA ROLLIN' WHEN THEY'RE **BLOWIN'** ME.
BET YOU CAN SUCK A MEAN **DICK**, BITCH...

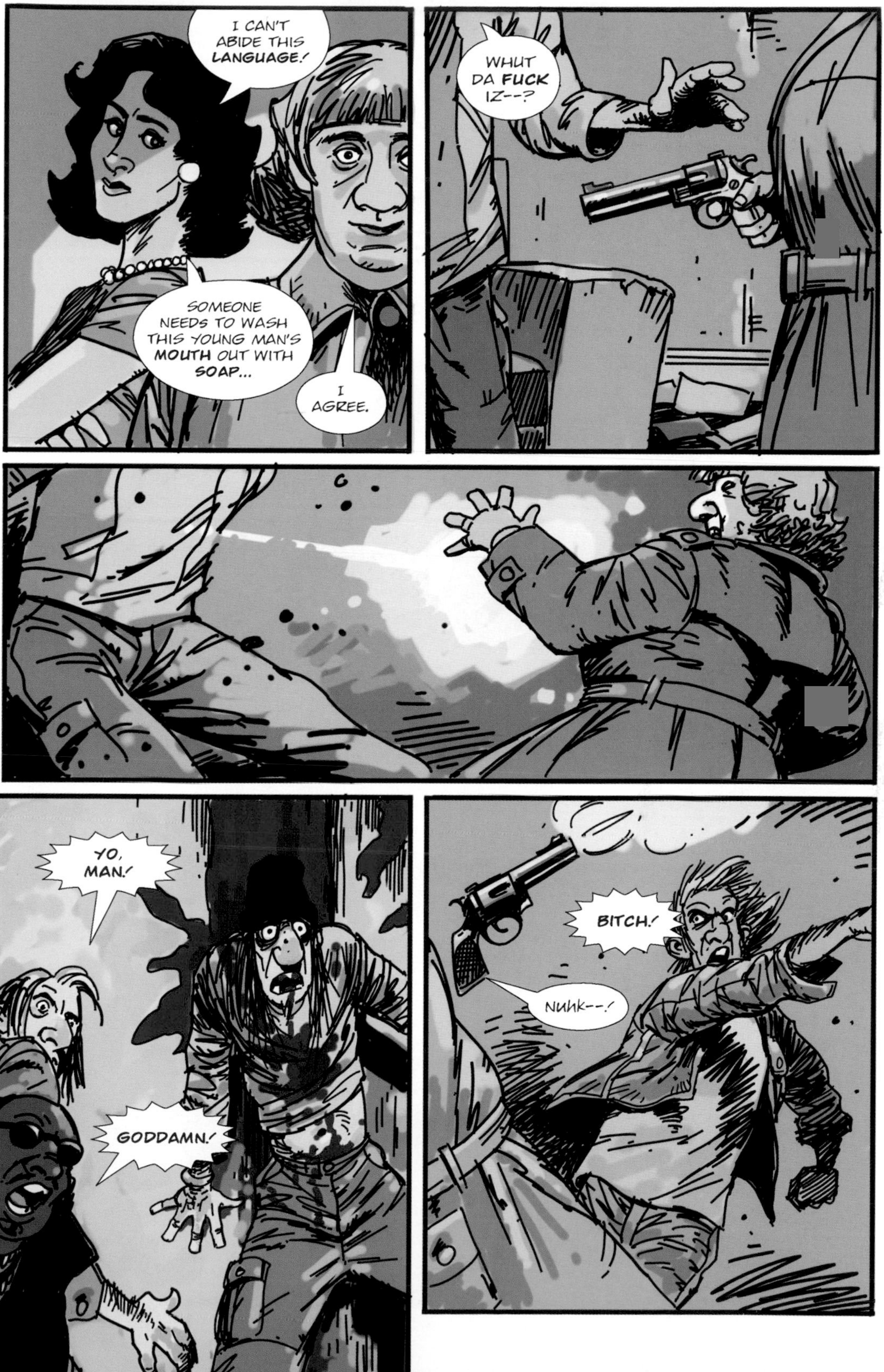
I CAN'T ABIDE THIS LANGUAGE!
SOMEONE NEEDS TO WASH THIS YOUNG MAN'S MOUTH OUT WITH SOAP...
I AGREE.
WHUT DA FUCK IZ--?
YO, MAN!
GODDAMN!
BITCH!
Nuhk--!

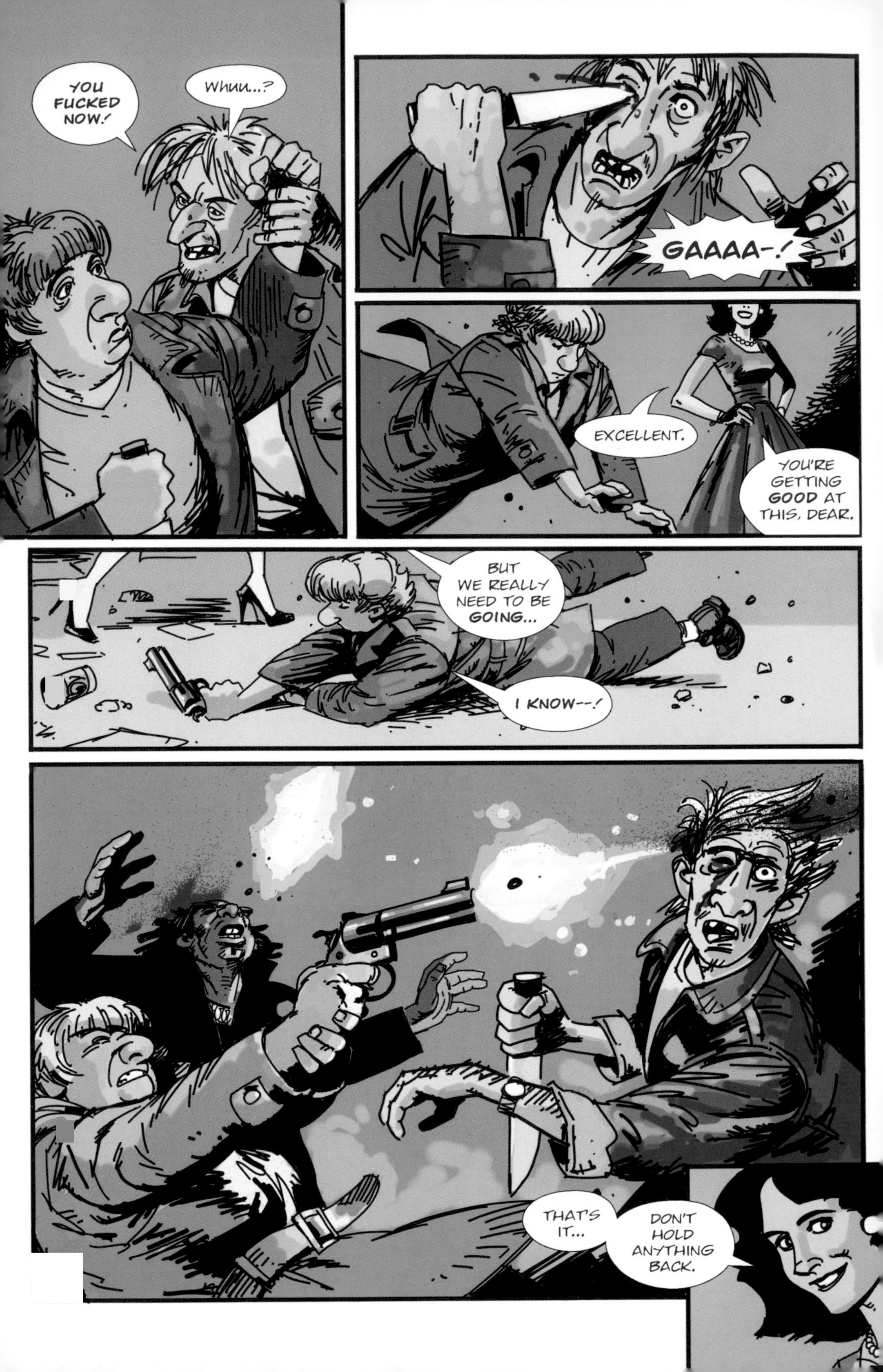
YOU FUCKED NOW!
Whuu...?
GAAAA-!
EXCELLENT.
YOU'RE GETTING GOOD AT THIS, DEAR.
BUT WE REALLY NEED TO BE GOING...
I KNOW--!
THAT'S IT...
DON'T HOLD ANYTHING BACK.

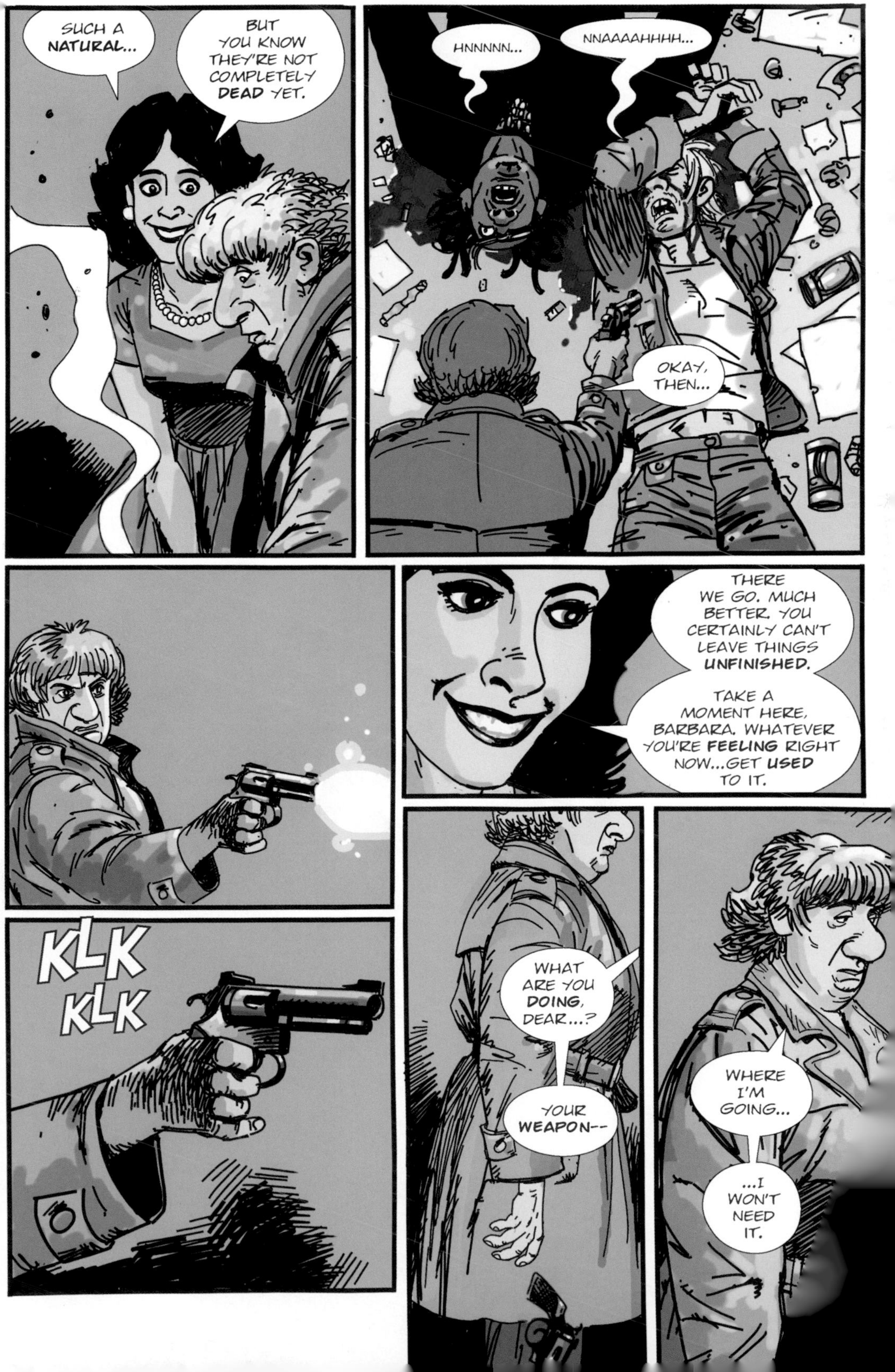
SUCH A NATURAL...
BUT YOU KNOW THEY'RE NOT COMPLETELY DEAD YET.
HNNNNN...
NNAAAAHHHH...
OKAY, THEN...
THERE WE GO. MUCH BETTER. YOU CERTAINLY CAN'T LEAVE THINGS UNFINISHED.
TAKE A MOMENT HERE, BARBARA. WHATEVER YOU'RE FEELING RIGHT NOW...GET USED TO IT.
KLK KLK
WHAT ARE YOU DOING, DEAR...?
YOUR WEAPON--
WHERE I'M GOING...
...I WON'T NEED IT.

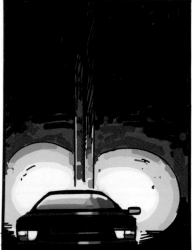

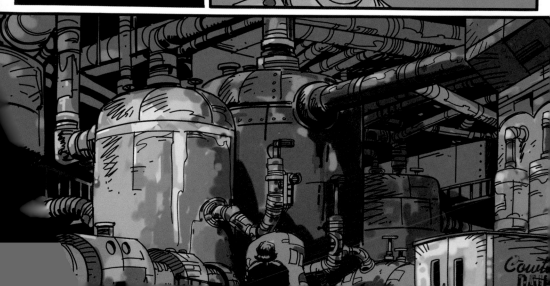

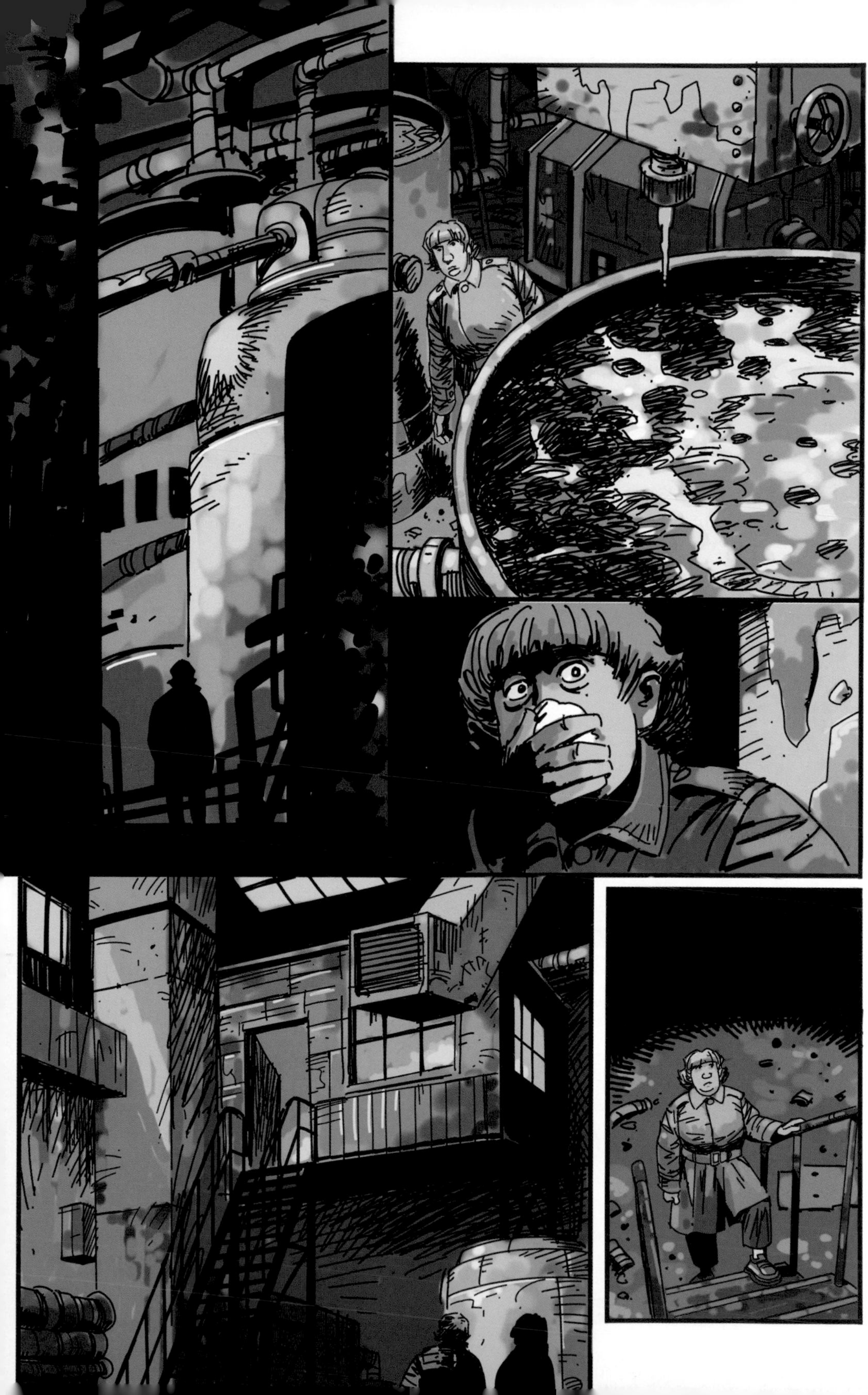

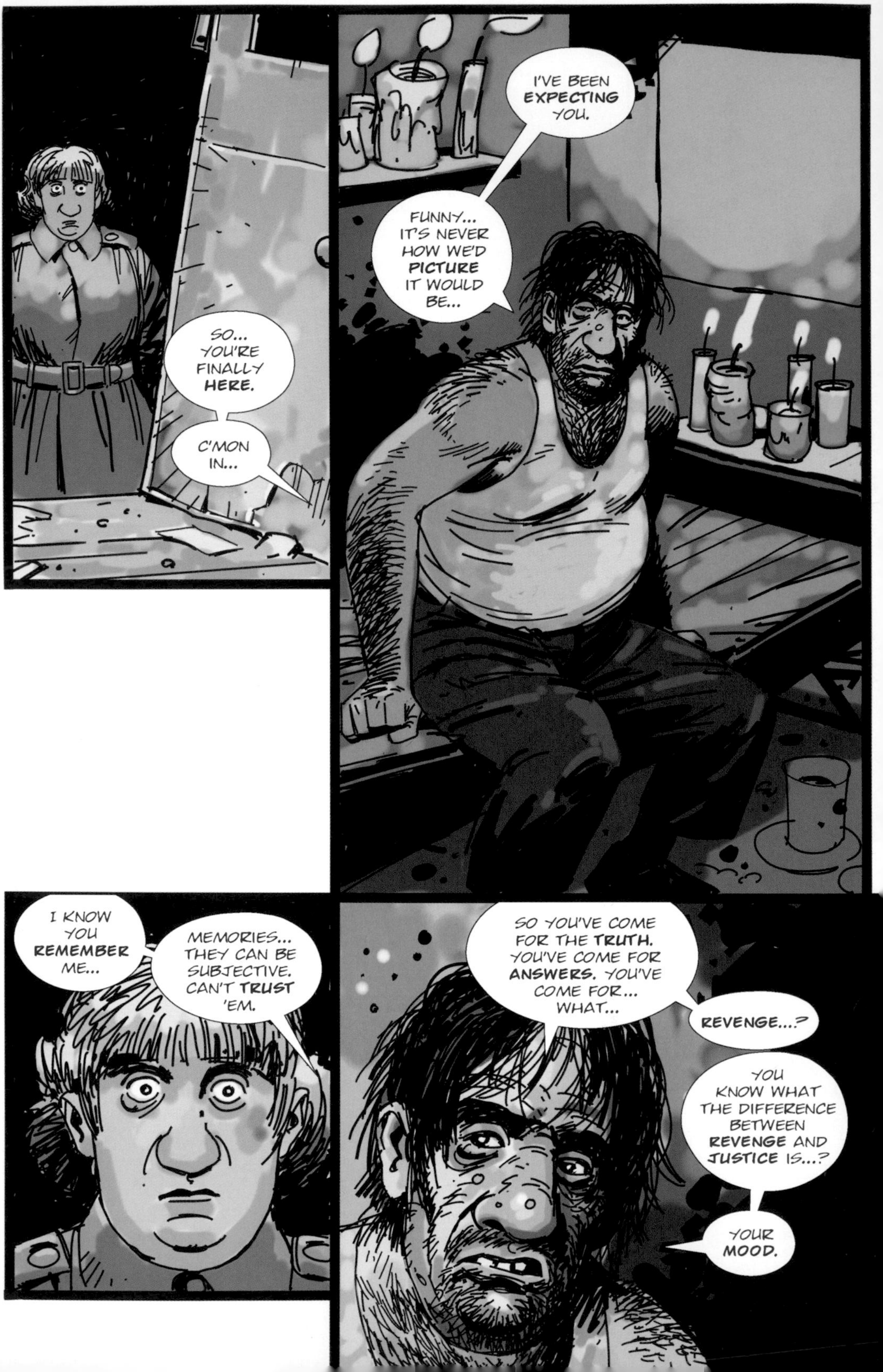
SO... YOU'RE FINALLY **HERE.**
C'MON IN...
I'VE BEEN **EXPECTING** YOU.
FUNNY... IT'S NEVER HOW WE'D **PICTURE** IT WOULD BE...
I KNOW YOU **REMEMBER** ME...
MEMORIES... THEY CAN BE SUBJECTIVE. CAN'T **TRUST** 'EM.
SO YOU'VE COME FOR THE **TRUTH.** YOU'VE COME FOR **ANSWERS.** YOU'VE COME FOR... WHAT...
REVENGE...?
YOU KNOW WHAT THE DIFFERENCE BETWEEN **REVENGE** AND **JUSTICE** IS...?
YOUR **MOOD.**

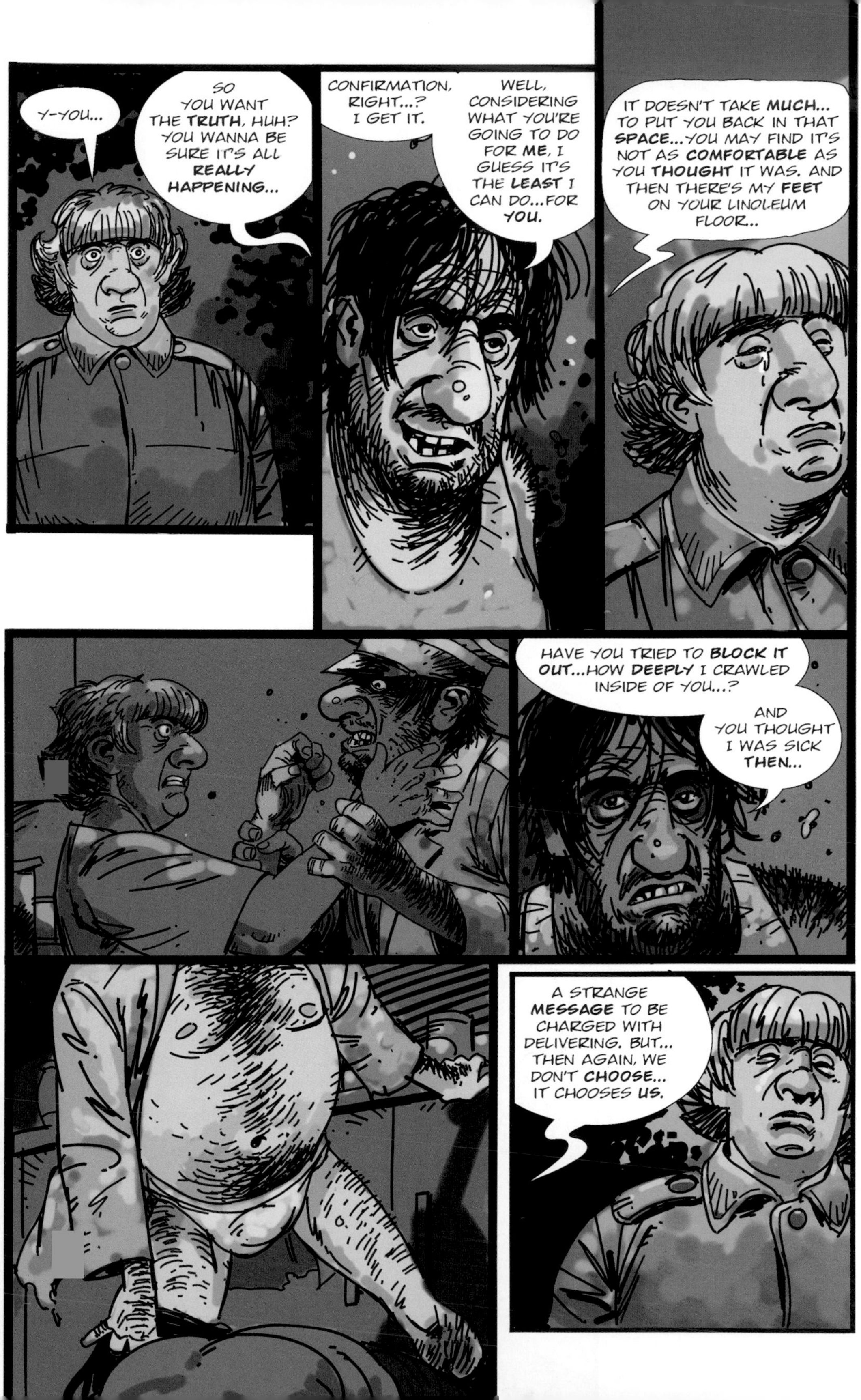
Y-YOU...
SO YOU WANT THE TRUTH, HUH? YOU WANNA BE SURE IT'S ALL REALLY HAPPENING...
CONFIRMATION, RIGHT...? I GET IT.
WELL, CONSIDERING WHAT YOU'RE GOING TO DO FOR ME, I GUESS IT'S THE LEAST I CAN DO...FOR YOU.
IT DOESN'T TAKE MUCH... TO PUT YOU BACK IN THAT SPACE...YOU MAY FIND IT'S NOT AS COMFORTABLE AS YOU THOUGHT IT WAS. AND THEN THERE'S MY FEET ON YOUR LINOLEUM FLOOR...
HAVE YOU TRIED TO BLOCK IT OUT...HOW DEEPLY I CRAWLED INSIDE OF YOU...?
AND YOU THOUGHT I WAS SICK THEN...
A STRANGE MESSAGE TO BE CHARGED WITH DELIVERING. BUT... THEN AGAIN, WE DON'T CHOOSE... IT CHOOSES US.

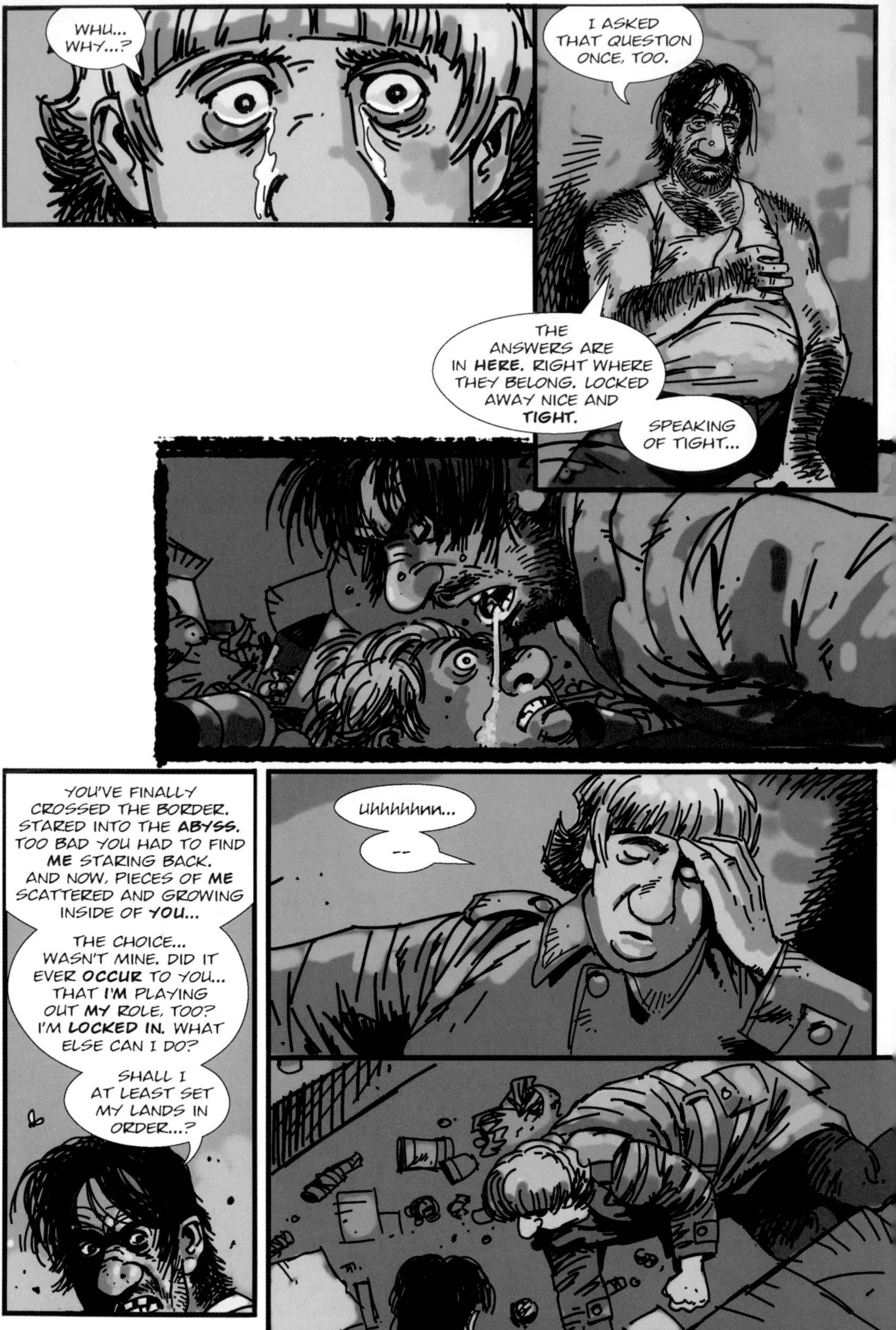
WHU... WHY...?
I ASKED THAT QUESTION ONCE, TOO.
THE ANSWERS ARE IN **HERE.** RIGHT WHERE THEY BELONG. LOCKED AWAY NICE AND **TIGHT.**
SPEAKING OF TIGHT...
YOU'VE FINALLY CROSSED THE BORDER. STARED INTO THE **ABYSS.** TOO BAD YOU HAD TO FIND **ME** STARING BACK. AND NOW, PIECES OF **ME** SCATTERED AND GROWING INSIDE OF **YOU...**
THE CHOICE... WASN'T MINE. DID IT EVER **OCCUR** TO YOU... THAT **I'M** PLAYING OUT **MY** ROLE, TOO? I'M **LOCKED IN.** WHAT ELSE CAN I DO?
SHALL I AT LEAST SET MY LANDS IN ORDER...?
Uhhhhhnn...
--

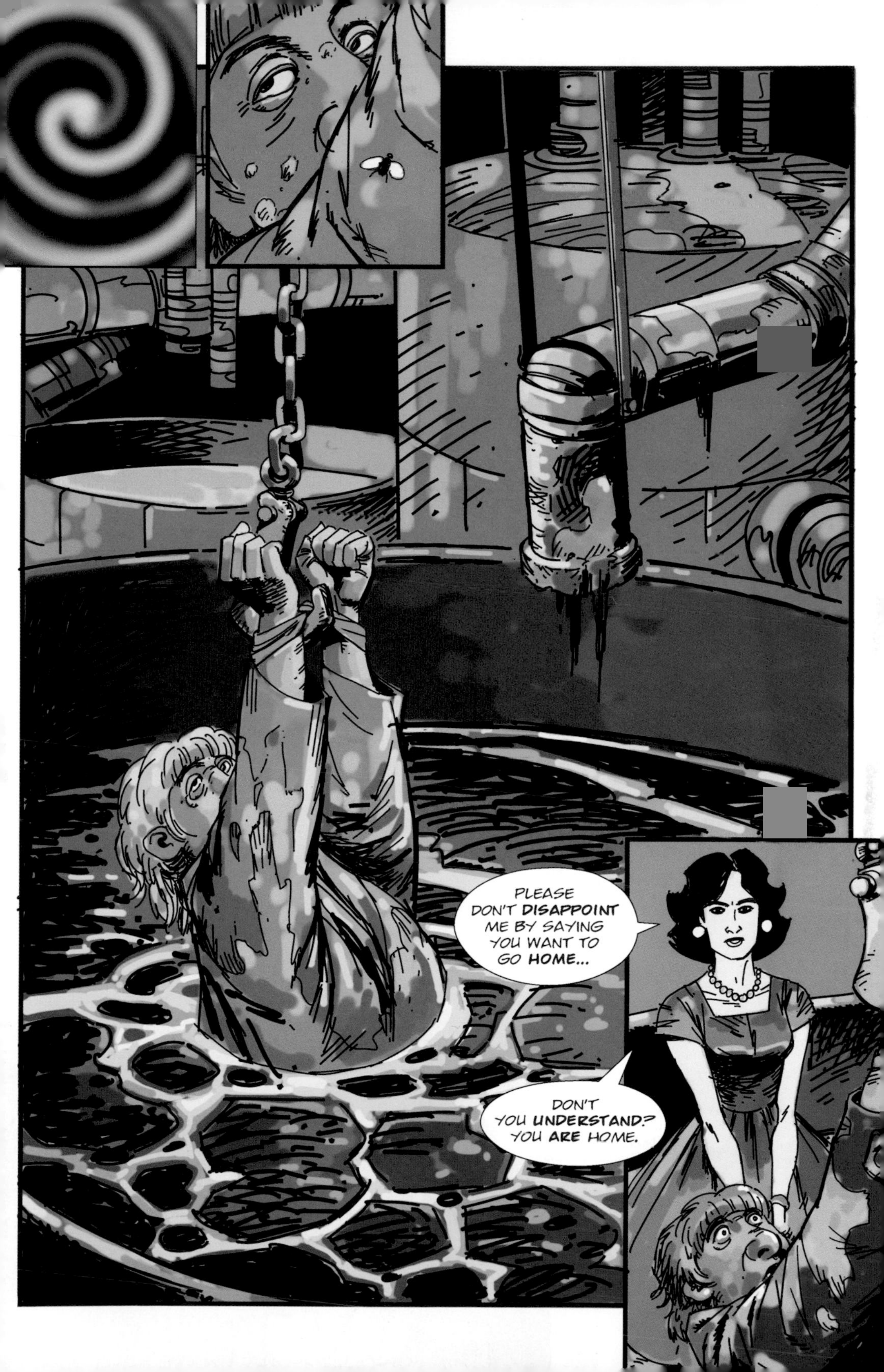
PLEASE DON'T DISAPPOINT ME BY SAYING YOU WANT TO GO HOME...
DON'T YOU UNDERSTAND? YOU ARE HOME.

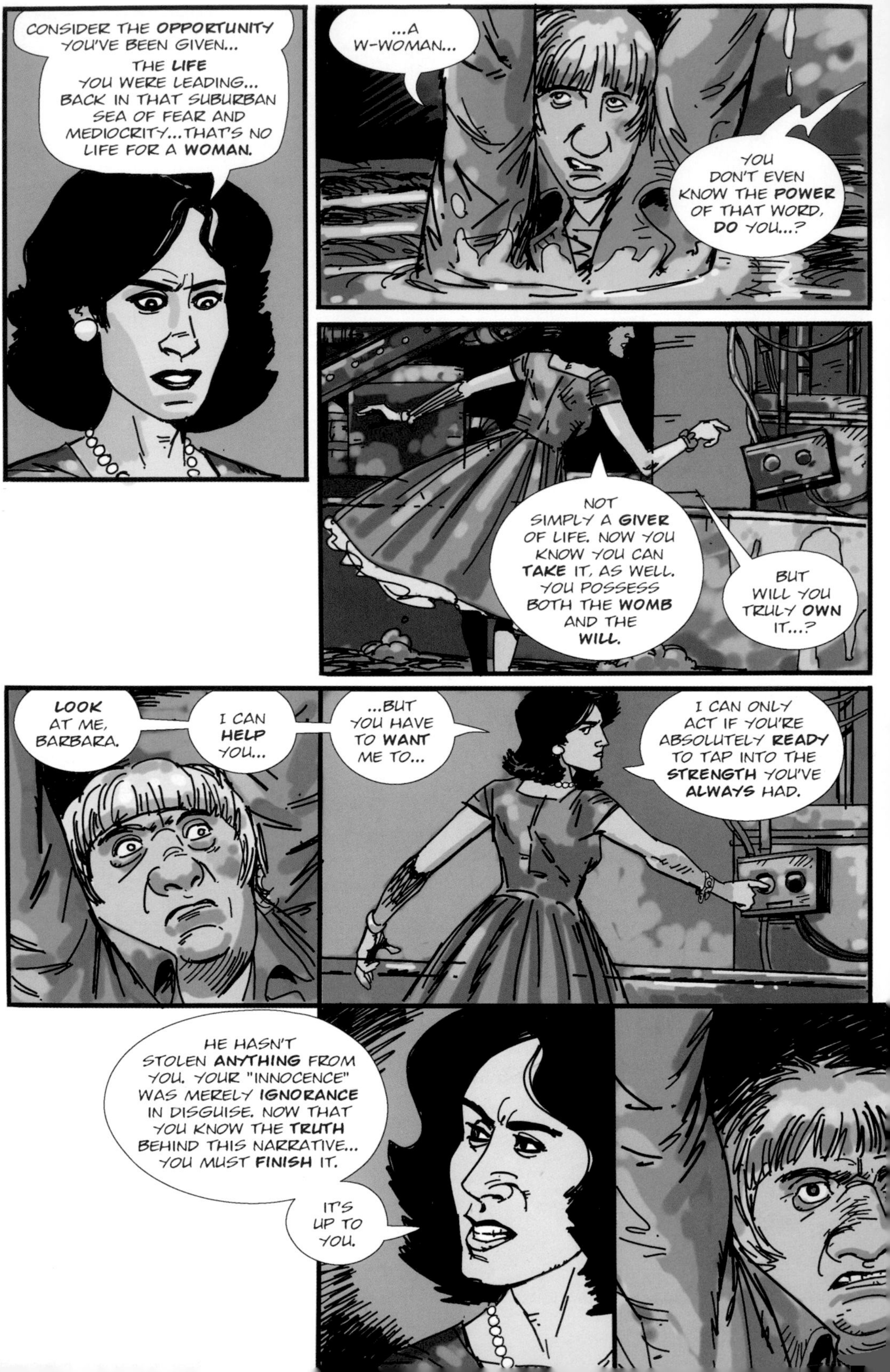
CONSIDER THE **OPPORTUNITY** YOU'VE BEEN GIVEN...
THE **LIFE** YOU WERE LEADING... BACK IN THAT SUBURBAN SEA OF FEAR AND MEDIOCRITY...THAT'S NO LIFE FOR A **WOMAN.**
...A W-WOMAN...
YOU DON'T EVEN KNOW THE **POWER** OF THAT WORD, **DO** YOU...?
NOT SIMPLY A **GIVER** OF LIFE. NOW YOU KNOW YOU CAN **TAKE** IT, AS WELL. YOU POSSESS BOTH THE **WOMB** AND THE **WILL.**
BUT WILL YOU TRULY **OWN** IT...?
LOOK AT ME, BARBARA.
I CAN **HELP** YOU...
...BUT YOU HAVE TO **WANT** ME TO...
I CAN ONLY ACT IF YOU'RE ABSOLUTELY **READY** TO TAP INTO THE **STRENGTH** YOU'VE **ALWAYS** HAD.
HE HASN'T STOLEN **ANYTHING** FROM YOU. YOUR "INNOCENCE" WAS MERELY **IGNORANCE** IN DISGUISE. NOW THAT YOU KNOW THE **TRUTH** BEHIND THIS NARRATIVE... YOU MUST **FINISH** IT.
IT'S UP TO YOU.

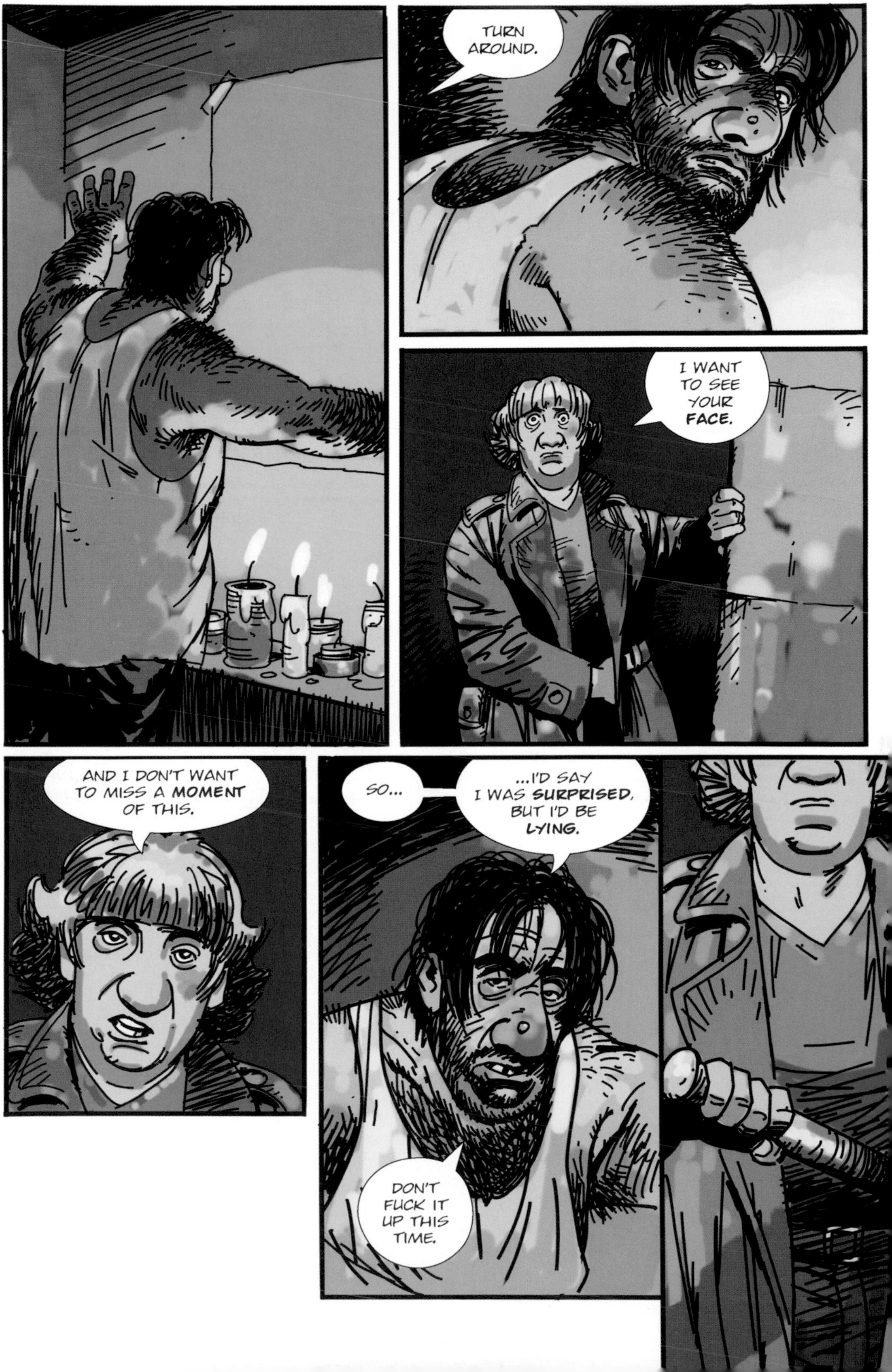
TURN AROUND.
I WANT TO SEE YOUR FACE.
AND I DON'T WANT TO MISS A MOMENT OF THIS.
SO...
...I'D SAY I WAS SURPRISED, BUT I'D BE LYING.
DON'T FUCK IT UP THIS TIME.

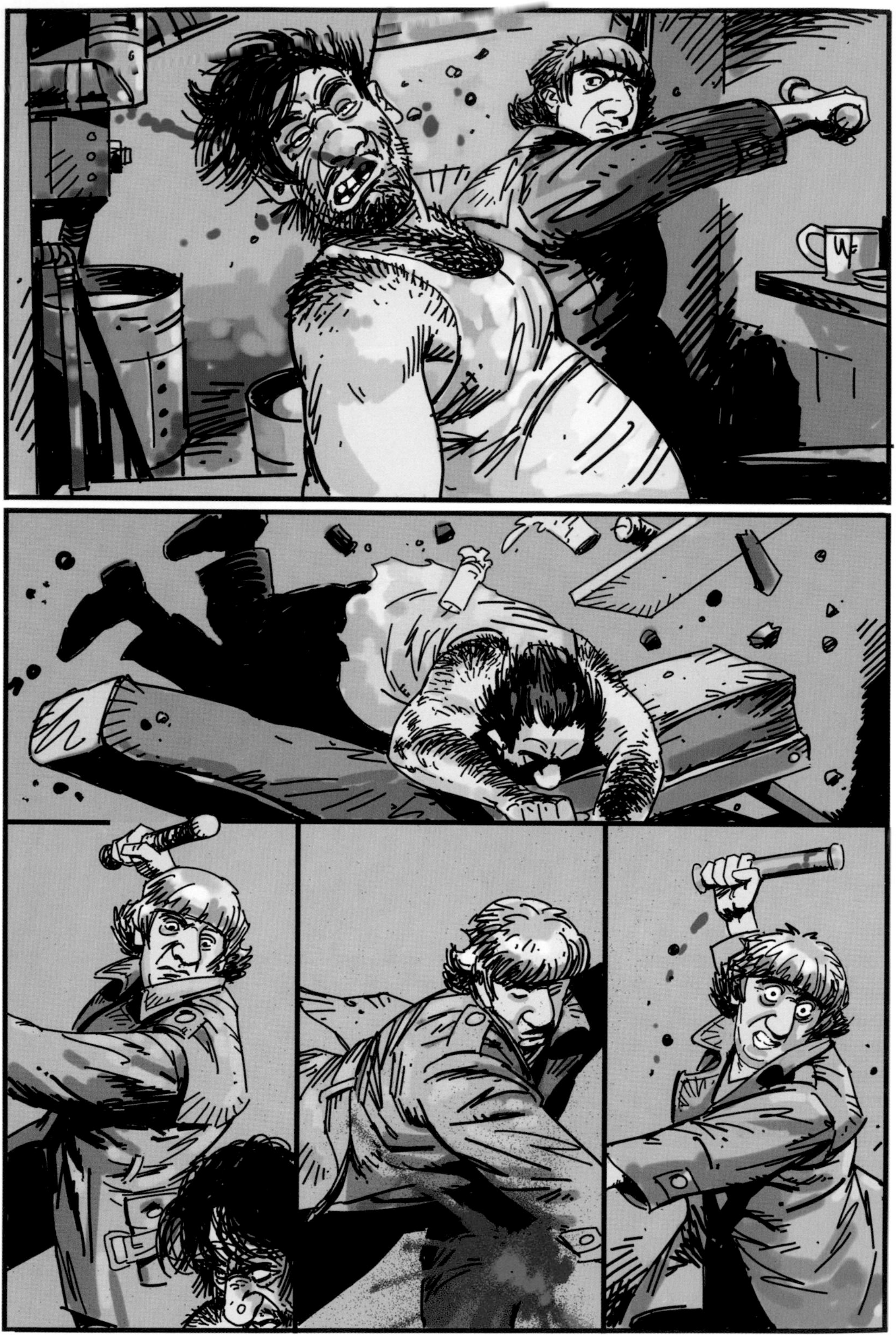

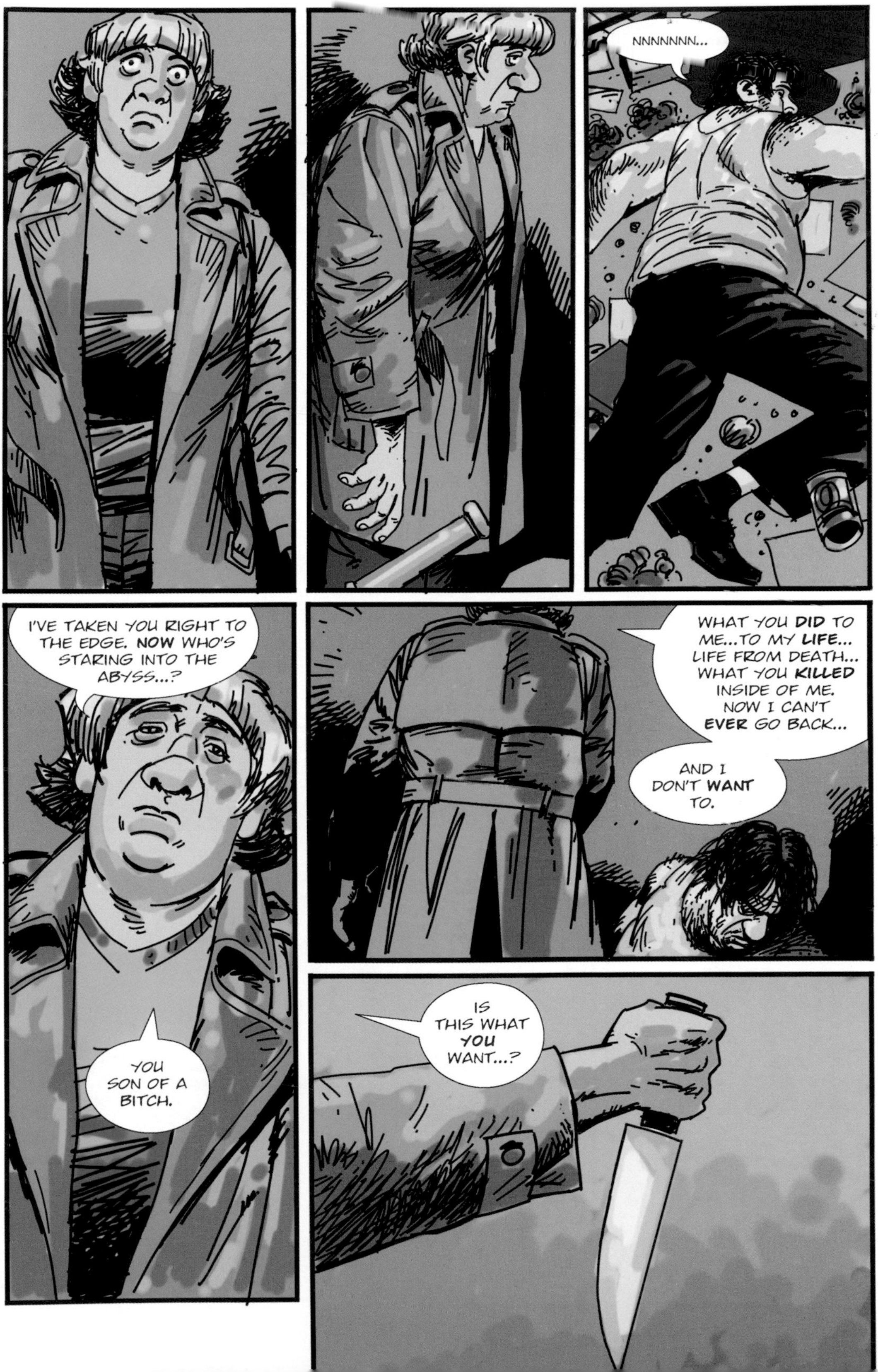
NNNNNNN...
I'VE TAKEN YOU RIGHT TO THE EDGE. NOW WHO'S STARING INTO THE ABYSS...?
YOU SON OF A BITCH.
WHAT YOU DID TO ME...TO MY LIFE... LIFE FROM DEATH... WHAT YOU KILLED INSIDE OF ME. NOW I CAN'T EVER GO BACK...
AND I DON'T WANT TO.
IS THIS WHAT YOU WANT...?

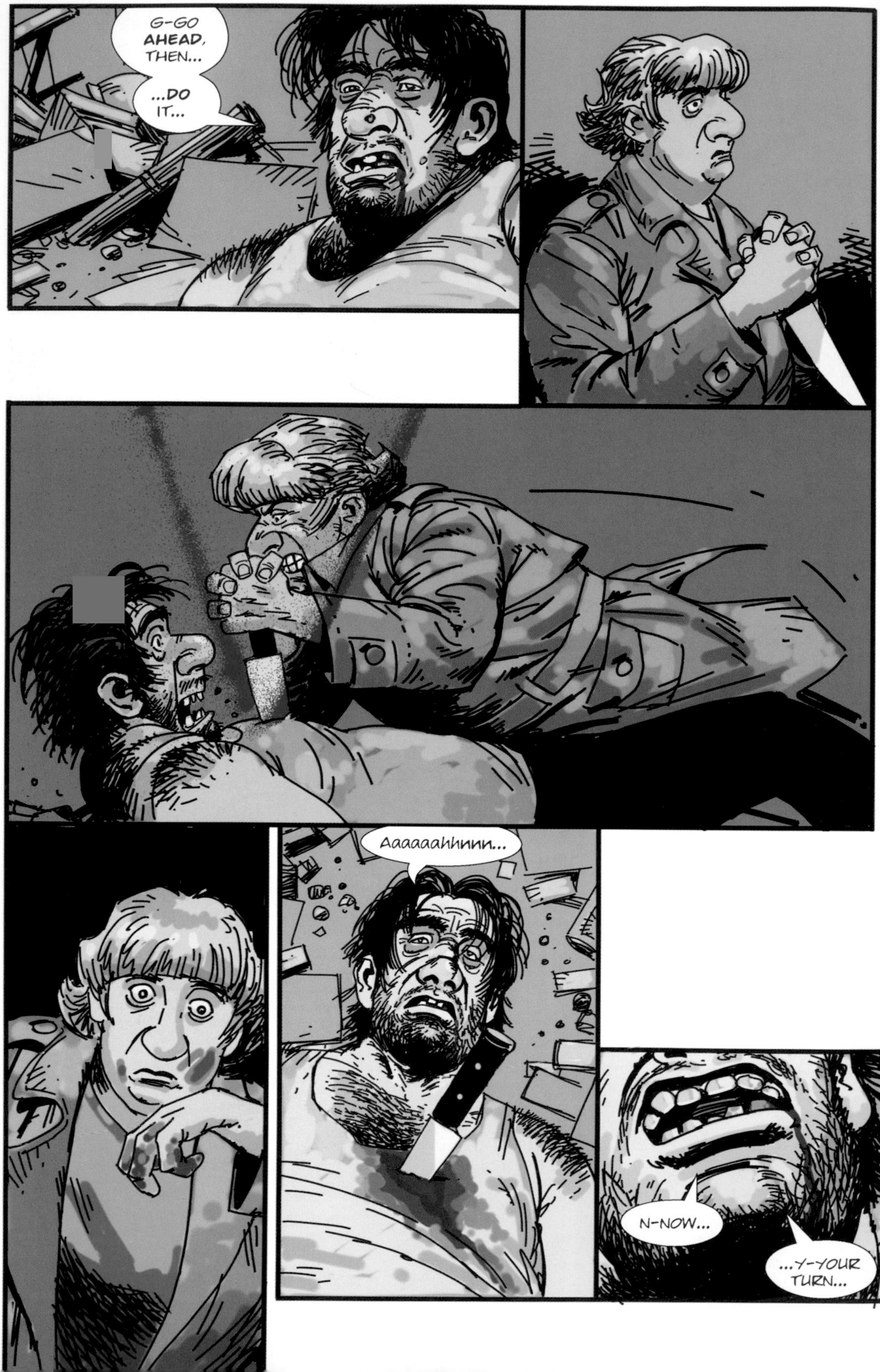
G-GO AHEAD, THEN...
...DO IT...
Aaaaaahhnnn...
N-NOW...
...Y-YOUR TURN...

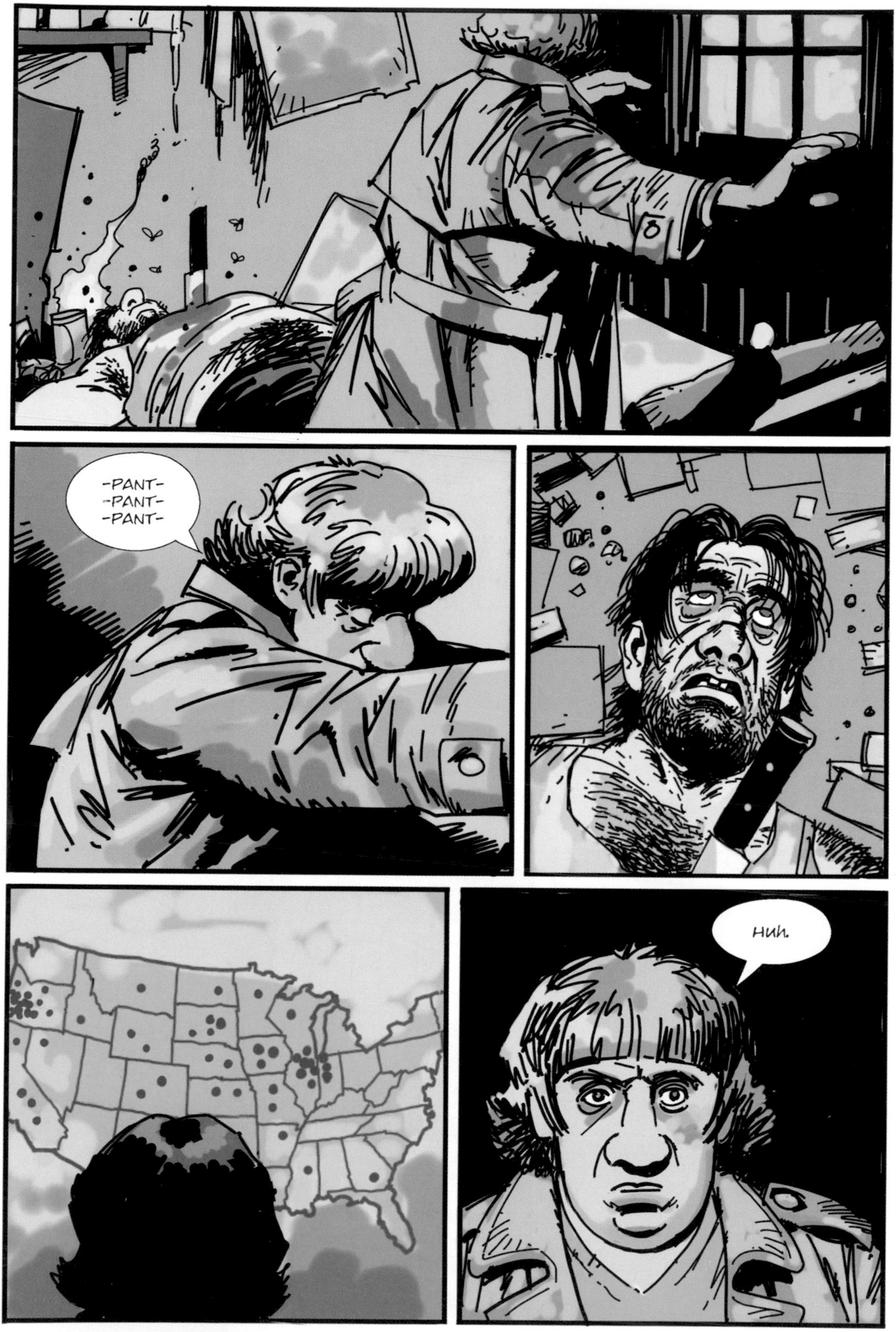
-PANT-
-PANT-
-PANT-
HUH.

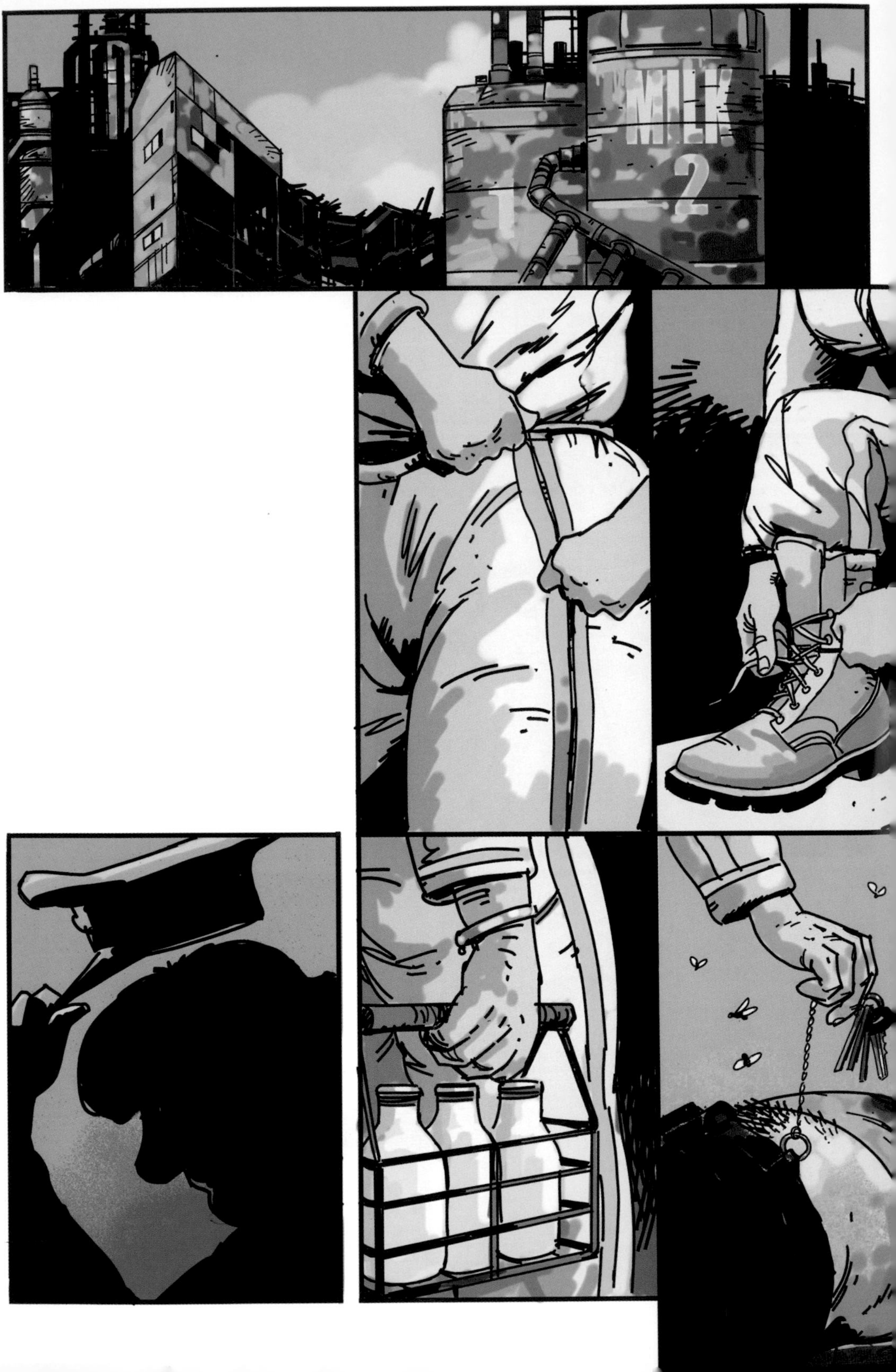
MILK
2

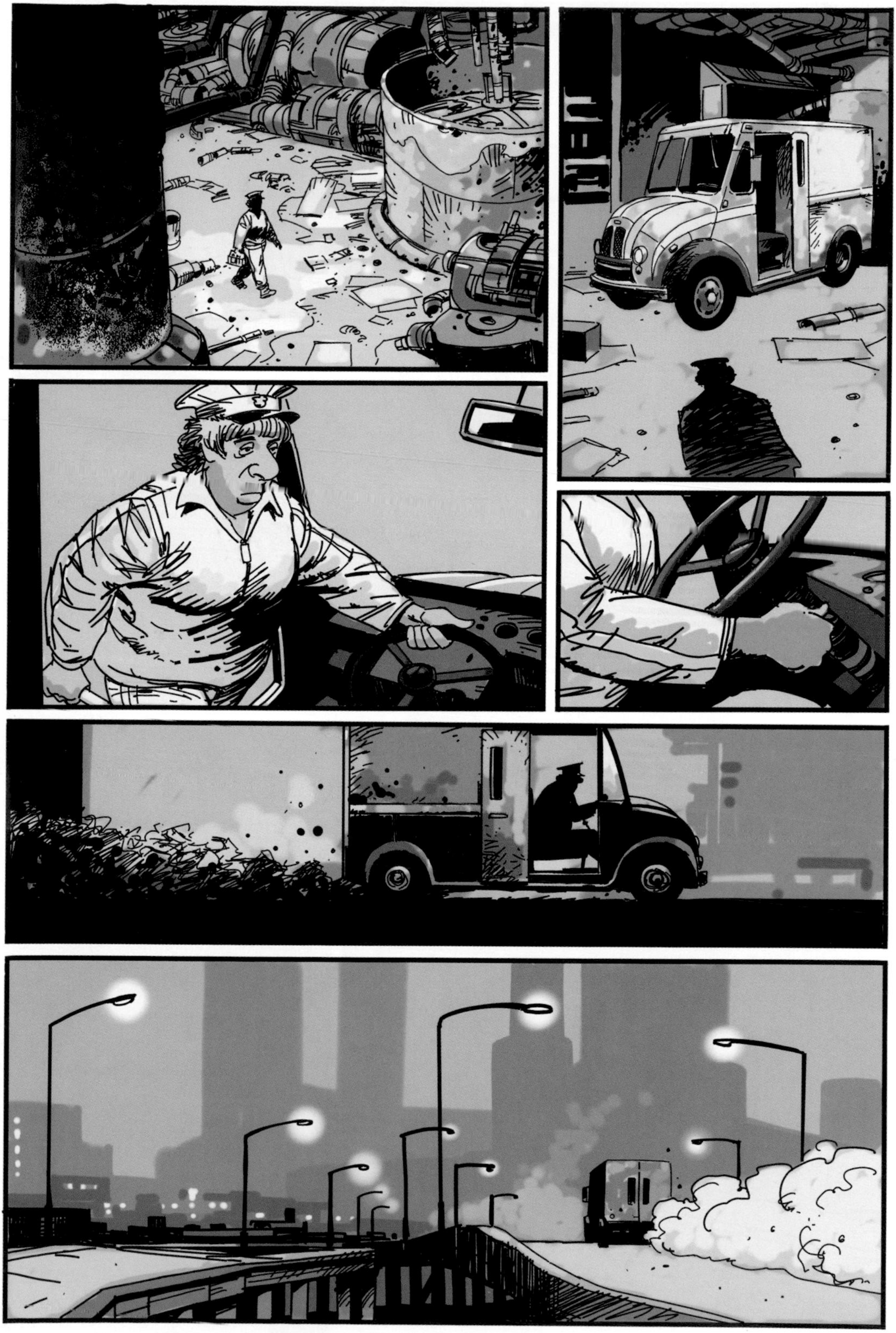

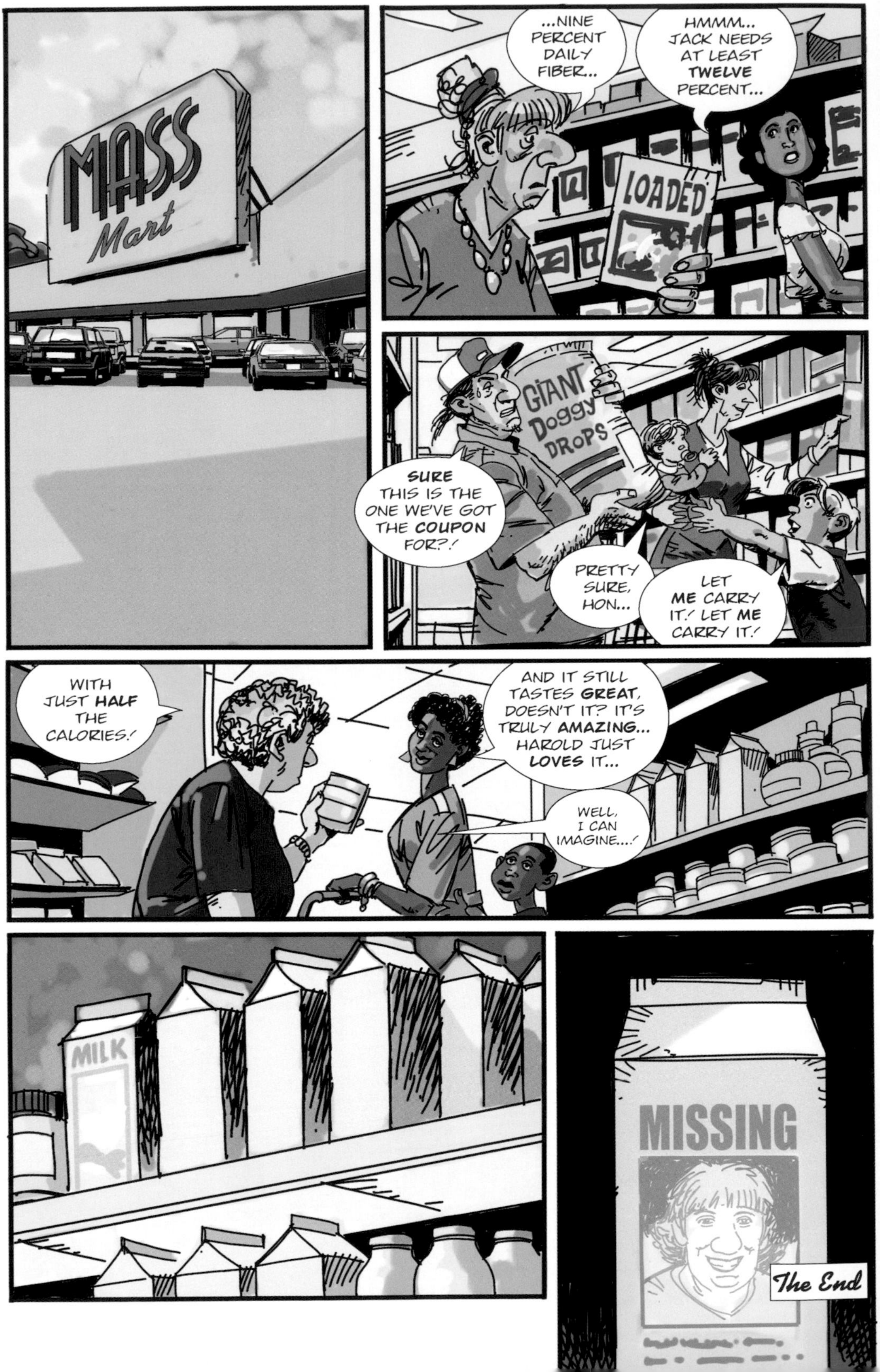
MASS
Mart
...NINE PERCENT DAILY FIBER...
HMMM... JACK NEEDS AT LEAST TWELVE PERCENT...
LOADED
GIANT Doggy DROPS
SURE THIS IS THE ONE WE'VE GOT THE COUPON FOR?!
PRETTY SURE, HON...
LET ME CARRY IT! LET ME CARRY IT!
WITH JUST HALF THE CALORIES!
AND IT STILL TASTES GREAT, DOESN'T IT? IT'S TRULY AMAZING... HAROLD JUST LOVES IT...
WELL, I CAN IMAGINE...!
MILK
MISSING
The End

AFTERWORD

Every once in a while—if you're a comic-book artist—a script comes along which has the same emotional impact as a message in a bottle to a shipwrecked mariner.

These scripts are rare. And the writers who produce them are rarer still. Too often, writers of the genre are obsessed with the desire to make movies. They are closet screenwriters (or worse: directors), hacking out what they consider to be cool movie shots, which cannot possibly work on the printed page.

BONE TO PICK WITH WRITERS DEPT.:

Have you guys ever stopped to think that it takes over four hundred people to make even a basic Hollywood movie? An artist is a single person. Does the equation balance? The fuck it does. The only reason that artists manage to incorporate your excessive ideas is because they work every hour God sends and are consigned to an early grave. And it's all your fault! Next time you want a crowd scene with two hundred extras—think about it.

Or they long to be novelists, and their scripts are full of whole-page monologues or scene descriptions that are patently un-illustratable. In other words, they are in love with their own writing. My advice to you—fuck off and write novels but leave comics alone.

Joe Casey's not like that. Joe is comics through and through. (That's not to say he's not capable of writing a novel or a screenplay—he just understands the difference.) Not only are his scripts a joy to read—they translate to the page with the economy and impact of a fighter in the ring. Joe's ringcraft is awesome. I hope

the comics industry has the good sense to hang on to him. Pay him huge amounts of money or whatever he wants. The man is a contender.

The message that Joe put in the bottle was as clear as day. Nothing ambiguous about it.

Our world is built on a Big Lie.

In our hearts we all know it.

The Vale family knew it, but chose to ignore it. They chose to be complicit in the half-truths that fed their withered souls. They gave their power away willingly for life inside a cage. This message gave me the energy and relish I needed to depict these people as they truly are: caricatures.

But caricatures with a difference. My background is suburbia, too. Vincent Vale is based on my own father, but with added charm. Barbara is a hybrid of family members, various aunts and others who struggled to bring some kind of civilization to a situation devoid of it. They failed because nobody took them seriously. Where I come from, women are not taken seriously. They're just part of the furniture.

I loved drawing this book because it gave me permission to draw from life. I didn't have to consult a model sheet for some crap superhero costume, or fake up a spaceship, or pump up some bimbo's jugs to be ogled by the "average reader." Even though I love doing those things, too. This time around I could draw to my heart's content and nobody could tell me it was wrong.

Thanks, Joe. And thank you, Scott. It was a great gig. I hope the audience enjoyed it.

Steve Parkhouse
Somewhere in England
Somewhere in the 21st Century

ALSO FROM DARK HORSE COMICS!

MIKE MIGNOLA'S
HELLBOY
WEIRD TALES
Volume One

HELLBOY: WEIRD TALES VOLUME ONE
By Joe Casey, John Cassaday, Steve Parkhouse, Alex Maleev, Eric Powell, Leinil Francis Yu, and many more! Cover by Mike Mignola

Some of the top writers and artists in today's world of comics provide their take on Hellboy and the B.P.R.D. Old-fashioned pulp fun featuring one of the greatest heroes of modern comics.

Soft cover, 128 pages, Full color
$17.95, ISBN: 1-56971-622-6

THE GOON
NOTHIN' BUT MISERY
by Eric Powell

THE GOON, VOLUME 1: NOTHIN' BUT MISERY
By Eric Powell

An insane priest is building an army of the undead, and only one man can put them in their place: the Goon. This volume collects *The Goon* issues 1-4 and *The Goon Color Special*, originally published by Albatross Exploding Funny Books.

Soft cover, 136 pages, Full color
$15.95, ISBN: 1-56971-998-5

Mike Mignola
P. Craig Russell
Jill Thompson
Evan Dorkin
Paul Chadwick
Gary Gianni
and others
The Dark Horse Book of
HAUNTINGS

THE DARK HORSE BOOK OF HAUNTINGS HC
Featuring Mike Mignola, P. Craig Russell, Paul Chadwick, Evan Dorkin, Jill Thompson, and others. Cover by Gary Gianni

Mike Mignola's Hellboy investigates a haunted house and discovers his own unexpected connection to the spirits within. P. Craig Russell and Mike Richardson tell the story of a child who vanishes into an abandoned house, and Paul Chadwick and Randy Stradley team up for a creepy short about a haunted suit. Jill Thompson and Evan Dorkin recount the legend of a haunted doghouse.

Hard cover, 96 pages, Full color
$14.95, ISBN: 1-56971-958-6

MIKE MIGNOLA JILL THOMPSON EVAN DORKIN SEAN PHILLIPS
SCOTT MORSE TONY MILLIONAIRE GARY GIANNI AND OTHERS
The Dark Horse Book of
Witchcraft

THE DARK HORSE BOOK OF WITCHCRAFT HC
Featuring Mike Mignola, P. Craig Russell, Paul Chadwick, Evan Dorkin, Jill Thompson, and others. Cover by Gary Gianni

Mike Mignola returns with another Hellboy story, and Jill Thompson (*Scary Godmother*) and Evan Dorkin (*Hectic Planet*) return to their stunning "Stray" story. Scott Morse Morse (*Soulwind*) presents a tale of old Salem. *The Dark Horse Book of Witchcraft* conjures up weird tales of horror and magic the likes of which one seldom sees in graphic novels.

Hard cover, 96 pages, Full color
$14.95, ISBN: 1-59307-108-6

DARK HORSE COMICS™ *drawing on your nightmares*
darkhorse.com

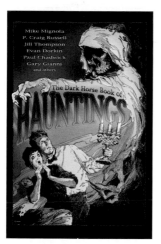

THE RING, VOLUME 1
By Hiroshi Takahashi and Misao Inagaki

The Ring, a Japanese multi-media frenzy based on the best-selling horror novels by Koji Suzuki, has already made its way to America in both a Western adaptation of the film, and an equally popular dubbed Japanese version. Now Dark Horse brings you the critically acclaimed manga, published in the original Japanese format!

Soft cover, 304 pages, Black & White
$14.95, ISBN: 1-59307-054-3

SCATTERBRAIN HC
By Mike Mignola, Steve Parkhouse, Craig Thompson, Killian Plunkett, Jim Woodring, Sergio Aragonés, Evan Dorkin, Jay Stephens, Dave Cooper, and others
Features: Preview, 1 Ecomic, 1 Game, 1 Trailer

This praised anthology features the monocular adventures of Steve Guarnaccia's award-winning *Kid Cyclops*, along with delightful tales from Mike Mignola, Jim Woodring, Sergio Aragonés, Steve Parkhouse, Killian Plunkett, Evan Dorkin, Jay (*Jetcat*) Stephens, Dave (*Weasel*) Cooper, and more.

Hard cover, 128 pages, Full color
$19.95, ISBN: 1-56971-426-6

THE DEVIL'S FOOTPRINTS
By Scott Allie, Paul Lee, Brian Horton, and Dave Stewart

Brandon Waite investigates his dead father's study of witchcraft. But his desire to protect loved ones forces him to cover up his own tentative steps into the black arts, leading him to mix deception with demon conjuration, isolating himself in a terrible world where his soul hangs in the balance.

Soft cover, 144 pages, Full color
$12.95, ISBN: 1-56971-933-0

THE BLACKBURNE COVENANT
By Fabian Nicieza and Stefano Raffaele

Someone is following novelist Richard Kaine. Someone interested in finding out how Richard came up with his best-selling first novel; because unbeknownst to Richard, his fantasy novel was non-fiction. Could Richard have written about an event that had been meticulously eradicated from human history? Who are the Blackburne Covenant? Why are they willing to kill Richard Kaine in order to keep him quiet?

Soft cover, 104 pages, Full color
$11.95, ISBN: 1-56971-889-X

AVAILABLE AT YOUR LOCAL COMICS SHOP OR BOOKSTORE

To find a comics shop in your area, call 1-888-266-4226 • For more information or to order direct visit darkhorse.com or call 1-800-862-0052 • Mon. - Sat. 9 A.M. to 5 P.M. Pacific Time • Prices and availability subject to change without notice